Collaborating to

Meet Standards:

Teacher/Librarian

Partnerships for K-6

Second Edition

Toni Buzzeo

Linworth Books

Professional Development Resources for K-12
Library Media and Technology Specialists

The Board of Education of Blue Valley Unified School District No. 229, owner of the unit, does hereby grant permission to Linworth Publishing, Inc., to use and publish a unit titled "If These Walls Could Speak," by Blue Valley librarian, Ronda Hassig, including portions of the School District's curriculum standards which are included within the unit. The unit may be published only in a book titled "Collaborating to Meet Standards: Teacher/Librarian Partnerships for K-6, Second Edition."

Library of Congress Cataloging-in-Publication Data

Buzzeo, Toni.
  Collaborating to meet standards : teacher/librarian partnerships for k-6 / Toni Buzzeo. -- 2nd ed.
    p. cm.
  Includes bibliographical references and index.
  ISBN 1-58683-302-2 (pbk.)
  1. High school libraries--United States. 2. Junior high school libraries--United States. 3. Library orientation for high school students--United States. 4. Library orientation for junior high school students--United States. 5. Information literacy--Study and teaching (Secondary)--United States. 6. Information literacy--Study and teaching (Middle school)--United States. 7. Curriculum planning-- United States. 8. Teacher-librarians--United States. I. Title.
  Z675.S3B88 2007
  027.8'223--dc22

                                        2007015406

Published by Linworth Publishing, Inc.
3650 Olentangy River Rd., Suite 250
Columbus, Ohio 43214

ISBN: 1-58683-302-2

5 4 3 2 1

Table of Contents

Table of Figures

Figure A-1 Page 1 Matrix of Learning Activities by Content Standard

Units

Content Area		Unit 1 Kinder Quest	Unit 2 Fishing for Facts	Unit 3 Geology for First Graders	Unit 4 Who's That by the Pond?	Unit 5 Superbugs!	Unit 6 The World Beyond Our Neighborhood	Unit 7 All About Exploring the Internet	Unit 8 Biography Bash
Grade		Kindergarten	Kindergarten	1	1	2	2	3/4/5	4
English Language Arts	Reading	X	X				X		X
	Writing	X	X	X		X	X		X
	Speaking					X	X		X
	Listening								
Science	Processes		X	X	X	X			
	Concepts: Biology	X	X		X	X			
	Concepts: Earth Sciences			X					
Technology			X		X		X	X	X
Social Studies	History							X	
	Citizenship Skills								
	Geography						X		X
	Culture						X		
Mathematics				X					
Physical Education	Health and Fitness								
	Dance								

Units

Content Area		Unit 9 Cultures of the Sun	Unit 10 History Fair	Unit 11 Canyons by Gary Paulsen	Unit 12 Food for the Community and You	Unit 13 PQI	Unit 14 If These Walls Could Speak
Grade		4/5	5	6	6	6	6
English Language Arts	Reading	X	X	X		X	X
	Writing	X	X	X		X	X
	Speaking		X	X		X	
	Listening			X			X
Science	Processes						
	Concepts: Biology				X		
	Concepts: Earth Sciences						
Technology		X		X	X		
Social Studies	History	X	X	X	X		X
	Citizenship						
	Skills						
	Geography	X		X			
	Culture						X
Mathematics					X		X
Physical Education	Health and Fitness						
	Dance						

About the Author

About the Author

Toni Buzzeo is a veteran library media specialist as well as an author. She holds an M.A. from the University of Michigan in English Language and Literature and an M.L.I.S. from the University of Rhode Island. In 1999, she was named Maine Library Media Specialist of the Year by the Maine Association of School Libraries and currently serves on the executive board of that organization. As an educator, she worked as a library media specialist for sixteen years and previously taught both high school and college English. As a writer, she is the author of professional books for librarians and teachers as well as twelve children's books. She is a frequent presenter at library, reading, and writing conferences as well as a district in-service trainer across the country. Her Web site, www.tonibuzzeo.com, offers additional insight into her many professional interests as well as her books. She can be reached at tonibuzzeo@tonibuzzeo.com.

Speaking Engagements

Librarians and educators who wish to contact Toni Buzzeo about conference and staff development speaking engagements related to teacher/librarian collaborations may visit her Web site at www.tonibuzzeo.com

Acknowledgments

Thanks go to my colleagues and friends who developed all of the units you find in this book. They and their collaborating teachers are, by far, the most dedicated of educators. I also want to thank my wonderful assistant, Robyn Foss, who put in many long days of work to format all of the units and to untangle the unfathomable tangles I had introduced. As always, I owe gratitude to my publisher and chief cheerleader, Marlene Woo-Lun, to my funny and supportive editor, Cynthia Anderson, and to my dedicated partner and idea-guy, Ken Cyll, who knew just what the first four chapters needed.

Dedication

To four of the most generous educators on this spinning planet, Laurie Dunlap, Mary Semons, Dolores White, and Carole Thomspon, co-authors of Unit 9: Cultures of the Sun, who share their knowledge and experience with me, guide me, and, above all, let me work and play with their kids so that I can learn, grow, and practice what I preach. With the very deepest appreciation, I dedicate this book to you.

Introduction

In early 2002, when the first edition of *Collaborating to Meet Standards: Teacher/Librarian Partnerships for K-6* was published, we taught in a much different educational world. As library media specialists, then, as now, we carried our 1998 "collaboration" mandate from *Information Power: Building Partnerships for Learning*: "Collaboration for authentic, information-based learning--through shared planning, teaching, collection development, and management strategies--provides the model for all the program's connections to the larger learning community (AASL 123)." We hadn't yet realized the significant changes that the newly signed *No Child Left Behind* (*NCLB*) federal legislation would visit upon our libraries, our schools, our educational world.

Now, as "literacy" has become the new buzzword of education under *NCLB*, especially in elementary buildings, our schools have turned all eyes and hands to the work of improving reading instruction in order to help students read better as measured by higher scores on mandated standardized tests. Our classroom teachers have found their literacy instruction more and more tightly controlled, in both method of delivery and time spent teaching. For our part, librarians have been challenged to learn new methodologies (often in response to schoolwide adoption of new literacy models), adjust our schedules, and maintain our ties to those classroom teaching partners as they ford new instructional streams. And in some schools that are recipients of Reading First grants under *NCLB*, classroom literacy instruction has risen to even greater prominence with the influx of monies for materials, staffing, and training. Library media specialists in those schools are all the more challenged to remain involved as the spotlight shines brightly on improving classroom literacy learning and purchasing *classroom* literacy materials.

With reading (and sometimes numeracy) in the spotlight and the need for schools to make Adequate Yearly Progress as measured on standardized tests, one might surmise an ascendancy in library importance. I certainly would have naively predicted that outcome back in 2002 as *NCLB* began to move in, unpack its bags (baggage, some might say), and settle in for an extended stay. After all, reading/literacy/libraries are incontestably joined. Or so we may have thought.

However, in the literacy-focused school, the drive to achieve higher scores has, in many instances, reduced the importance of the library and the librarian. In the worst of cases, we have been entirely written out of the literacy equation. One colleague reports that after the adoption of the Four-Blocks® Literacy Model in her school, some classroom teachers requested that she no longer read aloud to her students in the library, since that was already happening in the classroom. In another instance, an award-winning library media specialist colleague related her own astonishing experience. When her superintendent announced a newly formed district literacy committee, she was the first person in line to sign up. "No, no," her administrator responded. "This isn't about LIBRARIES. This is about READING!"

While we must see such attitudes for the challenges they are, and admit that we have our roadblocks cut out for us, there is no room or time to be discouraged. We know that we, and our library programs, are key contributors to student achievement--not only in reading but in all areas of instruction that require information literacy, critical thinking, and a knowledge-based approach to the subject matter.

Furthermore, despite recent educational changes, both library literature and library wisdom continue to hold collaborative teaching practice as a goal to strive toward. As a result, we must continue to dedicate ourselves to expanding our understanding, educating our classroom colleagues and special area teachers, and discussing methods for overcoming the roadblocks that litter our path. I speak across the country to my library colleagues at national and state conferences, as well as in district and regional in-service trainings, about their struggles and, above all, their victories as we all work to broaden and deepen our collaborative practice despite the traditional challenges and the new changes brought about by *NCLB*.

I advocate an approach that combines optimism with necessary realism. While mandated instructional time (particularly for literacy and numeracy) has changed the shape of our school days and the flexibility that collaboration often requires, we can still find ways to succeed at collaborative practice. If our classroom colleagues feel tied to schedules they no longer set, to expectations that come from the building administrator, the district administration, the federal government, we may offer new ways of working together that address their challenges.

Literacy as the undisputed central, and often exclusive, target of elementary education has definitely changed the landscape. We and our classroom colleagues find that this literacy focus in our elementary schools sometimes threatens to exclude teaching and learning in other content areas. Our teachers often miss the rewards and challenges of weaving science, social studies, and humanities teaching into their classroom instruction as they struggle to fit it all in. Luckily for them, for their students, and for us, creative planning and a genuine understanding of national, state, and local literacy standards allows us to engage our teaching colleagues and their students in meaningful standards-based collaborative units that will allow them to keep literacy and English language arts standards at the center while exploring other content areas and meeting those standards as well. Best of all, we can stir in a good dose of essential technology and information literacy skills our students will need throughout their education and have a great time in the process.

If you turn to the Matrix of Learning Activities by Content Standard at the front of this book, you will see that each unit included in Chapter Six covers a variety of content area standards. Choose your targets and get ready to adopt or adapt a fabulous unit submitted by practicing library media specialists and their collaborative teaching partners.

In the five years during which the first edition of *Collaborating to Meet Standards: Teacher/Librarian Partnerships for K-6* has been read and used by so many practicing and aspiring collaborative teaching teams, I have been delighted to hear, again and again, how helpful it has been for its readers. Writing the second edition has been exciting as I have anticipated the ways in which the content will help you to transform your practice or extend your currently successful collaborative teaching.

As always, this book is written for practicing elementary school library media specialists and their teaching partners. It is both a guide to collaboration and a collection of models of best practice, with a collection of fourteen excellent standards-based units written in a standardized template that you can borrow, adapt, and use in your own collaboration efforts. In addition, there are four meaty introductory chapters that include a round-up of opinions, research, and philosophy from the library literature--and from working library media professionals--about collaboration and, in this volume as in *Collaborating to Meet Literacy Standards: Teacher/Librarian Partnerships for K-2*, about literacy as well. It also includes practical suggestions for the implementation of collaboration and working around the roadblocks.

Chapter One takes a look back at the history of collaboration from Loertscher's taxonomies to Library Power and *Information Power*. Chapter Two looks closely at our age of literacy and the library media program, from initiatives and legislation to the role of the library media specialist. Chapter Three examines the definitions and benefits—to administrators, to teachers, to library media specialists, and above all, to students—of collaboration and the studies that have proven its value, quantitatively. In Chapter Four, you will read about the factors necessary for success and the keys to overcoming roadblocks, including current roadblocks posed by national legislation and the introduction of new literacy and classroom instructional time mandates. Included are the stories of many practicing library media specialists who have struggled and succeeded with sticky scheduling problems, overwhelmed teaching partners, and challenging school cultures. I hope they will inspire you. Remember, if necessary, you can even work with restrictions.

Following the introductory chapters, you will find a common template for use in planning collaborative units. It is clear, comprehensive, and easy to use. It is the template used in the wealth of standards-based collaborative units contributed by library media specialist-and-teacher teams all over the United States that follow. Six of these units are superb revisions of excellent units from the first edition. The other eight are new and original in this edition. These units are examples of best work, best thinking, and best practice. I encourage you to adopt them in whole or in part or adapt and adjust them (in time or in content) for your particular population. The Matrix of Learning Activities by Content Standard will allow you to search these units by grade level and content standard areas while an index will allow you to search the concepts and ideas in the introductory chapters.

As you read, I invite you to learn more about improved collaborative practice in order to affect student achievement in your school and employ standards-based collaborative units that address literacy as well as learning in many other content areas in meaningful and engaging ways. Finally, I wish you fun, excitement, and new energy in your teaching.

Resources

American Association of School Librarians and Association for Educational Communication. *Information Power: Building Partnerships for Learning.* Chicago: American Library Association, 1998.

Chapter One

Where We've Been— Where We're Going

New Roles

We have been at school librarianship for over a century now, since our career began at the turn of the twentieth century. Yet, for the past fifty years, we have struggled to find and stay the best course. That we have made enormous strides is clear, if one harkens back to the dusty book rooms of former days. Luckily, by the mid-twentieth century, the traditional role of the school librarian as "keeper of the books" had begun to change. AASL standards published in 1960 and 1969 contributed to this change, and by 1975, the publication of the AASL standards, *Media Programs: District and School*, identified two instructional roles: design and consultation. (6) As a designer of instruction, the librarian was charged with initiating and participating in curriculum development. As a consultant, the librarian was to recommend media applications for instruction (Pickard n. pag.). Jane Bandy Smith reports that during the 1970's our profession began to think seriously about the ineffective nature of our instructional efforts:

> Through study and experimentation, several important principles were discovered.
> ■ Information skills are best learned in the context of coursework.
> ■ A flexible schedule is more conducive to skill acquisition and application.
> ■ Collaborative planning ensures skills are learned and applied.
>   Library media specialists believe these three principles are valid, but
> many teachers and administrators do not know or do not accept them (60).

The Taxonomies

By 1982, the three elements of the library media program—traditional library services, audiovisual services, and instructional development—combined to create a new view of the role of the library media specialist (Loertscher, "The Second Revolution" 417). A variety of models for instructional development and design began to appear in the literature simultaneously with the first publication of Loertscher's library media specialist taxonomy in 1982. Collaboration had been formally named as a goal and has held sway in library literature ever since.

The 2000 revision of the taxonomy, published in *Taxonomies of the School Library Media Program*, 2nd edition, includes ten levels of involvement.

The Library Media Specialist's Taxonomy
by David V. Loertscher

1. **NO INVOLVEMENT**
   The LMC is bypassed entirely.

2. **SMOOTHLY OPERATING INFORMATION INFRASTRUCTURE**
   Facilities, materials, networks, and information resources are available for the self-starter delivered to the point of need.

3. **INDIVIDUAL REFERENCE ASSISTANCE**
   The library media specialist serves as the human interface between information systems and the user.

4. **SPONTANEOUS INTERACTION AND GATHERING**
   Networks respond 24 hours a day and 7 days a week to patron requests, and the LMC facilities can be used by individuals and small groups with no advance notice.

5. **CURSORY PLANNING**
   There is informal and brief planning with teachers and students for LMC facilities or network usage—usually done through casual contact in the LMC, in the hall, in the teacher's lounge, in the lunch room, or by e-mail. [For example: Here's an idea for an activity/Web site/new materials to use. Have you seen . . .? There's a software upgrade on the network.]

6. **PLANNED GATHERING**
   Gathering of materials/access to important digital resources is done in advance of a class project upon teacher or student request.

7. **EVANGELISTIC OUTREACH/ADVOCACY**
   A concerted effort is made to promote the philosophy of the LMC program.

8. **IMPLEMENTATION OF THE FOUR MAJOR PROGRAMMATIC ELEMENTS OF THE LMC PROGRAM**
   The four LMC program elements—
   > **collaboration,**
   > **reading literacy,**
   > **enhancing learning through technology,** and
   > **information literacy—**
   are operational in the school. The LMC is on its way to achieving its goal of contributing to academic achievement.

9. **THE MATURE LMC PROGRAM**
   The LMC program reaches the needs of every student and teacher who will accept its offerings in each of the four programmatic elements.

10. **CURRICULUM DEVELOPMENT**
    Along with other educators, the library media specialist contributes to the planning and organization of what will actually be taught in the school or district (Loertscher 17).

Reprinted here with permission from Dr. David V. Loertscher.

In his February 1982 *Wilson Library Bulletin* article, "The Second Revolution: A Taxonomy for the 1980s," Loertscher emphasized the merits of each level, saying there was no need for guilt. He felt that the first necessary step was to accept the entire list as a collection of legitimate roles of instructional involvement, each level being "good" (417-418).

Yet, the higher one goes on the taxonomy, the more collaborative is the relationship between teacher and library media specialist. While a brand new LMS in a building might work slowly to build from Level One to Six, during her inaugural years at a school (with an ever present dose of Level Seven Evangelistic Outreach), it is Levels Eight through Ten that hint at and then extend the role of "instructional consultant" first introduced in the 1988 AASL *Information Power: Guidelines for School Library Media Programs* document (26) to true collaboration. In other words, as Pickard pointed out in 1993, we were advised by our professional organization to stop being reactive, as described in Levels Three through Eight, and become proactive, as required by Levels Nine and Ten (n. pag.).

Josephine Dervan, Library Media Specialist, Strathmore School, Aberdeen, New Jersey

"ANY attempt toward collaboration with classroom teachers on the part of the librarian is a good one. That attempt should be showcased and talked up to use as an example of how we can work with the classroom teacher toward the common goal: producing literate students who can process and synthesize information properly.

So please do not despair if your initial efforts at collaboration are not on the highest levels of Loertscher's *Taxonomy*. Just keep your ears open for collaboration opportunities, offer to help your staff, and be flexible. You may be surprised how quickly other teachers will be interested in your help once they learn that you are available to help them" (n. pag.).

National Library Power Program

In 1988, through the National Library Power Program, the DeWitt Wallace-Reader's Digest Fund granted monies to New York City Public Schools to create library programs that improved the quality of education. By 1998, the program had been implemented at 19 sites (700 schools) nationwide serving more than one million children with an investment of over $40 million.

Collaborative planning was a major focus of Library Power professional development training sessions. In fact, the Library Power grant required that a site establish a totally flexible library program that employed collaborative planning. The fourth of six goals was to "Encourage collaboration among teachers, administrators, and librarians that results in improved teaching and learning" ("Library Power: A Report to the Community" n. pag.). Rusty Taylor, lead library media coordinator of Wake County Public Schools Media Services and formerly library media coordinator at the Aldert Root Elementary School, a Library Power school in Raleigh, North Carolina, says:

> Although funding from our Wake Education Partnership ended in 1998, we definitely have a Library Power legacy. When we started the Library Power program, only 7 of our 55 elementary schools had flexible access [a key factor in ensuring collaboration in elementary schools]—this year we have 88 elementary schools, and 78 have full or primarily flexible schedules—yet the actual four years of DeWitt Wallace funding affected only 20 of our elementaries (n. pag.).

According to Rhonda Butt and Christine Jameson, Library Power "became a formidable driving force for initiating and continuing support for professional collaboration between library media specialists and their classroom teachers" (n. pag.). And experience proved that the effects lasted long after the grant guidelines ended.

Collaboration and Information Power

During the decade from 1988 to 1998, the three roles of the library media specialist from *Information Power: Guidelines for School Library Media Programs*:

- ■ information specialist
- ■ teacher
- ■ instructional consultant (26)

had grown. When *Information Power: Building Partnerships for Learning* was published in 1998, four roles were recommended:

- ■ teacher;
- ■ instructional partner;
- ■ information specialist;
- ■ program administrator (4-5).

The old "instructional consultant" role had been replaced with the updated term "instruction and curriculum partner." The "consultant" role of the 1988 document was outdated, inferring an unequal status, with the library media specialist more qualified than other teachers on the planning team (Muronaga and Harada 9). Partnership, on the other hand, implies equal status and participation.

Diana Heimbrook, Media Specialist at Carver Elementary School in Florence, South Carolina (see sidebar) considers herself an instructional partner rather than a consultant. As Heimbrook points out, we've come a long way in this evolutionary process. By the turn of the twenty-first century, across the nation, library media specialists were actively involved in collaboration, working as equal partners with collaborative teachers to plan units of study that would be team-designed, team-taught, and team-evaluated. Then, a new age dawned, an age we might easily have construed as the answer to our dearest wishes, had we not encountered a complex reality. The age of literacy arose, and with it, a myriad of challenges for school librarianship, and particularly, collaborative practice.

Debra Gniewek, Librarian, CRHS South, Holland, Pennsylvania

"In my former school, PK-8 with 1100 students, we had a Library Power Grant. Teachers had to collaborate with me at least once a month. (We did this in grade groups during a common prep.) Because of a very strong teacher contract, the teachers were paid for lost prep time for that period. When the grant ran out and the prep payment stopped, all but one teacher continued the practice voluntarily" (n. pag.).

Debra Heimbrook, Media Specialist, Unit 1: Kinder Quest

"An instructional consultant means that the educational stakeholders (students, teachers, administrators, and staff) might ask for resources or ideas, but the media specialist is not part of planning. The media specialist is on the outside of the educational circle. An instructional partner means the media specialist is part of the educational circle, involved in curriculum and lesson planning and is an integral part of the process. Media specialists have evolved from the consultant to the partner role through understanding and practicing the integration of standards, resources, technology, and lesson planning with the teachers. Students have the opportunity to experience richer instruction when the media specialist and the classroom teacher work together in a collaborative process to provide resources and activities that meet curriculum standards." (n. pag.)

2

Collaboration, Literacy, and School Library Media Programs

What is Literacy?

Nowadays, we hear the word literacy on every educational news segment on radio or television, discuss it in nearly every educational conversation we engage in, and read it in nearly every educational article we encounter. Federal *No Child Left Behind* (*NCLB*) legislation enacted in 2001 put literacy center stage in American schools, American media, American homes.

Literacy Definitions

But what is literacy? Unfortunately, there is no single definition. *The American Heritage Dictionary of the English Language* defines literacy as "the quality of being literate, especially the ability to read and write." (Note that "literate" here has, as one of its meanings, "knowledgeable; educated"). And, indeed, the ability to read and write is at the heart of most traditional definitions of literacy. The United States Department of Education in its 2003 study of adult literacy published by the National Center for Education Statistics defines adult literacy as the ability to use "printed and written information to function in society, to achieve one's goals, and to develop one's knowledge and potential" ("Learner Outcomes: Adult Literacy" n. pag.).

Pam Wright, Library Media Specialist, The June Shelton School, Dallas, Texas

"Literacy is knowing what you do not know and how to find the answer when you want to know it. Not a traditional definition but I've always thought that being truly literate means that one realizes the limit of his literacy and can use prior knowledge to build a bridge to understanding" (n. pag.).

But do these definitions apply to children, especially young children? Some would say not. The Minnesota Early Literacy Training Project Center for Early Education and Development at the University of Minnesota, defines literacy as "the ability to talk, read, write, leading to the ability to communicate and learn" and the Public Library Association, in their initiative Every Child Ready to Read @ your library® offers a brochure for parents (*Early Literacy Begins with You*) that takes a step even further back in time to define early literacy as "what children know about reading and writing before they can actually read or write" (n. pag.).

Real Literacy Versus Decoding

Sharon M. Pitcher and Bonnie Mackey remark that 'real literacy' encompasses "literacy skills and strategies that are explicitly taught to children, who in turn can independently use these skills in their everyday lives. Children will naturally apply these strategies when taking any kind of assessment" (1). Yet academics and scholars worry that the "political" focus on literacy has limited its definition to the more mechanical work of decoding and encoding written language with a focus on transmission of knowledge from teacher to student, ignoring the wider and richer experience we know children have in early literacy. Iris Berger laments this circumstance.

> Unfortunately, a narrow definition of early literacy results not only in limitation to literacy instruction, but most importantly, as the quote above suggests, it inevitably leads to a limited and narrow view of literacy and learning by young children. It is ironic that early literacy—which was a term originally coined to reflect young children's intuitive capacities to learn and develop an understanding of the complex conceptual foundation for literacy learning without being formally taught—is now equated with the acquisition of basic literacy skills (n. pag.).

It is an interesting dilemma and one that points to the problem many elementary library media specialists face today. We—and our libraries—are being left out of the "literacy loop." And as we all know, that should not be.

There is certainly one place the library media specialist comes into the literacy equation. There can be many more, as well, as I will discuss in the following sections. Senator Barack Obama summarizes the importance of literacy, however we define it, but certainly to include the ability to read, in the article based on his speech delivered at the American Library Association 2005 annual conference in Chicago.

> Because I believe that if we want to give our children the best possible chance in life, if we want to open the doors of opportunity while they're young and teach them the skills they'll need to succeed later on, then one of our greater responsibilities as citizens, as educators and as parents is to insure that every American child can read, and read well. That's because **literacy is the most basic currency of the knowledge economy that we're living in today** (50).

Literacy in the Age of Standards

Of course, the focus on literacy is not simply a result of the *NCLB* legislation. Rather, it began with the standards movement in education. While there are standards written for every content area of the curriculum including English language arts, many schools and districts encouraged primary teachers to focus more closely on those reading, writing, listening, and speaking standards (along with mathematics standards) in their classrooms before moving on to the content areas. That focus then spread, in many schools, to the intermediate grades as well. We now hear many elementary teachers across the grades lament that there is no longer time in the day for science, social studies, or the humanities, as so much time is dedicated to literacy instruction.

Additionally, in its 2000 report, the National Reading Panel synthesized research on reading instruction and identified five essential components of effective reading instruction:

- phonics
- phonemic awareness
- vocabulary
- fluency
- comprehension

and determined that "to ensure that children learn to read well, explicit and systematic instruction must be provided in these five areas" ("Reading First" n. pag.). When its findings were later adopted by the *NCLB* Act (which supports scientifically based reading instruction programs in the early grades) as the basis for reading instruction, the change in reading instruction and the literacy focus in schools was complete.

Literacy Model

"Balanced Literacy"

A Research Based Approach

With the advent of *NCLB*, "balanced literacy" is American education's attempt to bring together reading research with tried-and-true or much-beloved past practices in literacy instruction. As Robyn M. Prince notes, balanced literacy is not just equal doses of phonics and whole language, stirred together. It is a research-based, integrative approach that responds to the literacy needs of individual students (27). In balanced literacy, attention to the five essential components is combined with authentic experiences in reading, writing, speaking, and listening. What results, educators hope, is a model of literacy that integrates all effective approaches.

 Jane E. Danielsons, Library Media Specialist, Veterans and Stowell Elementary Schools, Hannibal, Missouri

"One of the things that has happened as a result of balanced literacy is the use of a common language. For example: the teachers tell the kids to look for 'Just Right Books' and talk about how to choose using the five-finger test. We all also use SSR in library and in the classroom. Read alouds are frequent, so teachers are always looking for books. We have small children who come in almost daily to find another book... especially K-1" (n. pag.).

Professors Timothy Rasinski and Nancy Padak of the Kent State University Reading and Writing Center note the consensus among literacy scholars regarding balanced literacy and its effectiveness in improving student achievement in reading:

> In the spring of 2000, the National Reading Panel issued its long-awaited report, which appears to confirm what advocates of a balanced approach to literacy instruction have been saying—we need to try to provide students with a comprehensive approach to reading instruction, one that is more than authentic and holistic and more than skills-based. The panel noted that phonemic awareness, phonics and decoding, fluency in reading, and reading comprehension were important parts of the total reading process in the elementary grades and need to be emphasized in instruction (92).

The Affective Dimension of Reading

Yet Rasinski and Padak worry that "Even so-called 'balanced' reading programs do little to promote the affective dimension of reading," a dimension they define as "the love and appreciation for reading, writing, and the written word—a love that will span the school years and remain with students into their adult lives. This is no easy task, yet it is essential to a comprehensive literacy approach" (95-96). Interestingly, this is an essential element of the library media specialist's role in literacy education in the school.

Literacy Promotion Activities

Prince makes suggestions for the role of the LMS in the balanced literacy program. First, she suggests that we assist teachers in developing classroom libraries (a delicate matter that involves first ensuring that the school understands that classroom libraries do not supplant school libraries and serve a very different purpose). In order to guide teacher selections, Prince suggests that we host book open houses to share new materials (or, I would add, to introduce potential resources vendors have brought to share), design and present booktalks of new children's books to teachers, write and publish newsletters regarding excellent read-alouds and books to be checked out from the school library media center for the classroom library, and provide subscriptions to children's literature journals such as *Book Links*, *Bookbag*, and *Horn Book* (28).

She also suggests that we support balanced literacy by providing book talks for students, creating displays such as bulletin boards about themed books and popular topics, promote literary award winners and best books lists, deliver "book ads" during school announcements, sponsor book clubs, and encourage involvement in book award programs (28-29). Those looking for even more suggestions of ways to be intricately and specifically involved in shaping early literacy instruction will find a wealth of concrete suggestions to accompany each of the balanced literacy components in Bonnie Mackey and Maureen White's excellent article "Conversations, Collaborations, and Celebrations."

It is important, of course, for us to balance these "literacy promotion" activities with collaborative instruction. I have known many enthusiastic school librarians who are the primary literacy advocates in their schools but who, in order to fulfill that role, have set aside the collaborative teaching of information literacy skills. Beware of the necessary balance, even as literacy reigns supreme in your school. If you reflect carefully on your allocation of time, it is possible to do it all and to do it all well, for the benefit of your students.

The Four-Blocks® Literacy Model

A Literacy Framework for the Classroom

The Four-Blocks® Literacy Model is an example of a balanced literacy program that was developed by Dr. Patricia Cunningham and Dr. Dorothy Hall. This literacy framework incorporates four different approaches each day to teach children how to become better readers, writers, and spellers:

- Guided Reading
- Self-selected Reading
- Writing
- Working With Words

and acknowledges that not all children learn in the same way.

Four Blocks is a Framework for Reading and Writing that includes all the components of a comprehensive instructional program. We include teacher read-aloud and independent reading during the Self-Selected Reading Block. Comprehension instruction is included during Guided Reading. Phonics, including phonemic awareness, is taught during Working With Words. Fluency is developed as children learn to read and spell high-frequency words during the Word Wall activity and when we do Repeated Readings during Guided Reading. Writing instruction is included during the Writing block. Meaning vocabulary is taught during Guided Reading, especially when we include material during Guided Reading related to science and social studies. Meaning vocabulary is also developed during Self-Selected Reading as children listen to what the teacher reads aloud and engage in regular independent reading (Cunningham, Cunningham, and Allington n. pag.).

Rasinski and Padak report that such frameworks have been "demonstrated to lead to significantly positive outcomes in the primary grades. In the Four Blocks, students spend two hours per day in the reading curriculum. The two-hour block of time is divided into thirty minute segments that are devoted to self-selected reading, guided reading, word study, and writing" (92).

A Supportive Role for the LMS

Again, the library media specialist can play important roles in the Four-Blocks® Literacy Model as detailed by Cheryl M. Sigmon. She suggests that "media specialists can be critical to the success of

Vicki Krebsbach, Library Media Specialist, Wilderness Oak Elementary School, San Antonio, Texas

"It is critical that the LMS is familiar with the four components of the Four-Blocks® Literacy Model. Collaborating with the teacher and reading specialist to provide scaffolding in that instruction makes us partners in the 'bread and butter' of the language arts block. When we serve as partners in the role of reading instruction, the lesson and visit to the library is not perceived as an extra, or just a story time. I really do address all four quadrants in my library program as do the other librarians in my district. Our expertise in literature and literacy skills truly compliments and enhances the model. As a result, each component can have an effect on the library program and the role of the LMS" (n. pg).

4-Blocks in a school" and goes on to say, "When the partnership is strong between teachers and the media specialist, implementation can be so much easier and so much more effective" (n. pag.). She suggests that LMS's keep teachers updated on good read-alouds for the SSR block (as well as modeling read-aloud techniques at staff meetings), do the read-aloud portion of Self-Selected Reading block for classes on a rotating basis, help teachers decide on books for SSR or supply library books for individual book baskets, help with selections for the Guided Reading Block by making recommendations and housing multiple copies in the library, and furnish text for the Working with Words block (for example, rhyming texts or other texts that allow them to explore reading at the word level) (n. pag.).

An Instructional Role for the LMS

However, what I notice as I read the reflections of "reading" people, such as Sigmon, on the role of the library media specialist in the new literacy is that we are largely a) relegated to support for teachers, rather than collaborative partners, and b) primarily purveyors of reading materials rather than integral collaborative partners in reading instruction. It is up to us to take a meaningful role in Four-Blocks® as Krebsbach suggests (see sidebar), to determine the balance between our roles, and to seriously consider the effect each of our efforts has on student learning and achievement.

 Mary Birkett, Teacher-librarian, Richard Kane Elementary School, Bartlesville, Oklahoma

"My school has used Four-Blocks® as a framework for reading and writing instruction for the past several years. It is difficult to schedule classes in the library because the primary grades do their Four-Blocks® programming in the mornings. Consequently, everyone wants afternoon times—as if what we do in the library isn't related to reading which is part of the four blocks approach. My teachers are receptive when I suggest ideas for lessons that introduce or complement concepts included in reading, writing, or word study, but they still prefer to have me present the lessons outside of their usual Four-Block® time. They are not cooperative about sharing the teaching with me but often point out things I can do to reinforce topics they have covered in class" (n. pag.).

 Melissa P. Johnston, Media Specialist, Silver City Elementary, Cumming, Georgia

"It is up to the media specialist to play a proactive role in the Four-Block® program. It is crucial to educate yourself, learn the components of this program and then determine where you can provide support and instructional input. It is not only our role as media specialists to provide materials to support the Four-Block® program, but to work with teachers as instructional partners in the teaching of reading. The teaching of reading is one of our most important roles as school library media specialists. I plan and partner with the teachers to provide valuable instruction for students on the various reading comprehension strategies that they are working on in their classrooms. It is always helpful for students to hear something a different way and from a different person to reinforce learning and help make that connection for them" (n. pag.).

The Historic Role of Librarians in Literacy

Partners in Literacy

To be honest, of course, the roles mentioned by "reading people" were our traditional roles in literacy. We *were* the support team. We *were* the purveyors. We *were* sometimes the nearly-invisible element in schools. But that is no longer true. Today, we are partners in literacy. We do not just review the books, buy the books, catalog the books, shelve the books, circulate the books, dust the books, provide stacks of the books to teachers. Carol Simpson defines our changing role as a move from warehousing to consulting.

> School librarians expand their areas of influence to include the classroom when they collaborate with classroom teachers to meet the information needs of students. Moving beyond the "warehouse concept" of traditional libraries, librarians strike out into classrooms/departments to consult with classroom teachers. Suggesting resources, locating and acquiring needed materials, recommending strategies, facilitating use of technologies, and instructing students and teachers in optimal information-seeking methods replace the traditional librarian tasks of material circulation ("The School Librarian's Role in the Electronic Age" n. pag.).

We connect the contents of the books with their best readers and work collaboratively with our teachers to design units of study that incorporate literacy learning and meet content standards in information literacy as well as English language arts and other content areas. However, as the National Board for Professional Teaching Standards (NBPTS) points out:

> Today's library media specialists resemble the librarians of the past in at least one respect: They work to instill in their students a love of reading and a penchant for discovery. They teach students that reading is essential to learning and to success in life and that it is a fun and worthwhile activity in and of itself" (1).

And there we come full circle back to the point that Rasinski and Padak make about promoting the affective dimension of reading. Pitcher and Mackey say, "Lifelong literacy is what 'real literacy' is all about. Librarians provide literacy coordination and support that can make a big difference in changing the literacy focus of a school" (1). It is an important part of our mission, to be sure.

Lesley Levine, Library Media Specialist, Bedford Village Elementary School, Bedford, New York

"I do my part in supporting and supplementing the reading initiative in the district. I develop the collection to accommodate teachers' lessons, and I encourage the love of reading, literature and libraries in everybody that walks through my doors. By making the library a safe and emotionally comfortable place, books are sure to become friends to every child in my building. And that can only lead to good things from here on in!" (n. pag.).

The Library-Literacy Connection

How do LMS's fit into the literacy equation with the new emphasis on test scores, basic literacy, and accountability, one might wonder. I believe that in this age of high-stakes-testing, we make a critical error in disconnecting reading and literacy from the library. In order to love to read—and to read well—students require ready access to an excellent library collection that includes books in all genres and subject areas of appeal. The student who cannot read "at grade level" on a test may be the same student who is quite able to read an informational text such as a technical manual several "grade levels" above his when fixing the engine of a beloved car. Open access to libraries and active partnership between teachers and library media specialists will ensure that all of our students can and WILL read as adults. In fact, in *Texas School Libraries: Standards, Resources, Services, and Students' Performance*, Esther G. Smith reports, "Across all schools, 10 percent more students in schools with librarians achieved minimum TAAS (Texas Assessment of Academic Skills) expectations in reading than their peers in schools without librarians" ("School Libraries and Their Impact on Student Performance" n. pag). Again, our involvement in reading instruction makes a difference in our students' literacy levels.

Reading and Information Literacy

Furthermore, Carol Simpson notes that "the librarian has a storehouse of information. Information is the stock-in-trade of the librarian. While it is true that one who cannot read cannot access the information, it is also true that even those who can read well are not always intelligent consumers of information" ("Damned If You Don't" 8). Thus, the American Association of School Librarians *Position Statement on Resource Based Instruction: Role of the School Library Media Specialist in Reading Development* states that "The responsibility for successful implementation of reading development is shared by the entire school community—teachers, library media specialists, and administrators working together (n. pag)." It goes on to say that one of the elements integral to an effective reading program is that "Teachers and library media specialists share responsibility for reading and information literacy instruction. They plan and teach collaboratively based on the needs of the student" (n. pag.). The point made here is that reading and information literacy are married in collaborative practice between teachers and LMS's, which goes well beyond the historic role of the library media specialist.

The Changing Role of the Library Media Specialist in Literacy

A New Role for a New Era

Member of the Reading Team

So where are we now? What is our role in our educational world when basic literacy drives elementary education and test scores are beacons against which success is measured? Simpson notes that some advocate joining the "reading team," putting extra value on raising reading scores, since that is the currency of the day, and studies link strong library programs to reading achievement. They suggest making ourselves indispensable in this way so that teachers will not allow our positions to be eliminated. She ruminates about whether we should drop teaching information literacy all together and start teaching decoding. Anyone who knows Simpson and her firebrand approach to librarianship knows that this questioning is purely rhetorical. No, of course we should not. But, she agrees, we must document the impact we have on reading skills, let our communities hear about that impact, and join "the team."

No Librarian Left Behind

It will not be all that we do, of course, but if we are wise, we will "emphasize those highly visible efforts in the essential areas required by *NCLB*" so that *we* are not left behind. As Simpson says, "You're either there, or you aren't" ("Damned if You Don't" 8). And in an intriguing intellectual exercise, Christine Walker commands us, "Ask yourself—am I the gate keeper or the keymaster when it comes to unlocking the mysteries of reading for students?" (46). There is so much to juggle as we think about where we are now, whether we are doing precisely what we need to be doing to impact literacy while teaching collaboratively with our classroom and special area colleagues, and what our next steps might be.

Reading Achievement

Keith Curry Lance, our guru of student achievement studies and director of the Library Research Service, a unit of the Colorado State Library operated in partnership with the University of Denver's Library and Information Services Department, has significant findings to offer about reading achievement and the role of librarians and libraries.

> How much will a school's test scores improve with specific improvements in its library media program? The answer depends on the program's current status, what it improves, and how much it is improved. When library media predictors are maximized, reading scores tend to run 10 to 18 percent higher ("Libraries and Student Achievement" 9).

Certainly, an increase of reading scores by 10 to 18 percent will be meaningful to our administrators and teachers if they know. Gail Bush advises that we focus our efforts on informing our school communities about our impact. "We must make our role in reading development visible to the school learning community so that it is understood that support for the school library equals support for student achievement" (51).

Even the International Reading Association agrees that we are an essential component in the literacy effort in schools. The *In Support of Credentialed Library Media Professionals in School Library Media Centers* resolution states:

> WHEREAS, credentialed school library media professionals promote, inspire, and guide students toward a love of reading, a quest for knowledge, and a thirst for lifelong learning; promote creative and effective teaching; collaborate with classroom teachers to plan, design, deliver, and evaluate instruction using a variety of resources and information technology; provide leadership, expertise, and advocacy in the use of technology, print, and electronic resources; and manage the selection of, acquisition of, and access to high quality learning resources, be it therefore
> RESOLVED, that the International Reading Association recognizes the need for credentialed library media professionals and support personnel in schools worldwide (n. pag.).

We can be the heart of the reading program for the school, as Bush recommends (17). But it requires us to be proactive, to step forward to meet the task head on. The NBPTS states it strongly. "Accomplished library media specialists take an active role in promoting and advocating for a forward-looking approach to literacy that embraces the power and potential of information, multimedia, and technology" (2). In the changing role of the library media specialist in literacy, we must be:

- builders of quality collections for the LMC and the classroom;
- cheerleaders and promoters of the love of reading;
- creators and leaders of joyful reading environments and literacy centers;
- collaborative partners and knowledgeable teachers;
- designers of collaborative literacy engagements.

Builder of Quality Collections for the LMC and the Classroom

Quality Collections across the School

In keeping with our historic role as librarians, it is still our mandate, and an important aspect of our jobs as members of the reading "team," to build quality collections in our libraries. A newer aspect of the job is to help teachers and administrators to build quality classroom collections as well. Thus, when the American Association of School Librarians' *Position Statement on the Value of Independent Reading in the School Library Media Program* lists seven items necessary in order for students to become life-long readers, the first of these is "access to current, quality, high interest, and extensive collections of books and other print materials in their library media centers, classrooms, and public libraries" (n. pag.).

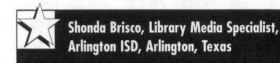

Shonda Brisco, Library Media Specialist, Arlington ISD, Arlington, Texas

"Our ultimate goal in collection development is to bring the world to our children, one book at a time. Building a library collection is more than aligning titles with the curriculum; it's also aligning the student with the world. Library collections should reflect more than just the curriculum; they should reflect the opportunities, interests, dreams, and goals of the students who use them" (n. pag.).

Even Secretary of Education Margaret Spellings acknowledges the essential nature of our role as builders of quality collections for the library and the classroom. "One of the main goals of *No Child Left Behind* is ensuring that all children learn to read on grade level by the 3rd grade and ensuring older students who are behind reach grade level. School libraries play a crucial role by providing children with books and resources so that they can strengthen their reading skills and achieve at high levels" (28).

Quality Collections across the Genres

In our role as Builder of Quality Collections, we will inevitably create rich print and electronic collections of materials to support the collaborative units we design, teach, and evaluate with our teaching colleagues. And if our collections are to serve the increasing attention paid to informational texts in reading instruction, we will develop strong nonfiction collections. Of course, building quality collections also goes beyond supporting the content areas of the curriculum. It speaks, as well, to meeting the personal reading interests of our students too.

The U.S. National Commission on Libraries and Information Science concurs. In a recent letter to President George W. Bush in support of school libraries, Chairman C. Beth Fitzsimmons writes:

> School library collections inform, educate, entertain and enrich students at all levels. They provide additional sources appropriate for a broad range of interests and reading levels. When children are able to read stories and explore information that is meaningful and appealing to them,

they not only learn faster but their library skills grow rapidly; they *learn how to learn* (n. pag.).

Quality Collections to Inspire

Most library media specialists understand the wisdom here immediately. We know that students become excited about reading when there is a wealth of reading material (particularly as a result of the work of Stephen D. Krashen in *Power of Reading: Insights from the Research.* 2nd ed.), when the books are new, when the topics of the books appeal to students' personal interests, and when there is adequate time devoted to self-selected reading of all of these materials. We cannot always control the time devoted to self-selected reading in our schools, but we have an enormous amount to offer in relation to the other three requirements. As Donna Shannon says, "While easily decodable texts can develop fluency, one cannot minimize a child's interests or preferences as motivational factors. After all, unless children see books as appealing, they may lose interest in or develop negative attitudes toward reading" (17).

I agree. It is about more than giving children leveled books—the ubiquitous "stapled" books. 'Just right' is not only about reading level. It is also about a child's experience, his knowledge, his interests and passions, his sense of himself as a reader and thinker and imaginer. A wise library media specialist can guide each reader to his own 'just right' book every day—a book that will make him curious or joyful or sad or smart, a book that will make him think and grow. And once the child has that 'just right' book in hand, we can engage him in conversation that lets him know that there are riches to be found there, intellectual and emotional journeys that are worth taking.

Chief Cheerleader and Promoter of the Love of Reading

The second aspect of our changing role as school library media specialists is not at all an unfamiliar one—to be the chief reading cheerleader and promoter of the love of reading in our schools. *NCLB* has mandated that all students *will* learn to read, which, of course, is a worthy goal. While we support learning to read *and* reading to learn in our role as educators, we have an additional responsibility. With the intense literacy focus that has taken hold of our schools, sometimes the joy students might take in reading has disappeared, or at least its flame is hidden a bit under the barrel of accountability. Therefore, in the best of situations, we are the one to whom all members of the community turn when they want to revel in talk about books, when they want to find books they will love, when they want inspiration and guidance about when, where, why, or what to read. Bush says it well when she remarks, "In the school library, we are in a position to feed the hunger for good stories and to try to satisfy each of our students' reading appetites" (32). As chief

 Hilda Weisburg, Co-editor of *School Librarians Workshop*

"I trust the classroom teachers to teach student HOW to read, and the reading teachers to help those who are challenged. It has always been my job to inspire a LOVE of reading—for that is what makes lifelong readers. We know that "kids who read, succeed." As Stephen Krashen keeps reminding us – the reading can take many forms, but young people need to be surrounded by a print rich environment—and in my opinion, a school library media specialist's love of reading is infectious. We share our favorites and encourage kids to talk with us about which ones they love. We don't just booktalk—we talk books" (n. pag.).

cheerleaders, it is our job to keep books front and center in our schools, not simply as objects filled with words to be decoded, but more importantly as treasures to be loved.

Ideas for Cheerleading in Your Library

How do we go about this job of cheerleading in our schools and libraries? Donna Reed suggests that we actively promote reading and raise our circulation statistics to boot. To that end, she offers some excellent suggestions:

- Allow more book checkouts. Who says your first graders can only check out one book? You do. So it is equally within your power to decide to allow first graders to check out five books (or ten). In addition, move books in and out of your library and into the hands of your readers by encouraging more frequent library visits.

- If you are on a flexible schedule (see Chapter Four for more about scheduling), encourage small groups and individuals to come more often to exchange books.

- If you are on a fixed schedule, establish small open blocks when possible to accommodate regular book exchange between visits.

- Work on book promotion, including new and themed book displays, monthly reading contests, statewide book award programs, circulating collections to classrooms, and newsletter reviews and announcements to students, teachers, and parents (57).

Maintaining a Balance

Of course, once again, we must remain aware of balance in our roles. These book promotion efforts alone could take up all of our time, if we let them, and our collaborative work with teachers would suffer. However, if you are wise, you will find ways to promote books *through* your collaborations.

Reading Aloud

Another essential aspect of our cheerleading role is reading aloud. While we are not in the business of sacrificing the teaching of information literacy skills, I will admit that sometimes that teaching has crowded out what for many of us has been the pure pleasure of sharing books aloud with our students. Juggling all aspects of librarianship is not an easy task, but I would encourage you to find time each week, if not each day, to share a book with kids in your library. As a busy collaborating LMS myself, I rarely met with classes to share a story, so busy was I collaborating and teaching information literacy skills embedded in content area projects. Periodically, though, I held an impromptu read-aloud when I saw one or more small groups of students in the library selecting books and knew they were not on a tight leash for time. I would grab a favorite picture book—sometimes right out of a student's hand—and begin to share it aloud. Before long, a crowd gathered and we all felt the deep satisfaction of story brought to life in the hands and voice of a skilled reader.

Free Reading

Finally, do not forget free reading. Become a champion of free reading (SSR, DEAR, FRED) in your school. One of the most important points that Krashen makes in his writing is that free voluntary reading is just as powerful a tool in developing readers and writers as is direct instruction. "In-school free reading studies and 'out of school' self-reported free voluntary reading studies show that more reading results in better reading comprehension, writing style, vocabulary, spelling, and grammatical development" (17) .

In summary, as Kathy Hirsh-Pasek and Roberta Michnick Golinkoff proclaim, "A librarian can be so powerful! Librarians who recognize that learning to read begins with a love of books and stories can do wonders for encouraging children to develop the emergent literacy skills they will need to become lifelong readers" (68). We have it in our power to instill the joy of reading that is the beginning of a lifelong reading habit. Follow Bush's outspoken advice. "Be proud and loud about the joy of reading. None of this invisible librarian stuff when it comes to reading. Lay it all out there" (16).

Creator and Leader of a Joyful Reading Environment and Literacy Center

The library in my elementary school in Dearborn, Michigan was a long, dim, dusty slice of space at the end of the upstairs hall. I do not have any idea what was its intended use, but it was certainly not designed as a joyful reading environment and literacy center. Did I find books there? Certainly I did, because I knew about books and libraries from my experiences in my hometown public library, filled with the magic that a children's library can hold. But what of the non-readers or those new readers in need of enticement? Did that deeply shadowed sliver of a room do the job? I wonder even now, decades later.

Create a Joyful Reading Environment

But you need not wonder on behalf of your students, for another aspect of your new role as library media specialist in the age of literacy is to be creator and leader of a joyful reading environment and literacy center. Some of that involves physical space, of course, and making the best library you can with the geography you have been granted in your building, a space that is bright, cheerful, comfortable, and inviting. But it goes beyond walls and windows, flooring and furnishings, book shelves, computer stands, and media storage. What this is really about is an intrinsic atmosphere of excitement and possibility and wonder and books—plenty of books. Bush charges you with the task of providing "a learning environment that supports and encourages free voluntary reading for your entire school learning community" (35), a heaven and haven for book lovers and readers of all ages.

Why is this book haven essential to your readers? Rasinski and Padak express concern about the missing affective domain in regards to reading in our schools. Even in balanced literacy programs, they say, we do not promote the affective dimension of reading.

> Students who like to read and write will read and write more and, as a consequence of reading and writing, develop fluency and grow as readers and writers. A truly balanced and comprehensive literacy program, then, must help develop in students a love and appreciation for reading, writing, and the written word—a love that will span the school years and remain with students into their adult lives. This is no easy task, yet it is essential to a comprehensive literacy approach (95).

And Peter Afflerbach, professor and director of the Reading Center in the Department of Curriculum and Instruction at the University of Maryland at College Park sees an essential role for the library media specialist in all of this as we "support students in their growth as strategic readers by providing a rich array of engaging texts and reading environments that encourage students to practice and use reading strategies while reinforcing the notion for students that reading is engaging and valuable" (Bush 12). As a result, those strategic readers you cultivate will be all the more successful in the reading they engage in during collaborative instructional units that focus on reading and making meaning of informational text in nonfiction print and electronic resources.

Connect with Students

I ask you to consider a strong emphasis on cultivating reading motivation that rises from that love of reading that is internal and personal for each reader. We can do that by getting to know our students, by talking to them individually and learning what makes their readers' hearts beat faster, and by providing them with a comfortable place to browse for their 'just right' books and to sprawl out and read them. In addition, encourage them to sample many books on each visit, as many as time will allow, for the 2002 student achievement study entitled *Make the Connection: Quality School Library Media Programs Impact Academic Achievement in Iowa* found that, "Comparing Iowa's elementary schools with the highest and lowest ITBS reading scores, the highest scoring students use more than $2\frac{1}{2}$ times as many books and other materials during visits" (*School Libraries Work!* n. pag.).

Highlight Your Treasures

Work also to spread the word about the treasures in your collection. As you employ booktalks and book clubs, author visits and reader's choice programs, book and library week celebrations, it pays to remember what Krashen has to say. "We don't need pizza, testimonials from basketball players, or quizzes, points, and prizes to create readers, just classroom, school, and public libraries filled with good books, and teachers and librarians eager to share their enthusiasm for reading" (Bush 32).

Create a Presence

In fact, say Mackey and White, this age of literacy focus demands the presence of a library media specialist who creates an exciting environment for reading in the library.

> The varied and interlocking components of a balanced literacy program provide the perfect keys for collaboration between SLMSs and classroom teachers. The emphasis upon quality children's literature to be used during readalouds, shared reading, and independent reading times warrants the expertise of the SLMS. By modeling excellent literacy centers and reading strategies, the SLMS reinforces classroom instruction (33).

What it comes down to, of course, is enticement, excitement, and involvement of the reader.

Collaborative Partner and Knowledgeable Teacher

A tension has certainly been created by the literacy movement about the role of the library media specialist beyond builder of quality collections, literacy cheerleader, and creator of joyful reading environments. That tension comes into play in our collaborative teaching role, a role that can be eclipsed by the first three and *should not be*. We are, above all, teachers. Our mission is to teach collaboratively with our classroom teachers and specialists. Our domain is broad, as the thinking, searching, and application skills that we teach cross content areas. The reading that we advocate is both reading to enjoy and reading to learn.

Establish Your Instructional Role

Yet as Walker notes, we face hotly debated questions about our role in literacy instruction within our collaborative work. Some have staunchly resisted taking on the role of reading teacher. Others, unluckier by far, have been replaced by reading specialists in their districts. However, for some LMS's such as Ann Schuster (see sidebar) who have been elementary classroom teachers, there is little tension. Even for those who have not been classroom teachers, Walker makes the point that we all offer instinctive aid, since helping is inherent to our profession. "Where there are children who need support to read, we should follow our instinct." She adds, "Adapting our teaching strategies so we can help students learn to read better fits with what we are drawn to do naturally" (46).

 Ann Schuster, Library Media Specialist, Blue River Elementary School, Overland Park, Kansas

"There is nothing I enjoy more than sharing my love of reading. However, I also strongly believe that, after 12 years in the classroom and 20 as a library media specialist, my abilities to teach reading, as an integral part of my lessons, continue to be enhanced by the fact that I am a teaching librarian. I hope I am a better teacher (in reading as well as in other areas) today than I was 20 years ago." (n. pag.)

Address the Cognitive Domain

Bush, taking it a step further, suggests that we relinquish our exclusive focus on the affective domain of reading and turn to the cognitive domain with our classroom teachers in the context of "collaborative units that have a strong reading component and independent reading programs that offer students a variety of ways to engage in literacy" (9). In fact, she says, "The more we learn about reading strategies that are developmentally appropriate for our students, the more confident we will feel sharing the responsibility for reading and information literacy instruction" (12). Think, for instance, about the literacy value we offer when we teach students strategies for encountering informational text features and interpreting informational texts. Bush offers additional guidance in our efforts to embed reading strategies in our collaborative teaching, suggesting that we provide guided and independent work that supplies our students with opportunities to practice reading strategies they have learned, remain with a student after locating information to be sure that he/she can engage with the materials, model interacting with information and think aloud as you do so, provide developmentally appropriate graphic organizers (13), and discuss and explore new vocabulary (15).

There are many options to consider in our role as collaborative partner and knowledgeable teacher within the framework of literacy instruction. In making her point to President Bush about the importance of school libraries, Fitzsimmons offers an important analysis of our role.

> When school librarians collaborate with classroom teachers to enrich the curriculum content, they help to create more authentic learning experiences. School librarians are the instructional backbone behind teaching 21st century learning skills (the ability to be discerning users of information and technology), as well as helping students' critical thinking skills. These information skills go beyond learning to read, they foster *reading to learn* (n. pag.).

Provide Instruction as Well as Tools

While Walker reminds us to ask ourselves, "Am I merely providing the tools, or am I furnishing the instructions on how to use the tools as well?" (46), Bush asks that we take the responsibility for teaching reading to learn seriously. "Be explicit. Be visible. Let the other educators in your building understand that you are a partner in developing strategic readers. Their mission is our mission. Learn the strategies that are used in your school. Reinforce them in the library media program" (15). And remember in the push to be visible and explicit to include your administrators and the school board, reminding them that you are an important instructional partner in supporting and expanding existing reading curriculum. Be clear about your role in supporting student learning and your affect on student achievement in reading. "Accountability carries credibility that serves to support our mission" (17).

Designer of Collaborative Literacy Engagements

Finally comes our role as designer of collaborative literacy engagements. While the focus on literacy has intensified across the educational landscape, our role as literacy supporter and collaborator has held steady. The AASL *Position Statement on Resource Based Instruction: Role of the School Library Media Specialist in Reading Development* outlines as one of seven elements integral to an effective reading program: "Teachers and library media specialists share responsibility for reading and information literacy instruction. They plan and teach collaboratively based on the needs of the student" (n. pag.). If we define the first four roles:

- Builder of Quality Collections for the LMC and the Classroom
- Chief Cheerleader and Promoter of the Love of Reading
- Creator and Leader of a Joyful Reading Environment and Literacy Center
- Collaborative Partner and Knowledgeable Teacher

as basics to our work, we can concentrate our next efforts on meeting our mandate to collaborate through our literacy initiatives with teachers. As Shannon points out:

> Most SLMSs in elementary schools were first attracted to their job
> because of a love for books and reading. With so much national attention
> (and funding) being devoted to reading, and with so much interest in inte-
> grating the use of children's books across the curriculum, SLMSs have
> ample opportunities for partnering with teachers and parents to provide
> rich literacy experiences for children. With their knowledge of their
> school communities, standards, and curriculum, and armed with the
> research on literacy learning, SLMSs are well-positioned to play an inte-
> gral role in their schools' early literacy initiatives (20).

Partners for Reading

Some of us see our teachers struggling—strangling, in fact—in this time of heightened urgency about literacy and test scores. Sometimes, they feel they do not have *time* to breathe, much less collaborate. It is our job, then, to ensure that they reframe their thinking. As Hirsh-Pasek and Golinkoff suggest, we need to encourage teachers to think of us as partners as they face the pressure to create "memorizers (with a focus on learning letters and sounds) instead of thinkers." As they strive to find extra time to allow children to breathe, a perfect opportunity is created "for teacher and librarian to collaborate so that children can enjoy reading for reading's sake and story for story's sake" (68).

The Wonder of Reading and Story

Many of the units in this book are superb examples of opportunities for students to enjoy reading and story. Units which build student learning and engagement in books through the use of quality children's fiction in the context of content-area-focused units include:

- Geology for First Graders by Linda Sherouse;
- The World Beyond Our Neighborhood; Part I: Where I Live; Part II: Children in Other Countries by Martha Taylor;
- History Fair by Abigail Garthwait;
- *Canyons* by Gary Paulsen: An Archaeological Study by Bernie Tomasso;
- If These Walls Could Speak by Ronda Hassig.

Peg Becksvoort, National Board Certified Teacher and Library Media Specialist, Falmouth Middle School, Falmouth, Maine

"Within our schools, librarians know all of the students; we are available to help all students; we want to share thinking, searching, and competency skills with all students, staff, and families in our districts; we recognize the importance of reading to future success in using all types of information resources; and we encourage good and ethical habits in using such resources" (n. pag.).

These units allow students to experience the wonder of reading and stories while meeting content standards in English language arts and other content areas as they work with both their classroom teachers and their librarians. Dorothy Strickland, past president of the International Reading Association and professor of education at Rutgers University, encourages this blending of reading instruction with content as a balanced literacy effort:

> Choose interesting activities that promote literacy skills and content knowledge. When you teach literacy and content together, you expand students' chances to learn both. Having students create their own information books, for example, is a collaborative activity that can be used in any content area. Not only does it build reading and writing skills, but it requires students to learn facts well enough to convey them to others. It also invites various kinds of inquiry, such as using the card catalog or Internet. Remember, everything we do to facilitate process helps students gain access to content (n. pag.).

Informational Texts

Shannon adds that "Instructing children in how to read and how to use informational text for authentic purposes are part of the information literacy skills that SLMSs are responsible for teaching. These strategies provide opportunities for collaboration with teachers of young children and for involving students in research projects using school library resources" (17-18). You will find examples of **learning to navigate informational texts** in several of the units in Chapter Five:

- Kinder Quest by Debra Heimbrook;
- Fishing for Facts: Exploring Ocean Animals by Yapha Mason;
- Who's That by the Pond? by Liz Deskins;

- Superbugs! by Margaret Hale;
- Biography Bash: A Study of Heroes by Dorcas Hand;
- Cultures of the Sun: Exploring the Aztec and Inca Cultures by Laurie Dunlap and Toni Buzzeo;
- Food for the Community and You by Faith A. Delaney;
- PQI (Personal Quest for Information) by Linda Sherouse.

While the tight focus on literacy in our K-8 schools—nearly a stranglehold of literacy instruction in our primary and intermediate grades—is new, collaboration remains a tried-and-true method for enhancing student learning, benefiting all teaching partners involved (both library media specialists and teachers), and adding pizzazz and excitement to the daily work of teaching and learning. Because literacy is a perfect match for our skill set, this book provides lessons to develop literacy K-6 and tie it to the national requirement for literacy for all. Even as we are federally required to test reading K-8, our new task should be to create joyful literacy collaborations.

Chapter Three

Collaboration: How it Looks and Who it Benefits

Collaboration: Examining the Definitions

Collaborative Planning

What IS collaborative planning? Peek ahead to the units included in this book and you can draw some pretty accurate conclusions. First, collaborative planning is two or more equal partners who set out to create a unit of study based on content standards in one or more content areas plus information literacy standards, a unit that will be team-

> **Dorcas Hand, Director of Libraries, Unit 8: Biography Bash**
>
> "Cooperation means I find out somehow what the teacher wants, and do what I can to help it along. Coordination means the teacher asks in advance for some ideas to help a project along, and maybe involves more than one teacher of different subjects. Collaboration means we work the entire plan out together, and then co-teach or alternate teaching sessions" (n. pag.).

designed, team-taught, and team-evaluated. Or, as the NBPTS defines it, "Accomplished library media specialists therefore collaborate with teachers to plan and develop units of study that integrate multimedia, research, and information literacy skills into classroom instruction, from the initial process of setting learning objectives to assessing student learning" (19).

Patricia Montiel-Overall elaborates in her discussion of the definition of collaboration. Her definition embraces my more focused collaborative planning definition (and that of the NBPTS) and looks at the emotional nature of the partnership as well as its process and goal:

> Collaboration is a trusting, working relationship between two or more equal participants involved in *shared thinking, shared planning* and *shared creation of integrated instruction.* Through a shared vision and shared objectives, student learning opportunities are created that integrate subject content and information literacy by co-planning, co-implementing, and co-

Bernie Tomasso, Library Media Specialist, Unit 11: *Canyons* by Gary Paulsen

"Cooperation is a very basic sharing and occurs when two parties get along. They may not necessarily be working on the same project but they stay out of each others' way. Think about two PE teachers who share a gym. Sometimes they cooperate and divide the gym according to the activity or equipment. Coordination occurs within a department or grade level and can occur when the library media specialist gets involved and provides the necessary materials and equipment for a project that might occur in the classroom but needs library resources. Think of a schoolwide reading program where the library media specialist might make materials available to a grade level or subject area that would be suitable to classroom activities. Collaboration—now that is the height of instructional practice because the two educators are co-teachers and use the knowledge and skills in their particular subject area to bring the students along in completing a successful exhibition" (n. pag.).

Linda D. Sherouse, Library Media Specialist, Unit 13: PQI

"In my LMC, I would define cooperation as the foundation of everything I do. It is why my LMC is open from 8 am to 3:30 pm. It is why we circulate materials to everyone who asks including community members, students, staff, and why we interlibrary loan to other schools in our school administrative union. Being of service to all of those populations both through our resources and the use of our facility is part of this foundation.

Coordination is why we purchase materials and services which match our curriculum as well as our students' interests. It is the reason why I am always happy to know what is being taught, what new areas are being explored, and to assist in any way possible with all aspects of the school culture. In an ideal world, no new idea would be tested without first passing it by the LMS. When teachers do that, and yes some do, I am always quick to ask good reference questions to really feel them out on what they are thinking and how they perceive the students accomplishing this new goal and where they see the connection to standards.

Collaboration can be initiated by a teacher or an LMS. It involves planning together with clear standards to achieve from the state or local curriculum as well as from *Information Power*. The refining is my favorite part of this process as, through the expertise of the teacher for the particular age of the students and the access to a wide variety of age appropriate resources, great activities are tried, revised, and continue to expand with each step of the process. Some of my favorite collaborative units are those which we change each year to fit the student population and the new resources—print, electronic, and human" (n. pag.).

evaluating students' progress throughout the instructional process in order to improve student learning in all areas of the curriculum" (n. pag.).

Furthermore, she identifies "shared vision" as the process by which "teachers and SLMSs jointly develop common plans for delivering instruction or have a common purpose for integrating content and information literacy in a teaching situation. Common plans include shared objectives for instruction" (n. pag.).

Levels of Instructional Partnership

However, there has been some confusion, since the 1980's, over the differences between three related concepts—cooperation, coordination, and collaboration. In *Collaboration*, a document in the ALA Learned Lessons series, Robert Grover makes the point clearly. While in cooperation, the teacher and library media specialist work independently but come together briefly for mutual benefit, their relationship is loose. Coordination means there is a more formal working relationship and an understanding of shared missions. The teacher and library media specialist do some planning and communicate more. However, in collaboration, the two partners have a prolonged and interdependent relationship. They share goals, have carefully defined roles in the process, and plan much more comprehensively (2).

Each stage of instructional partnership is an important aspect of the job of the library media specialist. Yet, in a recent *School Library Journal* interview, Todd, in reference to his and Kuhlthau's *Student Learning through Ohio School Libraries* study, notes that "one of the things that emerged out of the Ohio data was that while as a profession we've kind of built this mantra about collaboration—the classroom teacher and the school librarian collaborating together—my sense is that collaboration actually takes place at a very low level" (Kenney 47). Todd goes on to comment that "It's low even though we've consistently said this is one of the fundamentals of school library practice" (Kenney 47). We engage in cooperation and coordination as a matter of course as we serve our adult patrons' needs and provide instruction to our students that aligns with their classroom studies. Unfortunately, we sometimes call *that* collaboration.

Stepping Stones to Collaboration

Actually, though, cooperation and coordination can serve as stepping-stones to the ultimate goal of collaboration if we are purposeful about it. Sharon Coatney notes that "collaborative individuals look for openings to work with others. The beginning of collaboration is cooperation, a willingness to adapt, to be flexible, and to help others. Cooperation opens doors to the possibility of collaboration. When we abruptly close those doors, they may never open to that person again" (59). Sometimes, it is a three-step process. Cooperation is bumped up to coordination and from coordination we move on to collaboration. Coatney agrees. "Offering services helps build the collaborative culture. Cooperation leads to coordination as the teacher-librarian offers services in coordination with the school's learning calendar. The final step in the journey from cooperation to coordination is collaboration, and leadership is the key" (59).

While each stage in the instructional partnership continuum is, indeed, important, it is collaboration which defines a relationship that is focused, intense, and committed to improving student achievement. In her analysis of the literature, Montiel-Overall proposed four models of partnership. "The primary distinctions among the models are: (1) intent of the working relationship or reason for working together; (2) intensity or degree of involvement, commitment, or participation among participants (hereafter intensity); and (3) interest in improving student academic achievement or the extent to which the effort focuses on improving student outcomes" (n. pag.). Her fourth model, Integrated Curriculum is, of course, the model that exemplifies integration of content area instruction and information literacy skills through a collaborative partnership of equals.

Applying Loertscher's taxonomy, cooperation happens at Levels Three, Four, and Five; coordination happens at Levels Six and Seven; and collaboration begins with Level Eight, with full implementation at Level Nine (*Taxonomies of the School Library Media Program* 17), and an extension beyond the library walls and into the broader educational community at Level Ten.

True Collaboration

Are you still not sure you are really collaborating, working at Level Eight, Nine, or Ten? Consider using Smith's Checklist for Collaboration to take the measure of your practice:

- Planning is an ongoing activity through the year.
- The school administration endorses collaborative planning.
- A written lesson plan designates activities and responsibilities.
- Both professionals are responsible for planning, preparation, and instruction.
- Both professionals monitor progress in implementing the plan.
- Both professionals are responsible for assessment.
- Both professionals are responsible for group management.
- Both professionals reflect on the outcomes of the lesson.
- There is an avenue for either professional to address concerns or frustrations.
- There is a way to revise the lesson plan if needed by either professional.
- Library resources augment and enrich classroom materials.
- Students learn information skills.
- Students learn content and subject-related skills.
- Students are engaged in information retrieval as individuals and small groups.
- There is mutual regard for the collaborative partner.
- There is a shared vision about outcomes (79).

As defined by Smith's checklist, the library media specialist/teacher team is an educational gift. The library media specialist has familiarity with a broad range of resources as well as expertise in information skills and strategies, and the teacher has intimate knowledge of both the students and the content area. Pair them closely as equal partners in a supportive, trusting relationship from the inception of a unit through its execution and assessment, and the partners, the school community, and the students are the lucky beneficiaries of the union.

Reflection on the Process

In every educational endeavor, it is worthwhile not simply to plan forward, as collaborative partners do, but to reflect on the process once it is complete, to evaluate the outcome of the teaching and learning. Melody Thomas believes this is true and provides a set of questions to allow you and your partner to reflect on your own experience with the collaborative process.

- Did both educators teach the necessary skills?
- Did you meet the content area goals as well as the information skills goals?
- Were the lessons appropriate for the grade level and appropriately aligned with the content to be covered?
- Were you pleased with the process and the product?
- Did you and the classroom teacher equally share the planning, teaching, and evaluating processes? (18)

She adds that if any of your answers are "no," it is important to ask what can be improved next time to bring it to "yes" and make the lesson/unit more effective, and thereby, of course, improve student achievement.

Collaboration: Assessing the Benefits

The professional literature has paid much attention to touting the many benefits of collaboration during the two decades that it has been our focus. Early on, in *Collaboration*, Grover listed ten global benefits of collaboration:

- Students are more involved in learning, and their work is more creative.
- Collaboration "ignites" creativity among teachers, and the "creative fire" spreads to learners.
- Modeling collaboration results in more collaboration among faculty in the school.
- Modeling collaboration influences students, teachers and parents, who learn to share ideas.
- Teachers, principals and librarians communicate more frequently.
- When students work in teams, the role of the teacher changes to that of resource person and learning facilitator.
- When students work in groups, the student's role changes also.
- Students learn to interact with people outside of the school.
- The library media program is integral to the collaborative teaching model.
- Administrators benefit professionally from their participation in teaching teams (7).

The Nebraska Education Media Association (NEMA), on the other hand, focuses more closely on the outcomes of collaborative planning. They assert that collaborative planning:

- promotes student achievement;
- promotes library media centers as central to the learning environment;
- promotes innovative instructional design;
- strengthens critical thinking and problem solving skills;
- provides opportunities for interaction between library media specialists and teachers;
- promotes sharing of resources;
- promotes integration and instruction of information literacy skills with the curriculum;
- enhances relevant use of all resources in all formats;
- provides opportunity for teachers to be aware of available resources;
- promotes intellectual freedom and equitable access to information and ideas;
- strengthens connections with the learning community ("Collaborative Planning: Partnerships between Teachers and Library Media Specialists" n. pag.).

NEMA also looks at advantages of collaboration by listing the benefits to the various constituencies affected: administrators, library media specialists, teachers, and students. It is a useful way to scrutinize the perspectives set forth in the professional literature and expressed by practicing professionals while examining the benefits.

Benefits to Administrators

Administrators benefit in a variety of ways from the collaborative planning of their teachers and library media specialists:

- Beneficial instructional partnerships are developed.
- Information literacy standards and content area standards are integrated in a way that improves student learning of both.
- The time and energy of the library media specialist are used effectively.
- Flexible scheduling is supported, providing time for teachers and library media specialists to plan together as well as ensuring that the rich resource that is the library media center is used to address a variety of subject areas and content standards simultaneously.
- The school culture is enriched and deepened.
- Of primary importance, student learning and achievement is increased.

Furthermore, we benefit in concert with our principals, as Blanche Woolls, former program director and currently professor emeritus at the San Jose (CA) State University School of Library and Information Science wrote in 2003:

> When we help principals confront and tackle challenges, we take a leadership role. But most importantly, they'll become our biggest supporters, which means we have a better vantage point to begin collaborating with teachers—all of them. The benefits of coming together with your principal simply proves that he can't succeed without you (Whelan, "Greatest Challenges for 2003" 49).

Dorcas Hand, Director of Libraries, Unit 8: Biography Bash

"When teachers and librarians are collaborating, the kids are more engaged which makes administrators happier. The teachers are more engaged and better supported by the collaborative team they have built, so they are happier. The grades are good because the kids were more engaged and the teachers had a firm grasp of what they wanted and explained it well to the kids. The higher grades occur in more than one subject, so the report cards look better overall. Finally, the administrators get praise from happier parents because the kids had such a great time learning such difficult material!" (n. pag.)

Bernie Tomasso, Library Media Specialist, Unit 11: *Canyons* by Gary Paulsen

"Administrators are able to advocate at higher levels for more resources because collaboration implies that materials are not only being used but that the building can increase student achievement as staff members collaborate on projects and share their particular expertise. In addition, students work with adults who might have similar learning styles which reduces the child's frustrations and also educates the staff members" (n. pag.).

Benefits to Library Media Specialists

Of course, collaboration benefits library media specialists too, and the library literature reflects that. Collaboration allows us to use our wide-ranging skills in instructional design, teaching, assessment, information consulting, and program planning and administration. We also have the chance to facilitate partnerships, integrate our information skills curriculum into content area instruction, promote the use of our many print and non-print resources, develop a dynamic facility that serves as the instructional heart of the school, and of course, raise student achievement levels. As a side benefit, Debra Kay Logan points out in her *Information Skills Toolkit*, collaboration leads students, teachers, and administrators to better understand the role, expertise, and responsibilities of the library media specialist (3).

Peter Milbury, library media teacher at Chico High School, Chico, California, and founder of the LM_NET electronic discussion list, suggests that there are ten good reasons to take collaboration seriously, from the library media specialist's perspective:

1. Increases student achievement.
2. Allows you to model successful and desirable practices.
3. Reinforces your important and pivotal role as an educational leader.
4. Allows you to work in a non-clerical, non-stereotypical role.
5. Contributes to the quality of teacher training experience through working with student teachers, demonstrating the power of the SLMS.
6. Guarantees that ethical use of information is integrated into instruction.
7. Allows you to practice and hone important skills related to collaboration.
8. Allows you to showcase your important collaboration skills to other teachers.
9. Provides you with opportunities to search for, discover and make use of online information resources in context.
10. Allows you to expand and organize your online collections (30-31).

Janie Schomberg, former Urbana, Illinois elementary library media specialist and currently adjunct instructor in the School Library Media Certification Program at the University of

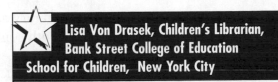

Lisa Von Drasek, Children's Librarian, Bank Street College of Education School for Children, New York City

"The most obvious benefit to me of collaboration is that I am part of the teaching team. My position, my job, my skills are part of everything that goes on in my school, from telling stories at a music assembly to providing the principal with his monthly required reading. Collaboration is invigorating. There is nothing repetitious about team teaching" (n. pag.).

Toni Buzzeo, Library Media Specialist, Unit 9: Cultures of the Sun

"I am, by my nature, a collaborative soul. I value the learning that I do when I work in concert with other professionals. I learn so much more about teaching, about ways to extend student learning in general and ways to address the needs and styles of individual learners. I have the wonderful experience, with great regularity, of something coming together because we are more-than-one at the table. Ideas grow and sparkle when they are tossed around and shared, and so the collaborative planning process produces wonderful units and projects that I might not have made so spectacular on my own. But above all, I value the actual TEACHING with a colleague. I love to interlace my skills and hers, my views with hers, my methods with hers" (n. pag.).

Illinois Graduate School of Library and Information Science has created her own list of benefits for library media specialists with some items not included on either mine or Peter's list.

- When you and the classroom teacher collaborate, the process leads to a better understanding of mutual roles and responsibilities.

- When you and the classroom teacher work as a team, the curriculum planning process is expanded and energized.

- When you and the classroom teacher identify the standards, concepts and skills for the unit together, information literacy skills can truly be integrated into the content curriculum.

- When you and the classroom teacher work together to develop the assessment instruments, you can address all the learning targets, including the process skills so often neglected in the assessment component of a content curriculum unit.

- When you and the classroom teacher co-teach and model throughout a unit, the students begin to look at you differently—not as that library teacher they see on Thursdays for library class, but as a full member of their instructional team.

- When you and the classroom teacher select instructional resources for a unit of study, resources are used to meet a wider variety of student needs.

- Collaborative unit development and implementation place you right in the middle of the student achievement picture (Schomberg, McCabe, and Fink n. pag.).

Undoubtedly, then, we are beneficiaries in the collaboration process.

Benefits to Teachers

Teachers are also beneficiaries of the collaboration model. As they struggle to ensure that their students meet standardized test goals, they look for meaningful assistance from knowledgeable colleagues. Nor should resource room teachers be left out of this equation as they endeavor to help their challenged students to meet those same standardized test goals, now that they are no longer routinely excluded from testing.

The benefits to teachers, both regular and special education, are many. Elementary classroom teacher in Urbana, Illinois, Lisa Fink reflects on some of the benefits of collaboration for her and her teaching colleagues across the nation:

Shonda Brisco, Library Media Specialist, Arlington ISD, Arlington, Texas

"If we collaborate with teachers, we help to alleviate the 'load' of the complete instruction and evaluation of the unit from just the teacher. And, thus, we make more time for the teacher. Good collaboration provides the teacher with a team member who helps with the instruction. The students are the ones doing all the work. The team shares the workload of planning and evaluating. We ALL win!" (n. pag.).

- When you and the teacher-librarian plan together, you each can draw from an expanded knowledge and experience base.

- When you and the teacher-librarian develop a unit, you gain a better understanding of information literacy and what that looks like in the classroom setting.

- When you and the teacher-librarian identify the standards, skills and concepts for your unit, you have the opportunity to analyze information literacy skills and break them into discrete blocks for effective teaching and learning.

- When you and the teacher-librarian work together, you have the opportunity to interweave instruction in the library with instruction in the classroom.

- When you and the teacher-librarian co-teach, you can provide direct modeling of the research process to your students at their point of need.

- When you and the teacher-librarian work together, you can design instruments for assessing the content, the product and the process components of your instructional unit.

- When you and the teacher-librarian are a team, your students have increased opportunities for success in a unit of study as well as to apply and transfer the skills and concepts they have learned to future activities and tasks (Schomberg, McCabe, and Fink n. pag.).

Teachers may not realize the benefits, however, unless you inform them. Thomas makes this point:

> Unless media specialists let teachers know what we can do and want to do for them and the school community, they cannot possibly know what we have to offer. If media specialists are to be considered professional educators instead of support personnel, then it is our role to let teachers know that we want to work with them and to remind them that we are professional teachers (17).

Recently, with colleagues on LM_NET who asked their collaborating teachers for input, I created a list of the advantages to teachers that you might want to share with your own teachers, as Thomas suggests, to let them know not only what we can do and want to do for them but how their buy-in will reap benefits:

- Increased access to books, online resources, and other materials to enhance learning and instruction
- Opportunities to communicate resource needs to LMS
- Professionally pre-searched topics ensure that appropriate materials are available for all learners
- Resource-based instruction
- Information literacy integrated into content area instruction

 Lauren Zucker, Teacher-Librarian, Unit 7: All About Exploring the Internet

"Teachers benefit from collaboration through assistance with handling their curriculum. They are so busy and have so much on their plates, that when they have the chance, they should take advantage of the help of the LMS. In addition, they also benefit through access to materials. The LMS is the specialist in both print and online materials to support the curriculum. It is much easier for the LMS to find quality supportive materials with quicker turn around during a collaborative project" (n. pag.).

 Faith A. Delaney, Library Media Specialist, Unit 12: Food for the Community and You

"Teachers benefit from collaboration because the LMS helps them plan their lessons and takes the role of collaboration guide in creating their lesson plans. Who wouldn't be appreciative of help with that? Teachers also benefit because the LMS helps to evaluate the students' work during and after the unit is taught, giving the teachers yet another tool to use in deciding a report card grade" (n. pag.).

- Suggestions of new project ideas
- A plan *in writing* (a road map) with goals/objectives articulated
- Reliable and age-appropriate resources in webquests
- Ensured reliability of Web sites
- Student instruction in evaluating Web sites, citing sources, and other information literacy skills
- Access to LMS expertise with technology, including new resources and searching strategies
- An extra pair of hands, eyes, and general help
- Opportunity to watch/learn how a colleague approaches/teaches a topic
- Opportunity to take some risks/try new things
- Lightened load with mutual support and fun
- Encouragement of higher level thinking skills
- Increased student learning and achievement

In putting forth these benefits to our teachers, it is obvious that we are serving them in a supporting role, and while I encourage you to take a leadership role in collaboration, encouraging teaching colleagues to join you in the collaborative model, as Montiel-Overall notes, this leadership position is not meant to detract from an equal partnership with your teachers once they are on board (n. pag.).

Benefits to Students

By far, the most important benefits of collaboration fall upon the students lucky enough to be taught by collaborating teachers and the library media specialists:

- Students learn independent use of relevant, integrated information skills;
- Students experience the excitement of resource-based learning;
- Students gain critical thinking and problem-solving skills, while increasing their creativity, and reading and writing skills;
- Students have the advantage of at least two teachers for collaborative units;
- Students experience at least two different teaching styles which address varying learning styles and intelligences.

Ronda Hassig, Library Media Specialist, Unit 14: If These Walls Could Speak

"Students benefit from collaboration in several ways. They see the library media center as another classroom and the library media specialist as another teacher. They get more bang for their buck! They also gain the life-long skill of being able to find and use resources for any topic, and this, in turn, helps to raise their test scores" (n. pag.).

Furthermore, Montiel-Overall points out:

> The synergy created from teacher and SLMS collaboration infuses instruction with new ideas. The intellectual stimulation of thinking with someone else and the process of integrating instruction may create the nurturing environment students need to develop a better understanding of how different pieces of the curricula fit together and how to create new knowledge from these pieces. Collaboration at this deep level of thinking

will have the most impact on student learning outcomes because it develops critical teaching, which results in critical thinking on the part of students (n. pag.).

It is, after all, student learning and student achievement that schools are all about. Donna Miller agrees and states the case in terms of information literacy in her book *The Standards-Based Integrated Library*:

> No matter how the planning team is organized and units of instruction are developed, at the center of every "framework" should be an information-literate child. Information literacy is the target. It is this focus that will enable building teams to 'flesh out' the details of exactly how their program should be developed (12).

In an interview with Todd and Kuhlthau in reference to the *Student Learning Through Ohio School Libraries* study, Debra Lau Whelan reports the authors as saying that the "study shows that school libraries are actively engaged as learning instructional centers to develop intellectual scaffolds for students and to help them engage with information meaningfully to construct their own understanding of the topic they're [studying]" ("13,000 Kids Can't be Wrong" 48). We collaborate, primarily, because as Jean Donham asserts, we want learning to be meaningful, authentic, and applied (20). Assignments created by teachers and library media specialists in concert are more likely to be authentic, complex, and significant. Montiel-Overall reflects on the impact collaboration makes on students:

Linda D. Sherouse, Library Media Specialist, Unit 13: PQI

"I believe that any time a student sees his or her regular classroom teacher working with another educator in their school, it opens the door for that student to feel comfortable using the other person as a resource. The act of collaboration brings the media center and its personnel into focus for a student in a new way. While they may see the 'library teacher,' as I am frequently addressed in the local supermarket, as an educator, the student's view of this person expands when he or she is actively teaching in their classroom and the media center with their primary teacher. Opening a student's mind to all the possible resources that are in their world is a by-product of collaboration. Life-long learners are those whose perspectives are broadened and know no bounds" (n. pag.).

Bernie Tomasso, Library Media Specialist, Unit 11: *Canyons* by Gary Paulsen

"In collaboration, students work with adults who might have similar learning styles to theirs which reduces children's frustrations and also educates the staff members about different learning styles" (n. pag.).

> Perhaps the power of collaboration lies in students' greater understanding of material from being exposed to diverse opinions and distinct teaching and communication styles. Students may develop a sense of importance in the collaborative effort when they witness deep commitment to innovative instruction from those responsible for their education. Students may also gain from integration of information that mutually reinforces learning and brings about a greater understanding of content and information literacy (n. pag.).

Through collaboration, information skills are taught in context of new and creative units of study. As a result, students benefit and achievement rises.

Collaboration and Student Achievment Studies

Keith Curry Lance Studies

Over the years, since 1993, the ongoing work of Keith Curry Lance and his associates has been the "voice" of student achievement through school libraries. Since the publication of Keith Curry Lance's "first Colorado study," *The Impact of School Library Media Centers on Academic Achievement*, many in our field have focused on establishing credible, data-based evidence that library media specialists and library media programs play an important role in student achievement. Lance notes:

> By 2005, the Colorado study model had been replicated and elaborated upon to a greater or lesser extent in Colorado and more than a dozen other states by five different researchers or research teams. Collectively, they have studied the impact of school libraries in approximately 8,700 schools with enrollments totaling more than 2.6 million students (Callison n. pag.).

The studies have returned similar results from state to state, from year to year, prompting Lance and other researchers to claim conclusively the positive impact of libraries on student achievement and to proclaim, "Enough already!"

> School libraries are a powerful force in the lives of America's children. The school library is one of the few factors whose contribution to academic achievement has been documented empirically, and it is a contribution that cannot be explained away by other powerful influences on student performance. If school decision-makers want to be sure that they leave no child behind, the best insurance is a strong school library program (Lance, "Libraries and Student Achievement" 8).

Luckily, says Mike Eisenberg, the library field has come to realize that we need to do more than simply "say" we make a difference. We need to focus on making changes that will demonstrate the effect (22). The Library Research Service of the Colorado State Library initiated a Web-based survey of library media specialists to answer the question: *What difference have all the studies made?*

> Three out of five respondents reported that, compared to before reading this research, they now spend more time planning collaboratively with classroom teachers (63 percent), teaching information literacy skills to students (62 percent), and identifying materials for teachers (60 percent). Almost half of respondents (48 percent) also reported spending more time teaching collaboratively with classroom teachers" (Callison n. pag.).

Since the same studies have shown that school library media specialists and library media programs influence student achievement when they "collaborate with classroom teachers to teach and integrate literature and information skills into the curriculum" (*School Libraries Work!* n. pag.), this increase in collaborative planning and teaching can only bode well for our students.

Collaboration Driven Achievement

A brief look back at the studies confirms this to be true. In *How School Librarians Help Kids Achieve Standards: The Second Colorado Study*, a central finding is "the importance of a collaborative approach to information literacy. Test scores rise in both elementary and middle schools as library media specialists and teachers work together" (7-8). Lance's Alaska study, *Information Empowered: The School Librarian as an Agent of Academic Achievement in Alaska Schools, Revised Edition* (2000) also found that regardless of the level of librarian staffing, the more library media staff time devoted to delivering information literacy instruction, planning cooperatively with teachers, and providing in-service training to teachers and staff, the higher student test scores (65-66). The Pennsylvania study, *Measuring Up to Standards: The Impact of School Libraries & Information Literacy in Pennsylvania Schools* (2000) found that test scores increase as school librarians spend more time, among other things, **teaching cooperatively with teachers**" (7).

All this research adds up to new and indisputable knowledge: school library media specialists, particularly those working in collaboration with teachers as teaching partners, have an impact on student achievement. Furthermore, as Ken Haycock says, "Collaboration between teacher and teacher-librarian not only has a positive impact on student achievement but also leads to growth of relationships, growth of the environment and growth of persons" (38). And as *School Libraries Work!* points out and as mounting evidence affirms,

> school libraries staffed by qualified library media specialists *do* make a measurable difference on student achievement. Whether that achievement is measured by standardized reading achievement scores or by global assessments of learning, school libraries and library media specialists are a powerful force in the lives of American children (n. pag.).

Evidence Based Practice

Todd and Kuhlthau at Rutgers University have taken a next-generation approach to the student achievement issue with an emphasis on Evidence Based Practice (EBP) and the published results of the *Student Learning through Ohio School Libraries* (2003) study in which they surveyed more than 13,000 students. This is the first time researchers have based a study on students' evaluation of their library media centers. Todd explains, "The question that has driven both Carol Kuhlthau and I is how do you move from saying, yes, good school libraries make a difference to student achievement to actually improving practice in an individual school?" (Kenney 45). Todd's answer is Evidence Based Practice, which focuses on two things: using evidence to make decisions about your role as a library media specialist and gathering evidence on teaching and learning in your library media center (Kenney 45).

> EBP is a kind of three-legged stool. One of the legs rests on the evidence information scientists have produced on the research process. Another leg stands on the librarian's understanding of how her individual patrons learn best—visually, aurally, by reading, or all three. The third leg consists of data, measurable proof that the librarian's guidance has a real impact on learning (Oatman 57).

Todd believes that we have to think about what the research is telling us and decide what steps we can take to enhance our roles as educators in our schools and libraries in ways that will positively affect student achievement. He also believes that each of us should be able to clearly articulate the learning outcomes of our library programs, to know and explain how our individual school practice contributes to the learning in our district (Kenney 47).

> Evidence-based research and evidence-based practice ask three things of each of us working in school libraries. First, it asks us to have a very clear and precise knowledge of and insight into the research of our profession that demonstrates the differences that an effective school library makes to the learning goals of the school. Second, it asks us to mesh that knowledge with our own wisdom and experience to build professional work practices that enable us to achieve significant student learning outcomes. Third, it asks us to look at our own school communities and work towards providing the evidence of how our local school library makes a difference—it asks us to articulate clearly and unequivocally how our school library helps students learn (Todd 13).

However, Todd bemoans the fact that few of us can do this articulating of knowledge and skills and attitudes and outcomes based on curriculum standards (Kenney 47). If that is so, we must take heed and focus our energies on becoming clearer—for our own benefit and for the benefit of our programs and, above all, our students.

Data Driven Collaboration

Finally, I would like to ask you to reflect on the use of student data to drive your collaborative practice. To be certain, we live and work in the age of testing and there is no dearth of standardized (and unstandardized) test data. If we are wise, we will make use of it to drive our instruction and to document our influence on student achievement. Todd says that "part of building a strong future is providing the evidence in our schools and districts that our school libraries make rich and transformative contributions to the learning and lives of our students" (17). One way to ensure that we have that evidence is to analyze the deficits in student knowledge and skills on those very tests and work, in concert with our teachers, to address those deficits in our collaborative practice.

- First, learn to read the test data.
- Second, identify areas where your students need to strengthen their skills.
- Third, think deeply about ways to embed student learning into collaborative units of study.
- Fourth, approach your teachers with a plan that will benefit students and prove your value as a collaborative partner who can produce demonstrated improvement in student achievement.

Collaboration: Ensuring Success in Collaboration Despite the Roadblocks

Examining Factors for Success

The Key to High Performance

In her thoughtful and strategic guide to libraries in the test-crazy twenty-first century, *Leverage Your Library Program to Raise Test Scores*, Audrey P. Church writes:

> We live in an information age, but in the K-12 environment, we also live in a standards-based, high-stakes testing age. We want our students to be independent, lifelong learners, but we also want them to perform well on standards-based tests. How do we achieve both? Where do these two goals meet? Where does it all come together? It comes together in the library media center with library media specialists collaboratively partnering with teachers in relevant, authentic instruction (34).

Linda D. Sherouse, Library Media Specialist, Unit 13: PQI

"The PQI unit in this book is a major piece of a three-year progression in grades 6, 7, and 8. Our Oratorical competition which comprises grades 7 and 8 involves students adopting a topic, researching, constructing a speech after an extensive study of public speaking, and then presenting their speech to their peers. Finalists then present their speeches on stage in January each year, and five winners are chosen. PQI is my most successful collaborative project because it is fully adopted by the sixth grade team and revised slightly each year. I look forward to this unit as much as the team does and it provides me a concentrated time to work with my sixth graders.

Students enjoy this unit because they are allowed to choose a topic of personal interest and investigate it. Presently we have the 'bare bones' version of this beginning in second and third grade classrooms. Teachers of these younger students are experimenting with how this personal investment influences motivation and the outcomes will naturally look different. Narrating the process for seven to nine year olds is a new challenge for me. As an educator who can see the global effect of this 'building block' activity, I look forward to working with these students as sixth graders" (n. pag.).

If we agree that collaboration is the key to creating independent critical thinkers who also perform well on standardized tests, it is worthwhile to ponder what factors determine success in the effort to implement or expand collaboration in our library media centers. Luckily, the library literature of the past two decades has much to offer in the way of wisdom.

Essential Ingredients for Successful Collaboration

Schomberg, McCabe, and Fink, as an elementary collaborative teaching team, describe their own collaborative venture from planning to assessment and reflection. They outline three essential ingredients for instructional collaboration:

1. There must be "real" time for collaborative planning. We did it before and after school, over lunch hours, on the weekend, whenever we could grab some time.
2. There must be flexible access to the library and teacher-librarian for collaborative units to be successful. Our school population allows for a combination of fixed and flexible scheduling but the time not scheduled does not always match with the schedule needs of the classroom.
3. There must be administrative support for a collaborative climate in which all instructional staff members are instructional partners. If that support is not present, collaboration will be very difficult to get off the ground (n. pag.).

In addition, I would add that it is important to share common goals about what students will know and be able to do. Design-down instructional development models ensure that we begin with instructional goals (in the form of learning standards), but in the absence of a design-down model, it is still worth taking time to ensure that all members of the planning team agree on the desired student outcomes as well as the process.

For her part, Carol Brown identifies ten key ingredients for successful collaboration. Drawing on interviews conducted with focus groups, conference attendees, public/school library partnership participants, and members of the LM_NET listserv, Carol Brown collected and analyzed responses to three key questions:

1. Can you tell me about your most successful collaborative project?

Ronda Hassig, Library Media Specialist, Unit 14: If These Walls Could Speak

"Several factors have contributed to the success of the If These Walls Could Speak unit. First, we sit down together from the very beginning of the project and plan what we are going to do—as a team. Then, every year, we sit down afterwards and reflect and make it better for the next year. We have done this project for almost 13 years and the original teachers are no longer teaching this unit; yet we keep doing it because we know it helps kids. Is it the same unit? Absolutely not. It has evolved and been done 13 different ways. Also, we make sure that the collaborative project meets standards on which students are tested. This enables us to do the project annually, making time for it each year, because the skills students learn will be carried over and reflected in their test scores" (n. pag.).

Dorcas Hand, Director of Libraries, Unit 8: Biography Bash

"Many years of a slow transition from a project taught solely in the library to one that migrated to include the teachers was one of the key factors toward success in Biography Bash. It took some personnel changes along the way, as well as changes in best practices as discussed in professional journals. And it has been a slow process of change over 10 years or more" (n. pag.).

2. Why do you think it was successful?

3. What contributed to the success? (n. pag.)

Her analysis identifies five environmental factors for success in collaboration and five social factors:

Environmental Factors
- Scheduled Planning Meetings
- Impromptu Discussion
- Administrative Support
- Defined Roles
- Flexible Scheduling

Social Factors
- Proactive Team Leader
- Shared Vision
- Self-Confidence in Contribution
- Open Communication
- Trust & Mutual Respect

She concludes:

By adopting the attributes of proactive (but flexible) leadership, trust, shared vision, open communication and self-confidence in one's contribution, teacher-librarians may be able to circumvent environmental factors not under their control. Lack of administrative support, time limitations and rigid schedules may remain as obstacles, but proactive attitudes are more likely to reach that most wanted group—teachers who will collaborate" (n. pag.).

Likewise, in *Collaboration*, Grover divides a similar list of fourteen factors for success (which he terms "lessons") into six categories:

1. Environmental Factors
2. Group Membership Characteristics
3. Process/Structure
4. Communication
5. Purpose
6. Resources

However, it is his four lessons under "Environmental Factors" that will speak most meaningfully to individual school library media specialists adopting a collaborative model:

Lesson 1. School culture must support collaboration.
Lesson 2. Flexible scheduling is a vital component of collaborative planning and work.

Lesson 3. The library media specialist can and should be a leader of the efforts to collaborate.
Lesson 4. Expect apathy and/or dissent among faculty.

Add to that Lesson 9 under Process/Structure: "School administrators and other decision-makers must support the concept of collaboration" (3-5) and it is a pretty complete list of the essentials: school culture, favorable scheduling patterns, levels of trust and commitment in collegial relationships, and administrative support. Haycock notes that "the characteristics and actions of the people involved [are] most important" to collaborative planning ("Collaborative Program Planning and Teaching" 38).

Positive Characteristics and Actions

If Haycock is right, what can we do to encourage positive characteristics and actions in the people involved? Small says that all participants must first see personal value in collaboration and must simultaneously believe that they possess the knowledge and skills necessary to make them successful in their attempts. She suggests that we not leave this all to chance but advises that "successful collaborative partners (teacher-librarians, classroom teachers, special area teachers such as for art and music, technology coordinators and administrators) require collaboration training during their professional preparation programs" (n. pag.). I might add that collaboration training for inservice teachers and librarians on the job is also beneficial. I spend a great deal of time in school districts training teacher/librarian teams in collaborative practice. It is rich and rewarding work.

Belle Sherman Elementary School (Ithaca, New York) teacher librarian Jennifer Groff concurs. She reports that attending a collaboration training I offered in her region was one of the best things on her road to collaboration as she and a teacher started with common understandings and then had an initial chunk of time to start their project. Groff also works in a district that is strong on staff development opportunities. She reports that her next plan will be "to look over the [staff development] offerings, go to a teacher and suggest we attend one together (some meet once a month for the year, for example), and then develop projects using that as a springboard" (n. pag.). What an excellent entrée into collaborative practice with a new colleague.

A final consideration is that much of the literature recommends the use of a planning form to ensure success. A form allows for efficient recording of goals, decisions, and responsibilities during planning sessions (I recommend that you be the recording secretary). The best planning forms are simple and straight-forward yet comprehensive enough to ensure that unit responsibilities, outcomes, and resources are clear and that the unit is easily replicable. The form on which the units in this book are recorded is one such template.

Overcoming the New Roadblocks to Success

Of course, knowing the factors for success does not automatically ensure that success. In fact, in some ways, it is equally important to know the roadblocks, both traditional and newly minted, and be prepared with methods to overcome them. We will begin with the new roadblocks imposed by federal education legislation and its fallout.

No Child Left Behind

A Changing Landscape

NCLB has definitely changed the landscape of American education in many ways. Unfortunately, it has erected roadblocks to teacher/librarian collaboration in many schools. Since it is unlikely that the legislation or its effects will disappear in the near future, we are best served by acknowledging it and establishing a plan.

Whelan advocates an optimistic and proactive approach:

> Although President Bush's education reform law [*NCLB*] is written with teachers in mind, media specialists have an equally important role to play in improving student achievement—particularly when it comes to reading. They simply need to carve out relevant tasks for themselves since the law doesn't spell them out (Whelan, "A Golden Opportunity" 40).

Ronda Hassig, Library Media Specialist, Unit 14: If These Walls Could Speak

"Time is a roadblock to collaboration posed by standardized testing. There are entire blocks of time during the year that have to be put aside for testing and that just makes time to collaborate more difficult to manage" (n. pag.).

Dorcas Hand, Director of Libraries, Unit 8: Biography Bash

"The gift of working in the private schools is the minimal effect of *NCLB* and standardized testing. We still give the tests—harder ones, in fact—but the assumption is that creative teaching will lead to deeper learning which will lead to better test scores" (n. pag.).

In fact, she believes that "No Child Left Behind is your chance to become indispensable" ("A Golden Opportunity" 41). To begin, she suggests that we become experts in *NCLB*. How many of us have read the law, looking for less obvious roles for ourselves inherent in it? You can read the law, print fact sheets, track new developments, and learn about Improving Literacy through School Libraries grant opportunities at the U. S. Department of Education Web site <http://www.ed.gov/nclb/landing.jhtml>. Once you have done your homework, Whelan recommends that you get involved at the district planning level. This is where decisions about *NCLB* funds are made, rather than at the individual building level. In fact, she says, do not wait to be invited to district planning meetings. Instead, request a place at the table ("A Golden Opportunity" 41).

Improving Literacy Through School Libraries

One aspect of *NCLB* that you are certainly familiar with, particularly if you are from a qualifying low-income school, is Title I, Part B, subpart 4 (Sec. 1251), the Improving Literacy Through School Libraries grant initiative:

> Sec. 1251. Improving Literacy Through School Libraries
> (a) PURPOSES- The purpose of this subpart is to improve literacy skills and academic achievement of students by providing students with increased access to up-to-date school library materials, a well-equipped, technologically advanced school library media center, and well-trained, professionally certified school library media specialists ("Elementary & Secondary Education: Subpart 4 – Improving Literacy Through School Libraries" n. pag.).

Fitzgerald Georges, library chairperson at Great Neck (New York) North High School Library, is enthusiastic about Sec. 1251:

> Using competitive project grants, the Literacy through School Libraries (LSL) objective is to facilitate the improvement of literacy skills and academic achievement of students by providing them with increased access to up-to-date school library materials and resources. We finally have a federally funded mandate to educate and positively impact local education agencies across the country about the important work we do (28).

American Association of School Librarians executive director Julie Walker takes a more cautious view, however, seeing *NCLB* as a mixed blessing. On the one hand, the Improving Literacy Through School Libraries initiative is the first designated federal funding for libraries in decades. But while some administrators, even without the aid of federal grant funding, are putting lots of money into library materials for students to read in an effort to improve reading scores (solid action based on proven reading theory), in other places, Walker notes that the curriculum has been narrowed as all available funding is spent on pre-packaged programs to raise scores. Even technology money in the library can go to software to track achievement-test data rather than to student resources (Goldberg 41). Michael Gorman, American Library Association president 2005-06, further bemoans, "One of the many shortcomings of the 2002 No Child Left Behind Act is that it largely ignores the role of School Libraries and credentialed school librarians in improving student achievement, increasing literacy, and equipping students for further study and an empowered life" (5).

A Potential Boon

Which leads to the most important point of all. *NCLB* can only be a potential boon for us if our communities understand our critical role in student achievement, a role that is created and proven though rich and effective collaborations with our classroom teachers and other faculty. According to Reed, "NCLB is a wake-up call for library media specialists. If their communities do not think of them as essential to the mission of improving student test scores, then library media specialists risk being seen as irrelevant and their budgets may be reduced or their positions eliminated" (56). Conversely, if we are seen as essential to that mission, we are likely to be not only the beneficiaries of increased funding but possibly in a leadership role in determining the direction the school community takes in committing money and time to improving student achievement.

A Proactive Stance

So what can a wise library media specialist do? First, of course, become a savvy grant writer if your school meets the guidelines for Improving Literacy Through School Libraries. Second, as Gerald Coles points out, recognize that "given the actual empirical evidence on the contributions that books and book reading make to reading acquisition, librarians should continue to feel confident that the tools of *their* trade are central to the reading process, regardless of assertions guiding *NCLB*" (22). You must not simply count on your administration and teaching colleagues to recognize that, however. A simple way to reinforce the idea is to suggest a faculty-wide book group to read and discuss the new edition of *The Power of Reading* by Stephen D. Krashen which makes the point solidly, repeatedly, and with an enormous amount of evidence.

Supply your principal with the AASL produced brochure, *Your School Library Media Program and No Child Left Behind*, which will make the case for you and your library as valuable assets in meeting the requirements of *NCLB*, including through collaborative practice.

Many state tests ask students to apply skills as well as recall facts. School library media specialists, by designing teaching information literacy units tied to the classroom curriculum, help all students learn to not only memorize information, but also to use it in meaningful and memorable ways. Which, of course, leads to higher test scores. We want to produce critical readers, real-world math users, and passionate, effective writers. Project-based learning that is planned, co-taught and assessed by your school's school library media specialist will always ask children to go beyond the minimum, and in doing so, they will have no difficulty in passing tests that measure just the minimum (n. pag.).

Former library media specialist and current director of technology for the South Portland, Maine, School Department, Andy Wallace (see sidebar) agrees that students should be required to use information in meaningful ways—even on the assessments themselves. He suggests that library media specialists work at a district level to get information literacy items embedded in the local common assessments to do just that. In addition, this will provide guaranteed opportunities to collaborate to improve student performance.

Data Driven Collaborative Units

Evan St. Lifer advises us to "ensure that the library is a vital resource for helping students succeed on high stakes tests" (13). I agree with both Wallace and St. Lifer and have been engaged in compelling staff development work with teacher/librarian teams to design data-driven collaborative units that begin with analysis of test data from district and state standardized tests to identify student deficiencies. These identified areas of concern then become our focus as we turn to the standards, using a design-down model of instructional planning, to create units of instruction that embed the necessary student learning that will increase student achievement on the tests. As Eisenberg notes, "we need to help students succeed at whatever has been set before them. Today, that means focusing on standardized tests and the relationship between information literacy skills instruction and student performance on these standard tests" (22).

Actually, it is a powerful opportunity that we must take advantage of if we are to prove our essential place in the student achievement enterprise. Collaboration is not just a more exciting, rewarding, and successful model for delivering content area teaching and information literacy skills teaching. It can and does affect student performance on standardized tests, and we can prove it. Eisenberg agrees and adds:

> It is possible to not only link information skills standards to content area standards, but to get much more specific in providing meaningful information skills instruction that helps students to succeed on standardized tests. I recognize that one lesson here and there will not have much of an

Andy Wallace, Director of Technology, South Portland School Department, South Portland, Maine

"A local common assessment, for example, need not be a pencil and paper (or online for that matter) exam, but can be a project or an essay, a performance or an artifact. Librarians would be wise to sneak library skills into these assessments, and make information literacy a required component. This way you will actually get to see and work with ALL the students, not just the ones whose teachers can find the time for the library. So, as rose-colored as it may sound, maybe common assessments can be an opportunity for librarians, just as they are a 'burden' to others" (n. pag.).

impact on student performance. However, over time, repeated lessons that focus on the same information skills—targeted to questions in the same format and style that appear on statewide tests, taught collaboratively by the teacher-librarian and classroom teacher—can make a difference (29).

Look at your test data with your teachers as a part of your collaborative planning. Identify those areas of weakness that can become a focus of your collaborative work and plan to incorporate a focus on those skills throughout the unit—and future units—in order to improve student performance.

Mandates of Classroom Instructional Time

A corollary effect of *NCLB* has been a restriction in the freedom teachers have to plan their instructional days. Both the increased time spent on testing and the mandates for dedicated literacy and numeracy blocks in the elementary school day have impacted the time teachers have available to collaborate with the library media specialist. According to the Center on Education Policy, "The No Child Left Behind Act holds schools and school districts accountable for improving student achievement in mathematics and reading/language arts. One strategy used by school districts to improve student achievement in these subjects is to increase the amount of instructional time spent on them" ("NCLB: Narrowing the Curriculum?" n. pag.). Of course, more instructional time spent *in the classroom*, focused on mathematics and reading, means less discretionary time in the day. In fact, the Center for Educational Policy reports that in one national survey of school districts, "64% of districts required elementary schools to devote a specific amount of time to reading and 53% required them to devote a specific amount of time to math" ("NCLB: Narrowing the Curriculum?" n. pag.). The average for districts receiving federal Title I funds is 94 minutes of instructional time in

Bernie Tomasso, Library Media Specialist, Unit 11: *Canyons* by Gary Paulsen

"Teachers are reluctant to give up class time because the administration has determined how time should be spent. Teachers are sent to workshops with little time to implement what is learned before the next workshop comes along. Schools are also buying into computer tracking programs which take time away from teaching and therefore time away from collaborative projects" (n. pag.).

Ronda Hassig, Library Media Specialist, Unit 14: If These Walls Could Speak

"I don't look at uninterrupted literacy time and other mandated classroom time blocks as separate from my goals. I try to find ways to make these initiatives part of my library objectives. Turn a negative into a positive. For most of these initiatives that's not hard to do" (n. pag.).

reading, more than an hour and a half, paired with an average of 64 minutes in math. No wonder teachers feel pressed for time to collaborate! Jennifer L Youssef, a Virginia classroom teacher studying to become a library media specialist, makes an encouraging point, however:

As a teacher after the 'No Child Left Behind' program has been established, I feel a little overwhelmed with all of the pretesting, quizzing, testing, writing portfolios, projects, post-testing, and state and nationally mandated tests. On top of the weeks lost to testing, we have a very rigid curriculum in which to teach an abundance of objectives in a little amount of time. How can teachers help students not just learn, but understand what we teach in so short of a time span? One strategy that I found to work very well is collaboration between a classroom teacher and a library media specialist (40).

This is the very point made by collaborating librarians across the country. It is our mission to help our teachers realize that collaboration is working smarter, not harder. In addition, requesting that time spent in the library be an important component of the literacy block is a wise move. Asking does not ensure a positive response, of course, and in many literacy models, all of the designated minutes must be spent in the classroom. However, as discussed in Chapter Two, there are often essential roles for the library media specialist during this block.

Overcoming Traditional Roadblocks to Success

Major Stumbling Blocks

As we look beyond the two new roadblocks posed by *NCLB* and mandated classroom instructional time for reading and math, we find that the library literature has long revealed three major stumbling blocks to collaboration in schools: lack of administrative support, difficult scheduling patterns, and school culture/teacher resistance. More recently, Brown's research has concurred with past findings.

Five social factors have been identified that affect success in collaboration. By adopting the attributes of proactive (but flexible) leadership, trust, shared vision, open communication and self-confidence in one's contribution, teacher-librarians may be able to circumvent environmental factors not under their control. Lack of administrative support, time limitations and rigid schedules may remain as obstacles, but proactive and positive attitudes are more likely to reach that most-wanted group— teachers who will collaborate (n. pag.).

One additional roadblock, lack of library media specialist interest, knowledge, or training, can also interfere, but as Brown notes, if you are a proactive team leader you are likely to succeed. To ensure a thriving collaborative practice, then, "the teacher-librarian will look for opportunities to develop collaboration instead of

Barbara Combes, Lecturer, School of Computer and Information Science, Edith Cowan University, Perth, Western Australia

"My advice is to watch and observe, target influential players and sympathetic teachers, begin small, always clearly delineate roles, and advertise your successes everywhere— as a guest at the parents meetings, in the school foyer, school newsletter, and reports to the principal and board. Document and program your involvement and set it in the core business of the school using that language, for example 'student learning outcomes.' Teacher-Librarians work at the big picture level—literacy and information literacy. Eventually they will come to you" (n. pag.).

Laurie Dunlap, Library Media Specialist, Unit 9: Cultures of the Sun

"I work with the willing and sometimes do more than I believe is my share of the work to move things along. Once we have had a successful collaborative unit, teachers look for more. I have one grade level that is very willing and quite open to collaborative projects, so I work with them a lot. All of the teachers in that grade level work well together and encourage participation in these projects. Each time we do a project, we get better at it and learn from our past work together" (n. pag.).

reacting to strategies or plans already in place" (n. pag.). We can often turn roadblocks around, work them to our advantage, and make them keys to success.

The Role of the Administrator

Administrative Support

In fact, your administrator is key to overcoming roadblocks in the other two areas as it is your administrator who has the most influence over school culture, whether negative or positive, and who has the final power to change the schedule. Unfortunately, your administrator can also be a roadblock to collaboration. Leonard and Leonard bemoan the fact that the roadblocks to collaborative practice, all within the realm of administration to work on and possibly to solve, are "hauntingly similar" to those that have been reported over the years.

> Teachers still complain that the scarcity of opportunities to collaborate is promulgated by increasing work demands and decreasing time availability. They also continue to lament persisting negative mindsets about the actual desirability of shared work and the resistance to moving beyond the traditional models of teacher relationships. While some schools seem to be headed by administrators who value and promote elements of the 'learning community,' others clearly are not. The distinction is important and it may be time for district level administrators and policymakers to unequivocally communicate expectations of the former to current and potential school-level administrators. School principals who continue to personify traditional leader traits in the currently emerging educational environment not only minimize professional growth, they may also optimize student mediocrity (n. pag.).

Haycock would agree. He writes that research findings show that "Collaborative planning requires a knowledgeable and flexible teacher-librarian, with good interpersonal skills and a commitment to integrated information literacy instruction, and **the active support of the principal**" ("Collaborative Program Planning and Teaching" 38). In fact, he says, "The role of the principal is so critical to the development of school priorities, culture, and resources that it would be fair to say the principal is the key factor in developing an effective and integrated school library program" ("Collaborative Program Planning and Teaching" 38).

Bernie Tomasso, Library Media Specialist, Unit 11: *Canyons* by Gary Paulsen

"I believe that administrators are not educated about the role of the library media specialist in learning and therefore sometimes disregard the enormous influence that the library media center can make on student achievement" (n. pag.).

Ronda Hassig, Library Media Specialist, Unit 14: If These Walls Could Speak

"My administrator is very supportive of any collaborative practice going on in the library media center. She truly believes that our library program is part of the reason we've made Standard of Excellence the past three years. If the lessons connect with the standards and assessments, that's optimum for my administrator. In fact, that's the case in many districts. Testing is a priority. The scores are even printed in the newspaper. Some may think their jobs are dependent on scores. It isn't said out loud, but everyone knows it" (n. pag.).

Lauren Zucker, Teacher-librarian, Unit 7: All About Exploring the Internet

"My administrators have been supportive in allowing for a schedule that enables me to collaborate and providing me with professional courtesy when trying new things" (n. pag.).

Montiel-Overall also found in her research that the principal is essential to collaborative practice:

> He or she is responsible for establishing a norm for the school environ-
> ment in which people work together. The principal can facilitate flexible
> scheduling, professional development, and distribution of resources that
> provide time for meeting and encourage classroom and library faculty to
> collaborate on instruction. The principal is responsible for opening up
> opportunities for faculty to take an active role in decisions involving cur-
> ricular planning through regularly convened discussions and meetings.
> The principal acquires needed resources for the library and the classroom.
> When collaboration is successful in improving student outcomes, the
> principal can use data collected to provide evidence to those who allocate
> resources that collaboration is worth continued funding. Most impor-
> tantly, the principal recognizes the SLMS as a co-equal to teachers who is
> capable of developing and implementing curricula (n. pag.).

Administrative Expectations

In addition to facilitating conducive schedules, professional development, and needed resources, and recognizing the value and stature of library media specialists in improving student learning and achievement, what are the ways a principal who understands the value of the collaborative model supports it? Chief among them are expectations. Van Deusen's 1993-94 AASL/Highsmith Research Award Study revealed that curriculum consultation was significantly higher when the principal expected teacher/librarian collaborative planning (n. pag.). This, of course, demands an administrator who is willing to offer strong leadership and take risks. He must be willing to design job descriptions, hire new teachers, and set goals with current faculty with explicit expec-tations for collaboration. "When an administrator asks classroom teachers how they are using the media center resources and the expertise of the teacher-librarian, the probability of collaboration between the teacher-librarian and classroom teachers is likely to increase" (Bishop and Larimer 20). In addition, principals can include collaboration expectations in evaluations, observe plan-ning sessions between teachers and library media specialists, monitor and log collaboration events, and provide inservice instruction in collaboration (Donham 24).

In fact, Wayne Hamilton, recently retired principal of Agnes MacPhail Public School in Toronto, Ontario and the 2005 Ontario School Library Association's School Administrator of the Year, includes in his "10 Things an Administrator Should Do to Support the School Library" a command to fellow administrators to require collaboration and a practical suggestion for ensuring its success:

> Insist on collaboration between the teacher-librarian and classroom
> teachers, and provide time for this collaboration. You may be aware of the
> literature on emotional intelligence and the incremental benefits of
> working collaboratively. Teacher-librarians have an extraordinary ability
> to work with students to take them to higher levels, and we need them to
> share their expertise to enhance all programs in the school. In order to do
> this, teacher-librarians must have available time that they schedule for
> collaboratively planned research units in various subject areas and grade
> levels. I generally set up the timetable so that 50% of my teacher-
> librarian's time is available for collaborative work with classes (71).

Becky McCabe, former principal of Leal Elementary School, Urbana, Illinois, currently on leave and serving on an Illinois State Board of Education leadership team, also has advice for administrators who wish to foster collaboration between teachers and librarians. Her suggestions focus on the affective realm, which will, in turn, foster a stronger, more collaborative school culture:

- Create a building focus on student learning;
- Build, nurture, and support trust at all levels;
- Establish and support an environment that defines professional growth as meaningful and purposeful to classroom work;
- Establish and support staff learning teams;
- Provide resources and feedback for staff learning teams to work well together;
- Keep professional work focused on school improvement; and
- Honor teachers' time and efforts (Schomberg, McCabe, and Fink n. pag.).

In addition to the suggestions by these forward-thinking administrators, I would add that for success, your principal must stay informed about collaborative planning and library media center usage through regular communication. In turn, you must keep your principal informed by sharing the weekly schedule, preparing monthly reports, and inviting the observations of or participation in library media center learning activities. We must play our role in this process if we expect to garner the administrative support that collaboration requires.

Time and Scheduling

Time Roadblocks

The issues of time and scheduling are the next big set of roadblocks to be overcome. How can we overcome the huge roadblock of time? The solution points back to the administrator. Smith makes this very point. "Successful collaboration needs administrative support because planning requires time during the regular school schedule, and collaborative activities do not always fit within the school structure" (70). This is all the more true as we struggle with protected classroom time for teaching reading and math, as noted above.

Possible variations for dealing with the time crunch are many, but the task requires creativity by administrators, librarians, and teachers who value collaboration. You will note that Vicki Krebsbach (see sidebar), working in a school with more than 1000 students, meets with grade level reps to plan a whole grade unit, rather than trying to get all of the players at the table. It is a practical and creative way to deal with a lack of adequate common planning time. Others, like Kim DeStefano (see sidebar), find that their most beneficial collaboration planning happens during the summer. And some-

Faith A. Delaney, Library Media Specialist, Unit 12: Food for the Community and You

"I allow the teachers who are collaborating with me to work out their own scheduling blocks of time, with give and take. For example, 'I'll take the class for a double period today and you can have a double tomorrow.' I let the teachers decide on the schedule and I make accommodations in mine. After all, I am more flexible than they are" (n. pag.).

Dorcas Hand, Director of Libraries, Unit 8: Biography Bash

"I deal with scheduling problems creatively. I can see ways around those problems, often by convincing teachers how spending this time on this project makes some other aspect of their day work better" (n. pag.).

times it is just a matter of coming in early or staying late to meet and take the most important first step—planning.

Scheduling Roadblocks

The much larger hurdle of the two, however, is scheduling. Because a flexible schedule benefits literacy throughout the school, our national organization names flexible scheduling as one of the integral elements of an effective reading program in its *Position Statement on Resource Based Instruction: Role of the School Library Media Specialist in Reading Development.* "The library media center is flexibly scheduled so that students and teachers have unlimited physical and intellectual access to a wide range of materials. Students are not limited to using only commercially prescribed or teacher-selected materials" (AASL n. pag.). Miller strongly agrees:

> As we struggle to raise literacy rates, denying children access to any library— much less their own 'academic' library media center—seems almost criminal. Yet, in many cases, we have allowed the library's schedule to drive the curriculum, rather than the reverse. An integrated library program rights this wrong by giving open access to the library media center. As more and more school library programs move toward flexible schedules, we will see children begin to have more access to information resources as well as books for pleasure reading, which is as it should be (3).

Furthermore, if the school is bound to a full, lockstep, rigid schedule, not only is there not time for teachers and library media specialists to jointly plan, there is also not time for them to jointly teach and to delve into a unit in ways that sometimes require much more than a weekly visit for a fixed time period. Bishop and Larimer point out that "a number of factors help facilitate successful collaboration between teacher-librarians and classroom teachers. Probably the

Vicki Krebsbach, Library Media Specialist, Wilderness Oak Elementary School, San Antonio, Texas

"It becomes very difficult to meet with 8 and 9 teachers to flesh out a project, so for several units I have met with 1 or 2 of the grade level reps. We have met after school, during the 'prep' period, before school, or just on the fly. We hash over ideas, come to a consensus and then they take it to the whole grade level" (n. pag.).

Ronda Hassig, Library Media Specialist, Unit 14: If These Walls Could Speak

"In order to deal with schedule and time constraints, I teach to more than one class. Instead of 28 students, I have 56 or 60. I am taking this approach next week with Civil War and artifacts/ primary sources. I have seven classes and five hours. So we'll do two classes together for two hours. It will be crazy, but we'll make it work so that all students benefit from the lesson" (n. pag.).

Kim DeStefano, Library Media Specialist, Daly Elementary School, Port Washington, New York

"I was able to get two half-days of paid workshop time for myself, three fifth-grade teachers, a special ed teacher, and an ELL teacher. We planned an entire I-Search project on 19th Century History for our 5th grade classes. Thanks to this summer planning, this turned out to be the best integrated project I have ever done!" (n. pag.).

Faith A. Delaney, Library Media Specialist, Unit 12: Food for the Community and You

"I keep a file of units that were done previously. I don't re-invent the wheel when there are collaboration books like Toni Buzzeo's and portfolios that librarians keep containing their successful collaborations. Of course the units are not only 'dusted off' but refined as they are re-used" (n. pag.).

most important factor is flexible scheduling" (19). In fact, as Gniewek points out, flexible scheduling makes teacher/library media specialist planning essential (34). With no set pattern or design for library media center use, all units become collaborations.

And it is collaboration that increases student achievement as measured by standardized test scores. In fact, in the 2003 Michigan study, *The Impact of Michigan School Librarians on Academic Achievement: Kids Who Have Libraries Succeed*, Lance, Rodney, and Hamilton-Pennell find that "at elementary schools with the highest Michigan Educational Assessment Program (MEAP) reading scores, teachers and students are 4 times as likely to be able to visit the library on a flexibly scheduled basis, as compared to their counterparts at the lowest scoring schools" (*School Libraries Work* n. pag.). Additionally, in their 2005 Illinois study, *Powerful Libraries Make Powerful Learners*, they find that "flexible scheduling continues to exert a positive effect on test scores, regardless of per pupil spending, teacher-pupil ratio, or students' race/ethnicity. Elementary schools with flexibly scheduled libraries performed 10 percent better in reading and 11 percent better in writing in the ISAT tests of fifth-graders than schools with less flexibly scheduled libraries" (*School Libraries Work* n. pag.).

Unfortunately, those with the power to adjust the library media center schedule are not always aware of the achievement studies. Nor are library media center schedules often the library media specialist's decision. Usually, scheduling decisions happen elsewhere. However, some library media specialists who have not been successful in switching to a fully flexible schedule have found a mixed schedule to be the answer. Van Deusen's study shows that "occurrences of all five curriculum consultation variables [gather, identify, plan, teach, evaluate] were significantly greater in schools employing flexible **or mixed scheduling** than in schools employing fixed schedules" (19).

While a mixed schedule is working for some library media specialists, nevertheless, there are schools in which no flexibility in the library schedule is possible at all. Butt and Jameson claim that even in these situations, collaboration is possible. "While flex scheduling offers the most supportive scenario for collaboration by the library media specialist and the classroom teacher, success within a fixed schedule is still possible" (n. pag.). They note that in order for it to happen, the teacher and the library media specialist must pre-plan the lesson and the teacher come to the library media center with her students. In order for pre-planning to take place, they say, professional planning times must coincide.

School Culture

A Collaborative Climate

The third potential roadblock to teacher/library media specialist collaboration is school culture. When a school lacks a collaborative work culture, teaching partnerships and collaboration have nothing on which to build. Consider Sybil Farwell's formula for successful collaboration. "The most promising formula for successful information literacy instruction is a combination of an energetic, knowledgeable, open-minded, and committed library media specialist; a flexible, confident, team-oriented staff; a risk-taking principal who understands change, how to manage both people and budgets, and the advantages and needs of an integrated resource-based instructional program;

Debra Heimbrook, Library Media Specialist, Unit 1: Kinder Quest

"I built trust slowly with the teachers. I was at my current school for two years before I felt I could approach the teachers with collaborative ideas. I had to prove myself first by providing materials they asked for and supplying them with applicable resources beyond their requests. When they began to think of me as someone who had a handle on their needs for teaching, I was able to become an instructional partner" (n. pag.).

and a system for providing regular, collaborative planning time during the school day" (30). Administrators, teachers, and library media specialists all must see collaboration as an effort worth a risk. The value of a collaborative climate in the school, then, cannot be underestimated.

Respect

Why is it so important? Smith notes that it all comes down to respect. Often, collaboration is a new venture, and, as with any new venture, there is a level of personal risk when one becomes involved. An underlying assumption of respect across the staff lowers the fear inherent in trying something new. "Successful collaboration . . . flourishes when there is a team spirit among the faculty because feelings of shared respect allow each individual to try something new and to falter or fail without fear of ridicule or rejection" (70).

In addition, a collaborative culture provides all faculty members with an inherent trust that they will derive something of value for themselves and for their students when working together. Small says, "To be motivated to collaborate, all participants must first see some personal value in collaboration and believe that they have the knowledge and skills necessary to be successful collaborative partners" (n. pag.). A collaborative school culture ensures these prerequisites.

However, a 2003 *School Library Journal* survey of 783 library media specialists nationwide uncovered a lack of collaborative culture in most schools if we are to read this evidence of barriers correctly: "68 percent of media specialists encounter . . . barriers to teaching information literacy, with the number-one obstacle being no support by teachers, closely followed by little knowledge of what information literacy actually is" (Whelan, "Why Isn't Information Literacy Catching On?" 51). The article goes on to report that only 15 percent of elementary school teachers collaborate with librarians to teach information literacy skills and of that 15 percent, "only 11 percent say they often design and teach information literacy units with teachers, while 51 percent say they sometimes do, and 35 percent say they rarely do" (Whelan, "Why Isn't Information Literacy Catching On?" 52).

 Teresa Wells, Librarian, J.R. Thompson Elementary School, Mesquite, Texas

"I've built on my background as a classroom teacher. I rely more on that one aspect of my librarianship than anything as I collaborate with teachers in my building. That and I listen. A very wise administrator once told me that people need to be heard, that their pain needs to be witnessed. I've found that if I listen to teachers talk about difficult kids, or gripey parents, and do nothing but nod, gasp, and say, 'You go, girl!' I've found a friend for life. When I go to those teachers with an idea for the library, they want to work with me, because I've witnessed their pain. I've stood with them in their uncomfortable shoes, and they will do likewise for me" (n. pag.).

 Faith A. Delaney, Library Media Specialist, Unit 12: Food for the Community and You

"Our teacher resistance can come from an older teacher not wanting to try anything new or from a new teacher just learning the ropes, and feeling overwhelmed by it all. Basically, I let the faculty members who have done collaborative units with me be my PR people. Older teachers and new teachers will respond to their peers who tell them success stories of their collaborative units. Many times a teacher will show up at the library asking me to 'do the unit with my class that you did with . . .'.

The challenging school culture in my district is the continuous overturn in faculty. New teachers don't stay in our schools very long for various reasons (child rearing, moving out of an inner city climate, or just feeling they need to get out of education). I work with new teachers every year to overcome their resistance. Actually, I have to become a PR person who convinces them that I can make their lives easier!" (n. pag.).

Collaboration is not happening very often and the reason seems to be lack of teacher interest and support.

The question is two-fold, then. How do we help to establish a collaborative culture and how do we garner teacher interest and support? In their article, "The Art of Collaboration," Karen Muronaga and Violet Harada begin by suggesting that the library media specialist must be willing to lead or to be an active team member as the situation requires (10). They outline eight steps to developing a collaborative culture:

1. building trust
2. developing collaborative relations
3. creating leadership teams
4. planning interactive meetings
5. valuing strengths
6. varying roles and responsibilities
7. emphasizing team work
8. viewing planning as a nonlinear, holistic, and dynamic process (10-14).

Nancy Braverman, Media Specialist, Chatsworth School, Reisterstown, Maryland

"I collect information about the units being covered in the classroom so that I can come up with collaborative projects to offer the teachers. While there are some teachers who approach me for collaboration, often the teachers who don't directly approach me for this purpose are willing to participate if I come to them. What is particularly appealing to teachers is that I offer variety in the ways that they can use me. Sometimes, we both work with the class simultaneously but other times, I take a portion of the students while they work with the other portion. This allows the classroom teacher an opportunity to work with a smaller group of students. Once one or two teachers in a grade level have a successful collaborative experience, others soon come seeking a similar experience" (n. pag.).

Many of the contributors to this book share Muronaga and Harada's beliefs and experiences.

Building trust goes a long way toward encouraging further collaboration. Developing collaborative relations over time is equally important. One avenue in this endeavor is the creation of and participation in leadership teams. If the library media specialist steps forward when there are building or district initiatives, she will have an opportunity not only to participate but also to collaborate. This has been especially true for many library media specialists who have served on district or state level teams who have written learning standards across the curriculum. If you become an expert in the content area standards for the committee on which you are serving, your teachers will be likely to trust your knowledge of the standards and be open to working with you to teach to those standards.

In instructional planning, librarians wishing to collaborate must allow for a variety of venues and be flexible. That flexibility with time, place, and even expectations is key to meeting the needs of the classroom teacher. Valuing strengths and acknowledging individual differences in our teaching partners is equally important; however, we should not overlook the fact that if we are doing good work with one teacher or team of teachers, word of that work will spread and create a demand. As the demand is created, it is important to be sensitive to the need for varying roles and responsibilities in collaborative partnerships. We must be sensitive to the individual needs, feelings, and attitudes of each of our teaching partners, watching for their comfort levels and gearing our projects accordingly. Finally, it is important to remember that the planning process and the development of collaborative partnerships do not always proceed in a lockstep, linear fashion.

Change Over Time

Over time, collaborative practice develops and grows in a trusting collaborative school culture that emphasizes and values teamwork. The library media specialist can become the cheerleader for team members' assumption of a variety of roles and responsibilities in the planning and execution of collaborative units. We can, in fact, support teacher self-efficacy by offering staff development that focuses on tools and strategies teachers need to effect student achievement and in that way, also, build a more collaborative school culture.

Working with Restrictions

Step by Step

You may have nodded in agreement and recognition throughout these sections, knowing you have done all you can by way of enlisting administrator and teacher support and developing a collaborative culture yet are still frustrated by the roadblocks you see in your way. How do you work with restrictions and still move forward? Remember, establishing collaboration takes time. Haycock claims, "Changes as complex as collaborative program planning and team teaching that reflect different approaches to teaching and learning do not take place quickly or easily; they are evolutionary, usually over two to five years . . ." ("Fostering Collaboration, Leadership and Information Literacy" 83). What, then, to do in the two to five years of change? How do you use those years to your best advantage?

Begin by remembering that trust is the bedrock of collaboration. The more trust you can engender in the teachers you hope to collaborate with, the more likely they are to meet you half way. Like Lisa Von Drasek (see sidebar), start by dropping off books that support curriculum and personal interests, presenting shared curriculum as a wonderful opportunity, making the rounds of your teachers every week, noting the teachable moment, and saying yes as much as possible. Be sure, as well, to assess the comfort level of various teachers and match the collaborative activity you suggest with that comfort level. Finally, it is also important, when starting out, to consider your own comfort

 Teresa Wells, Librarian, J.R. Thompson Elementary School, Mesquite, Texas

"There are some teachers with whom collaboration seems effortless. Both of us are excited about books and what they can do for the curriculum, hence what they can do for the kids in the classroom. It seems like every time we see each other, we're bubbling over with the new book we saw that will fit in with that unit from last year, or they ask whether I will order a certain book to go along with another unit. And then there are the people who are not so easy to work with, those you have to push a little more because they are not kindred spirits, for various reasons. It's those people I have to hunt down on e-mail or watch for in the hallway, and pass along books I know they will appreciate; or ask an extra 'favor' from that will enable their kids to have a freebie read-aloud time in the library. When I see them gathering huge stacks of books in the library, I pitch in with them or gather for them. Only after I have curried their favor do I then approach them with collaborative ideas. Sometimes they are receptive; sometimes they are resistant. But it's always work, even when things seem to be going well, because I want them to always continue to go well" (n. pag.).

level. Follow the advice of Bettie Fisher and Teresa Wells (see sidebars). Begin by approaching people with whom YOU are most comfortable working and move forward to the more challenging targets.

Group Psychology

Which leads me to a theory shared with me by my principal, Sheila Guiney, at the start of my first professional school library job, at Margaret Chase Smith School in Sanford, Maine. I was discussing the need to bring all staff members on board with flexible scheduling and collaboration. She told me that she had been in a workshop many years before in which she had learned a theory that applied to every situation in which a group of people are asked to change. In every group, she said, there will be three clusters, divided roughly into thirds. The first cluster is the "Oh yeah's!" These folks will instantly come on board for a change that they see as exciting, beneficial, and inspiring, even when there is a level of risk. The second cluster, she said, is the "Yeah, but's." This group watches and waits while the "Oh yeah's" jump on board and take the change for a test drive. After the change proves worthy, usually once a full year has gone by, they're willing to hop up to the wheel. Last are the "No way in heck's." This cluster holds stubbornly to the old ways. Even in the light of success experienced by the first two groups, they will not change until forced to change. That's where a risk-taking, forward-seeing administrator proves a wonderful ally.

Reaching the Goal

What are the keys to establishing a successful collaborative practice? First, respect individual strengths. Not every teacher is meant to be first up at bat. Form initial alliances with the collaborative superstars, the "Oh yeah's." Go for stellar collaborations with them and advertise these successes like a PR pro. Watch for opportunities to build on them with your "Yeah, but's." Keep your thinking about collaboration flexible. Do not expect everyone to participate at the same level. Learn to compromise for the sake of forward momentum. And last of all, remember that word of mouth is your best bet, with your teachers, of course, but with your students as well. Gather data, share your successes and your statistics, and encourage others to do the same. And by all means, keep trying, keep believing, and keep the goal in sight—increased student achievement.

 Lisa Von Drasek, Children's Librarian, Bank Street College of Education School for Children, New York City

"The teachers need to trust me, so I do as much as I can to offer whatever I can whenever they need it. It is important to build relationships, not just add work to their load. I practice patience, a willingness to be flexible, and bravery" (n. pag.).

 Bettie Fisher, Media Specialist, Eberwhite Elementary School, Ann Arbor, Michigan

"Mostly, when I've made suggestions to teachers about possible collaboration, I've found that, to start, it's easier with 'friends'—or those on the staff with whom I have the easiest relationships" (n. pag.).

 Laura Dunson, Library Media Specialist, Humphrey's Highland Elementary School, Amarillo, Texas

"Initially, I had to prepare the entire lesson myself and present it to one teacher at a time. I would show them the standards on which the lesson was based and how it was tied to their curriculum. Most lessons involved some kind of project, and I would show them a sample of the finished product with a grading rubric included. The rubric was especially persuasive because it did not require the teacher to come up with yet another grading criteria. If a teacher decided to do the lesson, we would meet and decide who would do what parts of the lesson unit (writing on a standardized form). Then they would feel like they were participating/collaborating. Once I did a lesson unit with one teacher, they would tell the other teachers in the grade level about the lesson, and the others would sign up to do the unit lesson. Word-of-mouth was the best method for getting teachers onboard" (n. pag.).

Using the Template

Elements of the Template

The template used in this book was designed after poring over numerous templates from professional resources and colleagues, and examining many more from my contributors. I borrowed the best elements from each source and then asked several of my contributors to "test drive" the result. We have found this template to be both comprehensive and user friendly and hope that you will too. The elements are as follows:

Header: Includes unit title, library media specialist name and title, teacher name(s) and title(s), school name, school address, school phone number, and library media specialist e-mail address.

Grade Level: Grade(s) that has/have participated in this unit.

Unit Overview: Description of the unit of study, focusing on goals, student learning, and student activity.

Time Frame: From start to finish, the unit takes this time to complete.

Content Area Standards: Exclusive of Information Skills Standards (listed above), content area(s) and standards targeted for each, drawn from local, state, or national guidelines.

Information Power Information Literacy Standards and Indicators: Drawn from IP Literacy Standards document in *Information Power: Building Partnerships for Learning* (AASL 1998). Information Literacy Standards are reproduced, with permission, here. To view the indicators, AASL invites you to read *Information Power: Building Partnerships for Learning*.

Cooperative Teaching Plan: Major teaching responsibilities of the library media specialist and teaching partner(s) for this unit.

>**Library Media Specialist Will:**
>
>**Teacher(s) Will:**

Resources: A list of outstanding resources for use in the unit and a summary of other helpful sources.

>**Print:**
>
>**Electronic:**
>
>**Audiovisuals:**
>
>**Equipment:**

Culminating Learning Product: A description of the student activity, product, or work that makes clear student learning.

Assessment Overview: A description of the student activity, product, or work that is assessed during the unit, with notation of who assesses it and how is it assessed. Assessment tool(s) (rubric, checklist, or other) are included where available.

Adaptations and Extensions: Suggestions of other activities that might extend from this unit (such as speakers or additional products) and how the unit might be adapted to meet the needs of students who are exceptional learners, whether challenged or gifted, as well as those with varied learning styles.

Attachments: Handouts, graphic organizers, and rubrics.

INFORMATION POWER

The Nine Information Literacy Standards
for Student Learning

Excerpted from Chapter 2, "Information Literacy Standards for Student Learning," of
Information Power: Building Partnerships for Learning (AASL 1998)

Information Literacy

Standard 1: The student who is information literate accesses information efficiently and effectively.

Standard 2: The student who is information literate evaluates information critically and competently.

Standard 3: The student who is information literate uses information accurately and creatively.

Independent Learning

Standard 4: The student who is an independent learner is information literate and pursues information related to personal interests.

Standard 5: The student who is an independent learner is information literate and appreciates literature and other creative expressions of information.

Standard 6: The student who is an independent learner is information literate and strives for excellence in information seeking and knowledge generation.

Social Responsibility

Standard 7: The student who contributes positively to the learning community and to society is information literate and recognizes the importance of information to a democratic society.

Standard 8: The student who contributes positively to the learning community and to society is information literate and practices ethical behavior in regard to information and information technology.

Standard 9: The student who contributes positively to the learning community and to society is information literate and participates effectively in groups to pursue and generate information.

Information Literacy Standards for Student Learning: Standards and Indicators may be found online:
<http://www.ala.org/aaslTemplate.cfm?Section=Information_Power&Template=/ContentManagement/
ContentDisplay.cfm&ContentID=19937>

Reprinted with permissions from American Association of School Librarians and Association for Educational Communication. *Information Power: Building Partnerships for Learning.* Chicago: American Library Association, 1998.

Unit Title

Library Media Specialist Name and Title

Teacher Name(s) and Title

School Name

School Address

School Phone Number

Library Media Specialist E-mail Address

Grade Level:

Unit Overview:

Time Frame:

Content Area Standards:

Information Power Information Literacy Standards and Indicators:

Cooperative Teaching Plan:

  Library Media Specialist Will:

  Teacher(s) Will:

Resources:

Learning Product:

Assessment Overview:

Adaptations and Extensions:

Attachments:

Collaborative Units

Unit 1
Kinder Quest

Debra Heimbrook, Library Media Specialist

Frances Parker, Kindergarten Teacher

Carver Elementary School

515 North Cashua Drive, Florence, South Carolina 29501

843-664-8156

<dheimbrook@fsd1.org>

Grade Level: Kindergarten

Unit Overview: Do all snakes bite? Do bugs have ears? How long do tortoises live? Kindergarten students are endlessly curious about the world around them. Inspired by an article in the AASL journal, *Knowledge Quest*, a library media specialist/kindergarten teaching team provide students with a rich variety of visual and audio resources that allows them to research in pairs and learn about animals while meeting science and English language arts standards. Students who are not yet readers feel accomplishment and excitement as they discover information and help to create a book to be enjoyed by other students, teachers, and parents.

Time Frame: Three weeks: three 30-minute library sessions with the media specialist; one initial 30-minute classroom brainstorming session and three 30 minute follow-up classroom sessions to write sentences after each library period; one final 30-minute classroom session for sharing; all classroom sessions with the classroom teacher.

Content Area Standards:
South Carolina K-8 Science Standards
<https://www.ed.sc.gov/apps/cso/standards/supdocs_k8.cfm>

Science Standards
K-1: The student will demonstrate an understanding of scientific inquiry, including the process skills, and mathematical thinking necessary to conduct a simple scientific investigation.
> K1.1 Identify observed objects or events by using the senses.

K-2: The student will demonstrate an understanding of the characteristics of organisms. (Life Science)
> K-2.1: Recognize what organisms need to stay alive (including air, water, food, and shelter).
> K-2.4: Compare individual examples of a particular type of plant or animal to determine that there are differences among individuals.

K-2.5: Recognize that all organisms go through stages of growth and change called life cycles.

South Carolina English Language Arts Curriculum Standards, Pre-K-2
<http://www.myscschools.com/offices/cso/standards/ela/documents/pk_2.pdf>

Writing Goal (W) The student will write for different audiences and purposes.

The Writing Process

W1 The student will apply a **process approach** to writing.

K-W1.1 Continue choosing topics and generating ideas about which to write.

Writing Purposes

W2 The student will write for a variety of **purposes**.

K-W2.1 Demonstrate the ability to use oral language, draw pictures, and/or use letters to explain and inform.

Research Goal (RS) The student will access and use information from a variety of appropriately selected sources to extend his or her knowledge.

Selecting a Research Topic

RS1 The student will select a topic for exploration.

K-RS1.1 Demonstrate the ability to ask *how* and *why* questions about a topic of interest.

Gathering Information and Refining a Topic

RS2 The student will gather information from a variety of sources.

K-RS2.2 Begin gathering information from a variety of sources, including those accessed through the use of technology.

The South Carolina English Language Arts Curriculum Standards are reprinted here with permission from Cathy Jones, Interim ELA Coordinator.

Information Power Information Literacy Standards and Indicators: 1.1, 1.3, 1.4, 1.5, 2.4, 3.2, 5.2, 8.3, 9.1

Cooperative Teaching Plan:

Library Media Specialist Will:
- Lead oral discussion with class, listing possible resources (books, encyclopedias, magazines, people, computers, videos, TV, etc.) used to locate facts about a topic.
- Demonstrate, using concrete examples, the difference between fiction and nonfiction.

- Add the "W" part of the **K**now-**W**ant to Know-**L**earned (K-W-L) Chart through guided discussion with the class, reviewing the "K" part that was created in the classroom.
- Pre-select appropriate reference resources and allow each pair of students to investigate the topic using one or more resources.
- Demonstrate appropriate and effective use of pictures, video/audio clips, and/or written words from pre-selected resources in order to gain desired information about a topic.
- After research is complete, guide discussion to list what was learned by each pair of researchers in the "L" section of the **K**now-**W**ant to Know-**L**earned (K-W-L) Chart.
- When chart is complete, orally review to discuss relationships among the **K**now-**W**ant to Know-**L**earned sections of chart.
- Assist each student pair in constructing at least one page for the class book, consisting of a complete sentence (fact learned about the topic) with an appropriate accompanying illustration.
- Laminate each completed page, bind all pages together, and create a cover to produce a class book about the topic that can be shared with others (see template).
- Share the completed work with the students who created the book and review the research process.
- Share the book with other classes of the same or different grade levels.
- Evaluate the student work with the Rubric.

Teacher Will:

- Brainstorm research topic possibilities with class and help students select one.
- Guide discussion to determine what students already know about the topic and list under the "K" portion of the **K**now-**W**ant to Know-**L**earned (K-W-L) Chart.
- Pair students for media center research.
- Following each library period, assist students who completed their research to construct a sentence about the topics.
- Assist each student pair in constructing at least one page for the class book, consisting of a complete sentence (fact learned about the topic) with an appropriate accompanying illustration.
- Share the completed work with the students who created the book.
- Evaluate the student work with the Rubric.

Resources:
Print

[Note: In addition to specific books listed, other books in the following series may also be used: New True, Let's-Read-and-Find-Out Science, My World, Life Cycles, Animal Opposites, Patterns of Life.]

Crewe, Sabrina. *The Frog* (Life Cycles series). Austin, Texas: Raintree Steck-Vaugn, 1997.
Heinemann First Encyclopedia. Des Plaines, Illinois: Heinemann Library, 2006.
Jenkins, Steve. *Actual Size*. Boston: Houghton Mifflin, 2004.
Johanasen, Heather. *About the Rain Forest*. San Anselmo, California: Treasure Bay, 2000.
Perkins, Wendy. *Animals Building Homes*. Minneapolis: Capstone Press, 2004.
Schlepp, Tammy J. *Minibeasts* (My World series). Brookfield, Connecticut: Copper Beech Books, 2000.

Schuette, Sarah L. *African Animals ABC: An Alphabet Safari*. Minneapolis: Capstone Press, 2003.

Sill, Cathryn. *About Amphibians: A Guide for Children*. Atlanta: Peachtree, 2000.

Zoobooks Magazine. [A selection of appropriate *Zoobooks* magazines]

Teaching Resource

Fisher, Penny, Ellen Heath, and Megan Price. "Kindergarten Research." *Knowledge Quest* 33:2 (November/December 2004): 36-39.

Electronic

"Animal Coloring Pages." *All About Coloring*. 11 October 2006 <http://www.coloring.ws/animals.html>.

"Animal Coloring Pages for Toddlers, Preschool and Kindergarten." *First-School*. 2001-2005. 11 October 2006 <http://www.first-school.ws/theme/animals/cpanimals.htm>.

Col, Jeananda. "Animal Printouts." *Enchanted Learning*. 1999-2006. 11 October 2006 <http://www.enchantedlearning.com/coloring>.

"Skeletons and Skulls." *Sir Robert Hitcham's Primary School*. 11 October 2006 <http://www.hitchams.suffolk.sch.uk/skeletons/index.htm>.

"Sound Safaris." *Wild Sanctuary*. 11 October 2006 <http://www.wildsanctuary.com/safari.html>.

Audiovisual

Photos and videos accessed via <www.unitedstreaming.com>. (subscription required— free to all South Carolina schools through etvStreamlineSC)

Equipment

- Chart paper and markers
- Computers for students to work at in pairs with cord splitters and headphones
- Printer for printing out information from the K-W-L chart and coloring pages
- Comb-style book binder (or other materials needed to bind the completed books)

Culminating Learning Product: Each pair of students will decide on the one most important or interesting fact they learned about their topic. With assistance from the media specialist or classroom teacher, each student pair will create a complete sentence stating the fact (printed at the top of a sheet of computer paper by an adult). An appropriate illustration (freehand drawing or a coloring page) will be added to the sheet by the same student pair. When all pages have been completed, the media specialist or teacher will create a cover page, laminate each page, and bind pages into a class book.

Assessment Overview: The lesson is jointly assessed by the media specialist and the classroom teacher using the Rubric.

Adaptations and Extensions:

- If a number of classes complete books, read each one to the students and compare/contrast information about mammals, reptiles, and amphibians.
- Before reading a book created by other class members, give clues about the type of animal the book is about. Invite students to guess the identity of the animal. Read the book aloud and then share some of the resources used with the students who did not research this type of animal so they can learn more about it.

- Ask academically challenged or ELL students to create their books with pictures only to represents a relationship between things pictured. For example, a student who discovered that kangaroos eat grass, roots, and leaves might use pictures to indicate the information.

- Steer academically challenged and ELL students toward resources with few words and clear photographs or nonfiction books with audiotapes.

- Invite students of all abilities to play a game created from the class book. Glue pictures of each of the topics in the book to one side of two index cards and the word for the picture on another card, then laminate the cards. Students shuffle the cards and play the game in many ways: place cards face-up and match the picture to the word; place the cards face-down and match the picture to the word or picture to the picture; use the picture cards only to play a charades game.

- Enlist gifted students to create the cards for the game above as well as make up their own game by using the cards.

Sample Template for Culminating Activity

Book Cover:	Page 2:	Page 3 to end:
Topic title (e.g. Snakes)	Ms. Smith's kindergarten class researched **Snakes**	Fact researched by student pair about the topic.
Appropriate student created illustration		
		Appropriate illustration
By Ms. Smith's Class Copyright 2007		Add names of students who researched this fact and illustrated.

For Page 2, the central table reads:

The students already **knew:**	The students **wanted** to know:
Snakes don't have legs.	How many babies do they have?
Snakes bite.	What do they eat?
Snakes live in the grass.	Do all snakes bite?

The students answered some of their questions and found out other information about snakes. They share what they have learned on the following pages.

Student Name _____

Rubric

Assessor	Activity	Activity Contribution	Attempted	Limited Understanding of Expectations
Classroom teacher	Participated in discussion to decide on research topic and information already known about topic.			
Library media specialist	Participated in class decisions about what to learn about topic.			
Library media specialist	Contributed to discussion of possible resources about the topic.			
Library media specialist	Distinguished between fiction and nonfiction materials about the topic.			
Library media specialist	Demonstrated the ability to use one or more of the pre-selected resources to gain information about the topic.			
Library media specialist	Made accurate inferences about the topic from the available resources.			
Library media specialist	Followed oral instructions for using resources responsibly and effectively.			
Library media specialist	Related information learned to prior knowledge about the topic.			
Library media specialist	Constructed (with assistance) at least one complete sentence and accompanying illustration about information learned to contribute to a class book.			

Unit 2
Fishing for Facts: Exploring Ocean Animals

Yapha Mason, Librarian

Jan Weissman, Technology Teacher

Abby Green, Kelly Henderson, Tracy Stern, Andy Strauss, Kindergarten Teachers

Jamie Chow, Kindergarten Associate Teacher

Yvette Piñon, Library Assistant

Brentwood School

12001 Sunset Blvd., Los Angeles, California 90049

310-471-1041

<yapha_mason@bwscampus.com>

Grade Level: Kindergarten

Unit Overview: What if you arrived on Earth from Mars and didn't know anything about our oceans, including what lives there? What questions would you ask? And where would you find the answers? During this ocean unit, kindergarteners bring their questions to the library for one of their language arts centers. With the librarian, each group of students explores its questions as students research and write a report on an ocean animal using a modified Big6™ protocol <http://www.big6.com/>. They then illustrate and type their final reports with the technology teacher.

Time Frame: Approximately 6 weeks. Three one-hour language arts periods with the librarian and teachers and 5 half-hour computer classes with the technology teacher.

Content Area Standards: Content Standards for California Public Schools <http://www.cde.ca.gov/be/st/ss/index.asp>

Please refer to the Web site for text of the standards and indicators.

English Language Arts Content Standards for California Public Schools

Reading: Kindergarten
1.0 Word Analysis, Fluency, and Systematic Vocabulary Development
Concepts About Print 1.3

Writing: Kindergarten
1.0 Writing Strategies
Organization and Focus 1.3
Penmanship 1.4

Science Content Standards for California Public Schools

Life Sciences: Kindergarten
2. a
2. c

National Educational Technology Standards for Students
<http://cnets.iste.org/students/s_stands.html>

Please refer to the Web site for text of the standards and indicators.

3. Technology productivity tools
Both indicators.

Information Power Information Literacy Standards and Indicators: 1.3, 1.4, 3.4, 9.3

Cooperative Teaching Plan:

Librarian Will:
- Meet for one hour with each group on a rotating schedule once a week for three weeks.
- Brainstorm questions and sources with students (Week One).
  - Write questions on a large sheet of butcher paper.
  - Explain what an encyclopedia is and why it is a great place to start research.
  - Briefly discuss evaluation of Web sites. Talk about how no one is in charge of the Internet.
- Begin to guide students in locating answers to questions (Week One).
  - Read aloud from the encyclopedia and instruct students to say "STOP" when they hear a fact that answers one of the questions.
  - After finishing the encyclopedia article, guide students to move on to books and other sources in order to research individually. If they are unable to read, ask them to find pictures that seem to illustrate answers they are looking for.
- Finish locating answers to questions (Week Two).
- Help students to rearrange questions and answers into a logical sequential order (Week Two).
  - Physically cut apart each question (with the answer attached) and then tape them back together so students can see and touch the new logical arrangement.
- With students, begin to write a rough draft of the ocean animal report (Week Two).
  - Solicit student help in converting questions and answers into sentences.
  - Write the new sentences on a whiteboard and have students copy them onto their own papers.
- Complete writing of the ocean animal report rough draft (Week Three).
- With classroom and computer teachers, evaluate student work using the Assessment Rubric.

Teachers Will:

- Engage students in an ocean study unit that is a framework for covering the content areas in the kindergarten curriculum, including math, language arts and science.
- With the librarian, one teacher from the kindergarten team will team teach the following tasks each day:
  - Brainstorm questions and sources with students (Week One).
  - Begin to guide students in locating answers to questions (Week One).
  - Finish locating answers to questions (Week Two).
  - Help students to rearrange questions and answers into a logical sequential order (Week Two).
  - With students, begin to write a rough draft of their ocean animal reports (Week Two).
  - Complete writing of the ocean animal report rough drafts (Week Three).
- With librarian and technology teacher, evaluate student work using the Assessment Rubric.

Technology Teacher Will:

- Support students as they draw a picture of their ocean animal using KidPix® and referring to pictures in the books and magazines used for their research.
- Introduce Microsoft® Word and the basics of typing.
- Guide students as they type the final version of their report in Microsoft® Word.
- Merge individual student drawings and reports.
- Print the final projects to go home.
- With librarian and classroom teachers, evaluate student work using the Assessment Rubric

Resources:

Print

Titles in the Rookie Read-About Science series (Children's Press) and the Ocean Life series (Capstone Press) including those listed:

Fowler, Allan. *Friendly Dolphins*. New York: Children's Press, 1997.

Fowler, Allan. *Stars of the Sea*. New York: Children's Press, 2000.

Rustad, Martha E. H. *Dolphins*. Mankato, Minnesota: Capstone, 2001.

Schaefer, Lola M. *Sea horses*. Mankato, Minnesota: Pebble Books, 1999.

Schaefer, Lola M. *Sea stars*. Mankato, Minnesota: Pebble Books, 1999.

Student Discovery Encyclopedia. Chicago: World Book, 2005.

ZooBooks Magazine.

Electronic

"Animal Bytes." *Sea World*. 21 September 2006
  <http://www.seaworld.org/animal-info/animal-bytes/index.htm>.

Equipment

Student-use computers with Kid Pix® and Microsoft® Word software
Data projector
White board
Butcher paper, student lined paper, and pencils

Culminating Learning Product: Students create a rough draft and final typed and illustrated copy of an ocean animal research report.

Assessment Overview: Because most of this project is done as group work, students are assessed on their participation within the group as well as their personal efforts. Students assess their own progress using the Student Checklist and their achievement using the Assessment Rubric. Student work is also scored by the librarian, classroom teachers, and technology teacher using the Assessment Rubric.

Adaptations and Extensions:

English Language Learners and other students challenged in the language arts are invited to:

■ create posters with their information instead of reports;

■ record the report onto audio tape instead of typing it;

■ break the report down into sentences, and ask each child to type and illustrate just one of the sentences, instead of the whole report, then bind these together into a book.

To meet the needs of developmentally young students:

■ use Scholastic Keys™ software to make Microsoft® Word more child-friendly.

To extend the unit for able learners, ask them to:

■ create an aquarium of their animals;

■ gather in groups of five (one for each animal) and present their findings to each other;

■ create additional illustrations to illuminate more of their facts.

To add to fun and involvement for all:

■ design T-shirts to be printed on iron-on inkjet paper;

■ create a slide show with Kid Pix® software.

Student Checklist

Name_____ Animal_____

Step	Task	Date Completed	Student Initials	Teacher Initials
1. Task Definition	• Create a list of the questions we will answer in our project.			
2. Information Seeking Strategies	• Brainstorm all possible sources of information and choose the best sources for this project.			
3. Location and Access	• Find the sources we are going to use. • Make a list of those sources. • Find the information within the sources.			
4. Use of Information	• Help take notes on the information in the sources. • Be sure that we find all the answers to our questions in Step 1.			
5. Synthesis	• Write report. • Type report.			
6. Evaluation	• Complete the evaluation checklist			

Assessment Rubric

Name_____ Animal_____

Teacher's Initials_____ Date_____

	Student's Evaluation		Teacher's/Library Media Specialist's Evaluation	
	MET	**NOT YET**	**MET**	**NOT YET**
I helped create a list of questions to be answered in my report.	☐	☐	☐	☐
I helped brainstorm a list of possible sources to use.	☐	☐	☐	☐
I helped choose the best possible sources.	☐	☐	☐	☐
I read through the sources to find information.	☐	☐	☐	☐
I helped find answers to the questions that I asked in Step 1.	☐	☐	☐	☐
I helped my group by making good suggestions.	☐	☐	☐	☐
I helped my group by being a good listener when other people gave suggestions.	☐	☐	☐	☐
I wrote a rough draft/sloppy copy of my report.	☐	☐	☐	☐
My writing was legible for others to read.	☐	☐	☐	☐
I typed up a final draft of my report.	☐	☐	☐	☐
My report answered all of the questions that we asked in Step 1.	☐	☐	☐	☐
Looking at my answers to the above questions, how do I think I did on this report?	☐ Did my best ☐ Tried my hardest ☐ Could have done better			

Unit 3
Geology for First Graders

Linda D. Sherouse, Library Media Specialist, BS, M.Ed., MLIS

Anna Spalding, Grade 1 Classroom Teacher, BA, M.Ed.

Laura Sher, Geologist/Science Consultant, BS, MS, M.Ed.

North Hampton School

201 Atlantic Avenue, North Hampton, New Hampshire 03862

603-964-5501

<lsherouse@sau21.k12.nh.us>

Grade: 1

Unit Overview: Geology for First Graders involves the collaboration of a library media specialist, a classroom teacher, and a geologist. It gives students a greater awareness of their natural world while satisfying their curiosity about rocks and minerals. Students become familiar with the layers of the earth, the rock cycle, and common rocks and minerals. They learn through experiential and interdisciplinary lessons that combine hands-on exploration of rocks and minerals with mathematics as well as language, visual, and creative arts. Students demonstrate critical thinking skills, communication skills, research skills, computer skills, math skills, and cooperation skills as they gain knowledge of new scientific concepts.

Time Frame: Thirty days: six 30-minute weekly library blocks with the LMS; thirty daily 30-minute language arts blocks with the classroom teacher; two 45-minute science blocks per week for 6 weeks with the classroom teacher and occasionally also with the LMS and consultant.

Content Area Standards: The New Hampshire Curriculum Frameworks
<http://www.ed.state.nh.us/education/doe/organization/curriculum/Curriculum.htm>

Uncopyrighted material available online from the New Hampshire Department of Education, Concord, New Hampshire.

Earth Space Science
ESS1 - The Earth and Earth materials, as we know them today, have developed over long periods of time, through constant change processes.

K-2 Grade Span Expectations (GSE's)
2. COMPOSITION AND FEATURES
S(ESS1)-2-2.2 Use observable properties, such as color and texture, to classify and organize rocks and minerals.

S(ESS1)-2-2.3 Recognize that Earth materials have a variety of properties, including size, shape, color and texture.

5. PROCESSES AND RATES OF CHANGE
S(ESS1)-2-5.1 Recognize that some changes are too slow or too fast to be easily observed.

6. ROCK CYCLE
S(ESS1)-2-6.1 Explain that large rocks can be broken down into smaller rocks.
S(ESS1)-2-6.2 Describe rocks and soils in terms of their physical properties.

Mathematics Local GLEs

Functions and Algebra
Grade 1
M(F&A)–1–1 **Identifies and extends to specific cases a variety of patterns** (repeating and growing [numeric and non-numeric]) represented in models, tables, or sequences by extending the pattern to the next one, two, or three elements, by finding a missing element (e.g., 2, 4, 6, ___, 10), or by translating repeating patterns across formats (e.g., an abb pattern can be represented as snap, clap, clap; or red, yellow, yellow; or 1,2,2).

Problem Solving, Reasoning, and Proof
K-2
M(PRP)–2–1 **Students will use problem-solving strategies to investigate and understand increasingly complex mathematical content** and be able to:

- Formulate and solve multi-step problems from everyday and mathematical situations.
- Solve problems using a variety of strategies (e.g., working backwards, looking for patterns and relationships; guess and check; making tables, charts, or organized lists; solving a simpler version of a problem, drawing a diagram; or creating a model).
- Verify and interpret results with respect to the original problem.
- Determine if the solution of a problem is reasonable.
- Solve problems using manipulatives, graphs, charts, diagrams, and calculators.
- Demonstrate that a problem may be solved in more than one way.
- Exhibit confidence in their ability to solve problems independently and in groups.
- Display increasing perseverance, and persistence in problem solving.

Communications, Connections, and Representations
K-2
M(CCR)–2–1 Students **will communicate their understanding of mathematics** and be able to:

- Demonstrate mathematical communication through discussion, reading, writing, listening, and responding, individually and in groups.
- Discuss relationships between everyday language and mathematical language and symbols (e.g., words that mean something different in mathematics and in everyday life).
- Explain conclusions, thought processes, and strategies in problem-solving situations.
- Discuss, illustrate, and write about mathematical concepts and relationships.
- Draw pictures and use objects to illustrate mathematical concepts.

English Language Arts
Written and Oral Language Grade Level Expectations (GLEs)
Grade 1
W-1-10 Students use pre-writing, drafting, revising, editing, and critiquing to produce final drafts of written products.

W-1-1 Students demonstrate command of the structures of sentences, paragraphs, and text by...
- W-1-1.1 Writing recognizable short sentences
- W-1-1.5 Distinguishing between letters, words, and sentences
- W-1-1.6 Applying directionality as appropriate to text (e.g., left to right, top to bottom)

W-1-3 In response to literary or informational text read aloud or read independently, students make and support analytical judgments about text by...
- W-1-3.1 Using prior knowledge or references to text to respond to a question (evidence may take the form of pictures, words, sentences, or some combination)
- W-1-3.4 Organizing ideas by using a beginning and an ending given a structure

W-1-5 Students demonstrate use of narrative strategies by...
- W-1-5.5 Writing about observations and experiences

W-1-6 In informational writing (reports or procedures), students organize ideas/concepts by...
- W-1-6.2 Representing facts through pictures, "words," "sentences," or some combination
- W-1-6.3 Listing steps of a procedure in a logical order, with instructional support

W-1-7 In informational writing (reports or procedures only), students effectively convey purpose by...
- W-1-7.1 Using pictures to create meaning

W-1-9 In independent writing, students demonstrate command of English conventions by...
- W-1-9.5a Using phonemic awareness and letter knowledge to spell independently (using phonetic or temporary spelling when needed)
- W-1-9.5b. Correctly spelling many common words (e.g., had, can, including own first name)

Information Power Information Literacy Standards and Indicators: 1.1, 1.2, 1.3, 1.4

Cooperative Teaching Plan:

Library Media Specialist Will:
- Utilize community resources to locate a geologist.
- Observe the content covered by the geologist's visits and reinforce vocabulary in the library media center.
- With students, view audiovisual resources that introduce rock formation and various earth processes.
- Provide students with multiple print resources to be used in the classroom as well as related choices for borrowing.
- Assist students with Internet use, exploring various Web sites for information and interactive activities.

- Assist students in generating and answering their questions using library media center resources.

- Engage students in edible hands-on activities that simulate the formation of the three igneous rock types. (Activity 5)

- Engage students in an edible hands-on activity that simulates the formation of sedimentary rock. (Activity 7)

- Engage students in an edible hands-on activity that simulates the formation of metamorphic rock. (Activity 8)

- Collaborate with classroom teacher and geologist on culminating activities (creating a *Rock Identification Game* and publishing a *Big Book of Rocks We Know*).

Classroom Teacher Will:

- Facilitate the unit, connecting science and literacy.

- Engage students in hands-on exploration of rocks and minerals.

- Read aloud *If You Find a Rock* by Peggy Christian and invite students to both tell and write a story about a rock they have seen.

- Read aloud *Milo and the Magical Stone* by Marcus Pfister and engage children in the "Shiny Rock" activity. (Activity 1)

- Read aloud *Elizabeti's Doll* by Stephanie Stuve Bodeen and make a "Rock Buddy." (Activity 2)

- Assist students with shared reading of nonfiction.

- Introduce scientific vocabulary.

- Generate discussion and inquiry.

- Engage the students in the construction of a clay model of the earth's layers. (Activity 3)

- Take students on a nature walk to explore the earth's crust.

- Enable students to differentiate between rocks and minerals by providing them with a concrete experience on how minerals form and how minerals combine with other minerals to create rocks. (Activity 4)

- Construct a center where students will sort and classify a variety of rocks based on attributes of their own choosing (i.e. shiny vs. dull, rough vs. smooth, angular vs. round, multi-colored vs. one color, etc.).

- Engage students in mathematics activities that build on rock study experiences using Geology for First Graders: Math Problems.

- Engage students in an edible hands-on activity that simulates the formation of the three igneous rock types. (Activity 5)

- Facilitate the sorting of rocks of differing sizes by hand and by using geologic sieves. (Activity 6)

- Engage students in an edible hands-on activity that simulates the formation of sedimentary rock. (Activity 7)

- Engage students in an edible hands-on activity that simulates the formation of metamorphic rock. (Activity 8)

- Guide students in creative and scientific writing (including collecting and recording data and journal writing).

■ Collaborate with library media specialist and geologist on culminating activities (creating a *Rock Identification Game* and publishing a *Big Book of Rocks We Know*).

Geologist Will:

■ Provide the class with igneous, sedimentary and metamorphic rocks, and common rock-forming minerals for comparison study.

■ Introduce the students to common rock-forming minerals, mineral properties and the difference between a rock and a mineral.

■ Present an overview on minerals and igneous, sedimentary, and metamorphic rocks.

■ Collaborate with the library media specialist and classroom teacher on scientific activities and experiments and provide technical support as needed.

■ Collaborate with library media specialist and geologist on culminating activities (creating a *Rock Identification Game* and publishing a *Big Book of Rocks We Know*).

Resources:

Print
Student Print Resources
Bial, Raymond. *A Handful of Dirt*. New York: Walker, 2000.

Bodeen, Stephanie Stuve. *Elizabeti's Doll*. New York: Lee & Low Books, 1998.

Bramwell, Martyn. *Rocks & Fossils*. London: Usborne, 1983.

Challoner, Jack. *Rocks and Minerals*. Milwaukee: Gareth Stevens, 1999.

Christian, Peggy. *If You Find a Rock*. San Diego: Harcourt, 2000.

Cole, Joanna. *The Magic School Bus: Inside the Earth*. New York: Scholastic, 1987.

Downs, Sandra. *Earth's Hidden Treasures*. Brookfield, Connecticut: Twenty-First Century Books, 1999.

Edwards, Ron and Lisa Dickie. *Diamonds and Gemstones*. New York: Crabtree, 2004.

Edwards, Ron and James Gladstone. *Gold*. New York: Crabtree, 2004.

Erickson, Jon. *An Introduction to Fossils and Minerals: Seeking Clues to the Earth's Past*. New York: Facts on File, 1992.

Flanagan, Alice K. *Rocks*. Minneapolis: Compass Point Books, 2001.

Fuller, Sue. *Rocks & Minerals*. London: Dorling Kindersley, 1995.

Gallant, Roy A. *Fossils*. New York: Marshall Cavendish, 2001.

Gallant, Roy A. *Minerals*. New York: Marshall Cavendish, 2001.

Gallant, Roy A. *Rocks*. New York: Marshall Cavendish, 2001.

Gibbons, Gail. *Planet Earth, Inside Out*. New York: Morrow, 1995.

Hurst, Carol. Otis. *Rocks in His Head*. New York: Greenwillow, 2001.

Kurlansky, Mark. *The Story of Salt*. New York: G. P. Putnam's Sons, 2006.

Lauber, Patricia. *Dinosaurs Walked Here: and Other Stories Fossils Tell*. New York: Bradbury Press, 1987. OP

Llewellyn, Claire. *Volcanoes*. Chicago: Heinemann Library, 2000.

Morganelli, Adrianna. *Minerals*. New York: Crabtree, 2004.

Morris, Neil. *Rocks and Soil*. North Mankato, Minnesota: Thameside Press, 2002.

Oliver, Ray. *Rocks & Fossils*. New York: Random House, 1993. OP

Parker, Steve. *Rocks and Minerals*. Milwaukee: Gareth Stevens, 2002.

Peacock, Graham and Jill Jesson. *Geology*. New York: Thomson Learning, 1995. OP

Pfister, Marcus. *Milo and the Magical Stones*. New York: North-South Books, 1997. OP

Polacco, Patricia. *My Ol' Man*. New York: Philomel Books, 1995.

Rosinsky, Natalie M. *Rocks: Hard, Soft, Smooth, and Rough.* Minneapolis: Picture Window Books, 2003. Also available as an e-book from Picture Window Books.

Simon, Seymour. *Danger! Volcanoes.* San Francisco: SeaStar Books, 2002.

Steig, William. *Sylvester and the Magic Pebble.* New York: Simon and Schuster, 1969.

Stewart, Melissa. *Fossils.* Chicago: Heinemann Library, 2002.

Stewart, Melissa. *Igneous Rocks.* Chicago: Heinemann Library, 2002.

Stewart, Melissa. *Metamorphic Rocks.* Chicago: Heinemann Library, 2002.

Stewart, Melissa. *Minerals.* Chicago: Heinemann Library, 2002.

Stewart, Melissa. *Sedimentary Rocks.* Chicago: Heinemann Library, 2002.

Walker, Cyril and David Ward. *Fossils.* New York: Dorling Kindersley, 1992.

Woolley, Alan. *Rocks and Minerals.* (Spotter's Guide series). London: Usborne, 2000.

Teacher Print Resources

Anderson, Alan, et. al. *Geology Crafts for Kids.* New York: Sterling, 1996. OP

Audubon Society Field Guide to North American Rocks and Minerals. New York: Alfred A. Knopf, 1978.

Geology (Grades 1-3). Science Works for Kids Series. Monterey, California: Evan-Moor, 1998.

Gibson, O. "The Building Blocks of Geology." *Science and Children* 39 (1): 38-41.

Lunis, Natalie. *Rocks and Soil.* New York: Newbridge, 1998.

Lunis, Natalie. *Investigating Rocks.* New York: Newbridge, 1999.

Sorel, K. "Rock Solid." *Science and Children* 40 (5): 24-29.

Stewart, Melissa. *Fossils.* Portsmouth, New Hampshire: Heinemann Library, 2002.

Stewart, Melissa. *Igneous Rocks.* Portsmouth, New Hampshire: Heinemann Library, 2002.

Stewart, Melissa. *Metamorphic Rocks.* Portsmouth, New Hampshire: Heinemann Library, 2002.

Stewart, Melissa. *Minerals.* Portsmouth, New Hampshire: Heinemann Library, 2002.

Stewart, Melissa. *Sedimentary Rocks.* Portsmouth, New Hampshire: Heinemann Library, 2002.

Varelas, M. and J. Benhart. "Welcome to Rock Day." *Science and Children*, 41(4): 40-45.

Wyler, Rose. *Science Fun with Mud and Dirt.* New York: Simon and Schuster, 1986.

Electronic Resources
Student-Use Websites

"Discover How Rocks Are Formed!" *Rock Hounds.* 29 January 1999. 21 September 2006 <http://sln.fi.edu/fellows/payton/rocks/create/index.html>.

"Fossil Matching Game." *Royal Ontario Museum.* 21 September 2006 <http://www.rom.on.ca/schools/fossils/game.php>.

Grolier Online. 21 September 2006 <http://auth.grolier.com/cgi-bin/authV2?bffs=N>. (subscription required)

"Kidspage." *NewsBank.* 21 September 2006 <http://www.newsbank.com/>.

"Mega Disasters: Volcanic Eruptions." *The History Channel.* 24 September 2006. <http://www.history.com/media.do?action=clip&id=Mdisasters_3Mi_broadband&gclid=COugwdf9yIcCFQvsPgodMw18Fw>.

"The Rock Cycle Experiments." *BBC Education.* 21 September 2006 <http://www.bbc.co.uk/education/rocks/rockcycle.shtml>.

"Sampling Rocks." *Science NetLinks.* 06 December 2000. 21 September 2006 <http://www.sciencenetlinks.com/lessons_printable.cfm?DocID=110>.

Sanders, Rex. "Ask a Geologist." *U.S. Geological Survey.* 08 April 2006. 21 September 200 <http://walrus.wr.usgs.gov/ask-a-geologist/>.

Professional-Use Websites

"The Learning Web." *United States Geological Survey*. 21 September 2006
   <http://education.usgs.gov/>.
   Dedicated to K-12 education in geology, geography and hydrology. Includes fun activities for students, project ideas, homework help, innovative lesson plans and activities for teachers, research tools and resources.

National Park Service. 21 September 2006 <www.nps.gov>.
   Provides information on curriculum based learning tools, parks as classrooms, teaching resources, workshops and skills development.

Rocks and Minerals. 21 September 2006 <www.rocks-and-minerals.com>
   Provides basic information about how rocks are formed, rocks that record the past, rocks that change into different rocks; concise text, great photographs and graphics.

Sanders, Rex. "Ask-a-Geologist." *United States Geological Survey*. 8 April 2006. 21 September 2006 <http://walrus.wr.usgs.gov/ask-a-geologist/>.
   Students and teachers can e-mail earth science questions to a geologist here.

Veins, Rob. "Student Resource Center." *Geology Link®*. 21 September 2006
   <www.geologylink.com>.
   Contains current news on geologic events, virtual classrooms, virtual field trips and resources for K-12 educators.

Audiovisuals

Digging up Dinosaurs. Videocassette. GPN Educational Media, 1986.

Hill of Fire, Videocassette. GPN Educational Media, 1998.

Inside the Earth. Videocassette. GPN Educational Media, 1989.

Magic School Bus Blows Its Top. Videocassette. Scholastic, 1996.

Real World Science: Rocks and Minerals. Videocassette. Sunburst Communications, 1999.

Culminating Learning Product: Students create a *Rock Identification Game*, based on the Fossil Matching Game <http://www.rom.on.ca/schools/fossils/game.php>. Students also create a *Big Book of Rocks We Know*. Each student chooses two to three rocks to write scientific observations for. They are accompanied by digital pictures taken of rocks found by students and contributed by the geologist.

Assessment Overview: The *Rock Identification Game* is self-corrected using an answer key while the *Big Book of Rocks We Know* is assessed using the Big Book Rubric.

Adaptations and Extensions:

Adaptations are naturally embedded into the unit:

- The Fossil Game and other picture and realia clues work to serve the needs of both ELL and challenged students.

- The bibliography includes books at a variety of reading levels to meet the needs of both gifted and typical first grade students.

To extend the unit:

- Suggest exploration of how crystals form and how to identify a rock that might be a geode.

- Allow students who pose specific questions to access the library resources with the LMS and explore beyond the class activities.

Observation Sheet Instructions

Mineral Observation Sheet—Figure U3.7

During the initial study of mineral samples brought in by the geologist, ask each student to select one mineral and describe the characteristics (listed on the left side of the observation sheet) in their mineral. If time permits, ask students to swap their sheets and minerals with a partner and compare findings. The geologist will help them add the name for the mineral under observation.

Igneous Rock Observation Sheet Instructions—Figure U3.9

After cooking up the Igneous experiment, have students circulate among the three types of cooked rocks. Caution them not to touch the trays or "rocks" as some may be eaten later. Ask students to help create a word list of descriptive words they might like to use. Then, request that they draw each type of rock and write sentences describing what they see. Introduce the transparent vs. translucent concept (using a piece of glass to demonstrate) at this time as a piece of obsidian will be quite translucent.

Sedimentary Rock Observation Sheet—Figure U3.12

After completing the experiment, when all layers have solidified and prior to eating, ask each student to observe the layers in the cup. Make a word list on the board of related terms and then ask students to draw what they see and create sentences describing their experiment.

Metamorphic Rock Observation Sheet—Figure U3.14

Once the actual "rock" has been created, prior to baking, pass these sheets out to students and tell them they are going to draw what they have created and write about the process on the Before side. Ask what words they would like on their word wall to help with their sentences. Also, once this part is complete, have them predict what changes will occur when 350 degrees of heat is applied to the "rocks." Talk about which "minerals" might change the most and add some additional words for their observations. Once the "rocks" are cooked, students can draw and complete the After side.

Math Problems

Exploring the Earth's Crust

The class collected so many things from the Earth's crust. We filled 19 plastic bags.
    Each bag had 3 things from the Earth's crust in it.
How many things did our class collect from the Earth's crust?
Show your math work and explain your math thinking clearly.

Rocks Go to School

Jillian collected lots of rocks and brought them to school. She had so many rocks, she
    filled up 3 cardboard egg cartons and half of another egg carton.
How many rocks did Jillian bring to school?
Show your math work and explain your math thinking clearly.

Collecting Rocks

Sarah collected rocks every day after school.
On the first day, she collected 4 rocks.
On the second day, she collected 8 rocks.
On the third day, she collected 12 rocks.
This increasing pattern continued for the 5-day school week.
How many rocks did Sarah collect on the fifth day?
How many rocks did Sarah collect in all over the 5 days?
Show your math work and explain your math thinking clearly.

Who Has More Rocks?

Everyone in the class is bringing rocks to school for the new unit.
Ricardo brought 17 rocks to school.
Katie brought 23 rocks to school.
Talisha brought 25 rocks to school.
Anthony brought 18 rocks to school.
Did the boys or the girls bring more rocks to school?
How many more did they bring?
Show your math work and explain your math thinking clearly.

The Lost Rocks!

Ashley put 26 rocks in a bag to bring to school. When she got to school she discovered
    a hole in her bag. Some of the rocks had fallen out. She only had 18 rocks!
How many rocks did Ashley lose?
Show your math work and explain your math thinking clearly.

How Many Rocks?

The class collected so many rocks. The rocks filled 11 plastic bags. Each plastic bag
    had 5 rocks in it.
How many rocks did the class collect?
Show your math work and explain your math thinking clearly.

Sharing Rocks

Each table of students was given 32 rocks to share and study. There were 4 students at
    each table. Each student received the same number of rocks.
How many rocks did each student get?
Show your math work and explain your math thinking clearly.

Special Rocks

The class made a table of "special" rocks.
There were 24 striped rocks!
There were 17 rocks with sparkles!
There were 26 super smooth rocks!
There were 15 rocks with bumps!
How many rocks were on the "special" table?
Show your work and explain your math thinking clearly.

Twice as Many!

The class counted out 37 rocks and put them on a table. The principal saw them and
    said, "I have **twice as many** rocks in my collection."
How many rocks does the principal have?
Show your math work and explain your math thinking clearly.

Types of Rocks

The class members sorted their rocks by type.
They had 35 IGNEOUS rocks.
They had 26 METAMORPHIC rocks.
They had 44 SEDIMENTARY rocks.
How many more sedimentary rocks were there than igneous rocks?
Show your math work and explain your math thinking clearly.

BONUS: Can you calculate how many rocks there were in all?

Being Generous

One class had 54 rocks. They gave 27 rocks to another class who did not have enough.
How many rocks did the generous class have left?
Show your math work and explain your math thinking clearly.

Big Book Rubric

Geologist_____ Date_____

	1	2	3	4
Science	Works with 1 or no rocks.	Works with 2 rocks.	Works with 3 rocks.	Works with 3-4 rocks.
	Does not yet describe any rocks accurately.	Accurately describes 1 or 2 rocks but may be inconsistent.	Accurately describes 2-3 rocks but may be inconsistent.	Accurately describes 3 rocks consistently.
	The rocks appear to have all of the same attributes.	The rocks are different in one of three attributes (color, size, texture).	2 of the rocks are varied in color, size, and texture.	All of the rocks are varied in color, size, and texture.
Writing	Uses 1 or no glossary words in written description.	Uses 2 glossary words in written description.	Uses 3 glossary words in written description.	Uses 4 glossary words in written description.
	Uses 1 or no adjectives correctly.	Uses 2 adjectives correctly.	Uses 3 adjectives correctly.	Uses 4 adjectives correctly.
	Writes 1 or fewer complete sentences.	Writes 2 complete sentences about each rock.	Writes 3 complete sentences about each rock.	Write 4 complete sentences about each rock.

Activity 1: Shiny Stone

Materials:
Book: *Milo and the Magical Stone* by Marcus Pfister
Smooth egg-shaped rocks (1 or 2 per child)
Newspaper
Dishwashing soap
Water
Pie tins (1 per child)
Clear nail polish

Teacher Set-up:
1. Cover a work area with newspaper.
2. Scrub rocks with soapy water, rinse well and let dry completely.
3. Fill pie tins with water (approx. $3/4$" deep).
4. Add one drop of clear nail polish into the water. The drop of nail polish will spread out over the surface and make a cellophane-like film.
5. Place one pie tin at each child's place in the work area.

Procedures:
1. Tell the children that they will be making their own shiny stones.
2. Next, ask the children to each choose a smooth rock and take it back to their work place.
3. Tell them that the pie tin in front of them is filled with water and a drop of clear nail polish and that it will transform their ordinary stone into a magical one.
4. Demonstrate the procedure for the children (hold the side of the rock with your fingers and roll it slowly across the bottom of the pie tin).
5. Direct the children to do the same and to put their stones on the newspaper to dry (it will take several hours to dry completely).
6. The children can then make a second magical stone by adding an additional drop of nail polish to the pie tin and repeating the rolling process.

Activity 2: Rock Buddy

Materials:
Book: *Elizabeti's Doll* by Stephanie Stuve Bodeen
Rocks of various sizes
Poster paint
Trays for paint (egg cartons)
Paint brushes (1 per child)
Water
Wiggly eyes
Tacky glue
Newspaper

Teacher Set-up:
1. Cover the work area with newspaper.
2. Place paint, a brush, water, wiggly eyes and glue at each child's place in the work area.

Procedures:
1. When you have finished reading the story, review the plot with the children focusing on the imagery (terms and expressions that appeal to the senses) and figurative language (symbolism).
2. Ask the children to imagine a rock buddy of their own and the kind of experience that they would have with it.
3. Next, ask students to each choose a rock and take it back to their work place.
4. Direct them to paint their ordinary rocks in any way they wish, thereby transforming them into special rock buddies. Wiggly eyes can also be added.

Activity 3: Directions for Clay Model of the Earth's Layers

Materials:
Modeling clay (4 different colors)
Pie tins (1 per student)
Plastic knives (1 per student)
Baggies (for completed models to be transported home)

Procedures:
1. Demonstrate how to create the inner core, and then the outer core which surrounds it, followed by the mantle, and then the relatively thin crust.
2. Slice the model of the Earth in half to show the cross-section of the finished model.
3. Invite the students to create their own model at their work place and slice it in half when completed.

Activity 4: Mineral Building Activity

Materials:

Mineral Observation Sheet
Mineral collection that includes:

Feldspar	Hornblende	Quartz
Galena	Magnetite	Sulfur
Graphite	Mica	Talc
Halite	Pyrite	

A large chunk of granite (igneous rock)
A large chunk of gneiss (metamorphic rock)
Hand lenses
Geology Journals
Pencils
Colored pencils
Lego® blocks (small size, 1000 piece container)

Preview:

1. Review with the children that minerals are the basic geologic materials that make up the solid part of our planet.
2. Ask the students to look closely at the different mineral samples. They may observe them with a hand lens, touch them and scratch and smell them.
3. Talk about the unique nature of each mineral and devise a simple classification based on color, hardness, shape (atomic structure) and luster (metallic or non-metallic).
4. Identify each mineral and its use.
5. Direct the students to illustrate the minerals and write brief descriptions of them on their Mineral Observation Sheets.
6. Review that when different minerals are combined, the result is a rock. Rocks look different from each other because they are formed in different ways (i.e. from the cooling of volcanic magma or molten rock deep within the earth, from the deposition of sediment from rivers, etc.).
7. Pass around a large piece of granite (igneous rock) and show the students how to recognize quartz, feldspar, mica, and hornblende (the minerals that make up this rock).
8. Pass around a large piece of gneiss (metamorphic rock) and tell the students that this rock is also made up of the very same minerals as granite, but it looks different from granite (it is banded) because it was formed in a different way.
9. Tell the students that they will now be building their own minerals out of Lego® blocks and that they will combine their minerals to form rocks.

Procedures:

1. Give each student 10-12 Lego® blocks of each color (red, blue, yellow, green, white). They can be of varying sizes. Each color grouping of Lego® blocks will represent a different mineral.
2. Tell the students that the Lego® blocks are atoms (the smallest building pieces of minerals), and challenge them to put together the Lego® blocks in any pattern they choose.
3. After the first attempt, direct students to take apart their creation and form a new mineral pattern.
4. Invite the students to then compare their Lego® models to others. Each different model represents the unique atomic structure of a mineral.
5. Next, ask the students to work in small groups to build more minerals and then combine them to create rocks. Give the groups additional Lego® blocks (20 of each color).
6. Challenge some of the student groups to combine their minerals to make granite and others to make gneiss. (Granite will be a random cluster of minerals; gneiss will be a banded, or striped cluster of minerals).

Mineral Observation Sheet

Geologist _____

Date _____

Mineral Observation

_____

_____

_____

_____

_____

_____

_____

_____

Look for...
- Color
- Shape
- Size
- Weight
- Texture

Activity 5: Cooking Up Obsidian, Pumice, and Granite: An Igneous Rock Activity

Materials:
Igneous Rock Observation Sheet
Cookie sheets (with sides) (3)
Cooking pots (3)
Measuring cups and spoons
Wooden spoons for stirring (3)
Sugar (6 cups)
Water
Rainbow sprinkles
Milk (1/4 cup)
Baking soda (4 Tbsp.)
Cooking spray (to grease the cookie sheets)
Stove top (or 3 hot plates)
Baggies

Procedures:
1. Review with the children that obsidian and pumice form from rapidly cooling lava on the surface of the earth and that granite forms slowly from the cooling of magma deep within the earth.
2. Set out the 3 cookie sheets on the table and lightly coat each with the cooking spray.
3. Set out the 3 cooking pots on the table.
4. Add 2 cups of sugar to each pot and just enough water to form a thick liquid. Stir.
5. Next, place each pot on a burner or hot plate and bring to a boil. Stir the pots until the sugar liquid becomes clear.
6. Take the first pot of hot sugar liquid and pour it onto a cookie sheet. Set aside. This mixture will cool rapidly and become smooth and glassy like **obsidian.**
7. Take the second pot of hot sugar liquid and add 4 Tbsp. of baking soda to it. Gas bubbles will appear, simulating the escaping gases on the top of a lava flow. Pour onto a cookie sheet and set aside. This mixture will also cool rapidly and be filled with air holes like **pumice.**
8. Take the last pot of hot sugar liquid and add $^1/_4$ cup of milk and rainbow sprinkles to it. Pour onto a cookie sheet and set aside. The added milk will make this mixture cool more slowly than the **obsidian** and **pumice**, and it will appear crystalline like **granite.**
9. Observe and record on Igneous Rock Observation Sheet.

Igneous Rock Observation Sheet

Geologist _____ **Date** _____

1. Draw a picture of what it looks like.
2. Write about what it looks like.

Name of Rock:

Activity 6: Sorting Weathered Rocks of Differing Sizes

Materials:
Geologic screens (2.0mm, 0.50mm, 0.125mm)
Weathered rocks ranging in size from large pebbles (>4mm) to fine sand (>0.125mm)
Paper plates
Metric rulers

Preview:
1. Review with the children that clastic sedimentary rocks are formed from pre-existing igneous, metamorphic or sedimentary rocks that have been broken up by weathering and then transported, deposited, and lithified (compacted and hardened) into rock.
2. Tell the students that they will be looking at and sorting weathered rocks of varying sizes from large pebbles to fine grained sand and that they must imagine that these weathered rocks have been transported and deposited right into their classroom and have yet to be lithified into a rock.
3. Tell the students that the size of these weathered rocks will determine the type of sedimentary rock that they will become (i.e. pebble sized rocks will be lithified into **conglomerate**; sand sized grains will be lithified into **sandstone**) and that their job of sorting is very important.

Procedures:
1. With students in small groups, give each group a bag of weathered rocks ranging in size from large pebbles to fine sand, and some paper plates.
2. Ask each group to sort their rocks into at least three different sizes.
3. Ask each group to explain the sizes they chose for sorting, whether they found it increasingly more difficult to sort the smaller sizes, and whether they can think of a different way to sort the rocks.
4. Explain to the children that geologists often use sieving screens to separate sediment into varying sizes.
5. Show them a set of screens and explain that each screen has a different mesh size, measured in millimeters. The screens are placed one on top of the other from smallest mesh size on the bottom to largest mesh size on top.
6. Demonstrate how sieving works by taking a sample of weathered rocks and pouring it onto the stack of sieves. Gently shake the stack.
7. Take off the top sieve. Show the students that everything trapped on this sieve is 2mm or larger in size (all the pebbles) and is classified as gravel. Take off the middle sieve. Show the students that everything trapped on this sieve (>0.50mm) is classified as coarse sand. Take off the bottom sieve. Show the students that everything trapped on this sieve (>0.125 mm) is classified as medium to fine sand. Anything that falls through the bottom sieve and collects on the tray is silt and clay.

Activity 7: Recipe for Edible Sedimentary Rocks

Materials:

Sedimentary Rock Observation Sheet
1 Large box each of raspberry, lime, and lemon gelatin
1 Package of Oreo® cookies
1 (8oz) container of whipped topping
7 Bananas
Large plastic cups, one for each child, plus a few extra
Paper plates

Plastic knives
Cooking pot (or something to boil water in)
3 Mixing bowls
Measuring cup
Mixing spoons
Rolling pin
Stove top (or hot plate)
Refrigerator/Freezer
Water

Teacher Set-up:

1. Place a paper plate, knife, and half of a banana at each child's place in the work area.
2. Crush the Oreo® cookies with a rolling pin, and set aside in several of the large plastic cups.
3. Make the raspberry, lime, and lemon gelatin in separate mixing bowls, following the package directions. Set the lime and lemon gelatin aside.
4. Pour the raspberry gelatin into the bottom of each plastic cup, measuring approximately one half inch thick. Place the cups in a freezer and set for 10-15 minutes.

Preview:

1. Review with the students that clastic sedimentary rocks are formed from pre-existing rocks that have been weathered, transported, deposited, and lithified (compacted and hardened). Sedimentary rocks made of **pebbles, sand, silt** and **clay** become cemented over time to form conglomerate, **sandstone, siltstone** and **shale**, respectively.
2. Tell the students that they will be creating edible sedimentary rocks that formed in a lake basin.

Procedures:

1. Give each student a plastic cup with the raspberry gelatin in it. Tell them that their cup represents a lake basin, and that the raspberry layer is **shale**, formed from the lithification of **clay** (mud) particles that settled quietly in the lake basin.
2. Have the students cut banana slices and put them on top of the raspberry layer. Tell the students that the bananas are fossilized remains of ancient fish, shellfish, and plants that once lived in the lake. Over time, the lake dried out and all the living organisms died.
3. Next, tell the students to imagine a river flowing into the basin and pour the yellow gelatin over the bananas. This represents a new layer of sediment carried in by the river (perhaps silt, that lithifies over time into **siltstone**).
4. Next, tell the students to imagine that violent spring rains bring boulders, pebbles, and coarse sediment cascading down a nearby mountainside and into the river that in turn carries this increased sediment load into the once quiet basin. Sand sized sediment particles are now deposited into the lake basin. Have the students sprinkle the crushed Oreo® cookies over the yellow gelatin, representing the **sand** layer that will lithify over time into **sandstone**.
5. Lastly, stir the whipped topping into the lime gelatin, and pour this on top of the Oreo® cookies. Tell the students that so much sediment has been washed into the basin from the eroding mountainside that the once clear lake is muddied with suspended silt and clay particles. Over time the rains cease and the lake once again dries up, leaving a fresh layer of **muddy sediment** that will lithify into **shale**.
6. Label each child's cup with his/her name and place in the refrigerator for several hours to "lithify."
7. Observe and record on Sedimentary Rock Observation Sheet.

Sedimentary Rock Observation Sheet

Date _____

Geologist _____

Activity 8: Recipe for Edible Metamorphic Rocks

Materials:
Metamorphic Rock Observation Sheet
1 Bag of peppermint candies, crushed
1 Bag of mini marshmallows
1 Bag of mini semi-sweet chocolate chips
1 Package of Oreo® cookies, crushed
Flour
Paper plates, 1 per student, plus extra
Cookie sheets (2)
Cooking spray (to grease the cookie sheets)

Cookie dough:
- ■ *½ cup butter*
- ■ *1 cup sugar*
- ■ *1 egg*
- ■ *2 cups flour*
- ■ *½ tsp. salt*
- ■ *2 tsp. baking powder*
- ■ *½ tsp. vanilla*

Cream together the butter and sugar. Beat in egg. Sift together dry ingredients and add to mixture. Add vanilla. Mix until well blended. Form into a ball and chill overnight.

Teacher Set-up:
1. Set a paper plate at each child's work area and put a little flour and 2 small balls of dough on each plate.
2. Set out crushed peppermints, marshmallows, chocolate chips, and crushed Oreo® cookies within the children's reach around the table.

Preview:
1. Review with the children that **metamorphic** rocks are formed from pre-existing **igneous** or **sedimentary** rocks and that **metamorphism means change in form**.
2. The cookie dough "rock" that they have in front of them will change form when baked due to the "**heat**" and "**pressure**" of the oven.
3. Metamorphism may also entail a structural change called **banding**, where light and dark minerals form alternating bands. Challenge the students to create a **banded metamorphic** rock, using the light colored and dark colored peppermints, marshmallows, etc.

Procedures:
1. Ask students to flatten their cookie dough and creatively add in the extras (crushed peppermints, marshmallows, chocolate chips, and crushed Oreo® cookies).
2. Place the creations on greased cookie sheets and bake in 350° oven for 10 minutes or until done.
3. Observe and record on the Metamorphic Rock Observation Sheet.

Metamorphic Rock Observation Sheet

Geologist _____ Date_____

Before	After

_____   _____
-    -
_____   _____

_____   _____
-    -
_____   _____

_____   _____
-    -
_____   _____

_____   _____
-    -
_____   _____

Unit 4
Who's That by the Pond?

Liz Deskins, School Library Media Specialist

Lisa Callif, Stacey Zawisza, Grade One Teachers

J.W. Reason Elementary School

4790 Cemetery Road, Hilliard, Ohio 43026

614-870-1641

<Lizabeth_Deskins@fclass.Hilliard.k12.oh.us>

Grade Level: 1

Unit Overview: Who's That by the Pond? guides students through a pond discovery process in keeping with a literature-based, constructivist methodology and employing an inquiry-driven curriculum. Students learn the difference between living and nonliving things, discover the importance of environment to sustain life, learn about life cycles and the role of people in aiding or destroying pond habitats. They "wonder and wander" through books, creating questions to be answered, conduct initial research on pond creatures, go on virtual field trips—as well as a real trip—make webs of life cycles and, ultimately, construct a pond creation on the hallway wall showing levels, layers, and life around and in the pond.

Time Frame: 4 weeks: 2 one-hour library periods with the teacher and the LMS, multiple small group 30 minute sessions to locate print and nonprint information and to begin research, and daily 50 minute blocks in science and/or writing workshop in the classroom with the teacher.

Content Area Standards: Ohio State Board of Education Academic Content Standards <http://www.ode.state.oh.us/GD/Templates/Pages/ODE/ODEPrimary.aspx?Page=2&TopicRelationID=305>

Ohio State Board of Education Science Academic Content Standards

Life Sciences Standard
Students demonstrate an understanding of how living systems function and how they interact with the physical environment. This includes an understanding of the cycling of matter and flow of energy in living systems. An understanding of the characteristics, structure and function of cells, organisms and living systems will be developed. Students will also develop a deeper understanding of the principles of heredity, biological evolution, and the diversity and interdependence of life. Students demonstrate an understanding of different historical perspectives, scientific approaches and emerging scientific issues associated with the life sciences.

Life Sciences Benchmarks K-2

A. Discover that there are living things, non-living things and pretend things, and describe the basic needs of living things (organisms).
B. Explain how organisms function and interact with their physical environment.
C. Describe similarities and differences that exist among individuals of the same kind of plants and animals.

Life Sciences Indicators Grade One

Characteristics and Structure of Life

1. Explore that organisms, including people, have basic needs which include air, water, food, living space and shelter.

Diversity and Interdependence of Life

4. Investigate that animals eat plants and/or other animals for food and may also use plants or other animals for shelter and nesting.
5. Recognize that seasonal changes can influence the health, survival or activities of organisms.

Scientific Inquiry Standard

Students develop scientific habits of mind as they use the processes of scientific inquiry to ask valid questions and to gather and analyze information. They understand how to develop hypotheses and make predictions. They are able to reflect on scientific practices as they develop plans of action to create and evaluate a variety of conclusions. Students are also able to demonstrate the ability to communicate their findings to others.

Scientific Inquiry Benchmarks K-2

A. Ask a testable question.
B. Design and conduct a simple investigation to explore a question.
C. Gather and communicate information from careful observations and simple investigation through a variety of methods.

Scientific Inquiry Indicators Grade One

Doing Scientific Inquiry

1. Ask "what happens when" questions.
2. Explore and pursue student-generated "what happens when" questions.
4. Work in a small group to complete an investigation and then share findings with others.
8. Use oral, written and pictorial representation to communicate work.
9. Describe things as accurately as possible and compare with the observations of others.

Ohio State Board of Education Technology Academic Content Standards

Standard 5: Technology and Information Literacy

Students engage in information literacy strategies, use the Internet, technology tools and resources, and apply information-management skills to answer questions and expand knowledge.

Students become information-literate learners by utilizing a research process model. They recognize the need for information and define the problem, need or task. Students understand the structure of information systems and apply these concepts in acquiring and managing information. Using technology tools, a variety of resources are identified, accessed and evaluated. Relevant information is selected, analyzed and synthesized to generate a finished product. Students evaluate their information process and product.

Benchmarks K-2

C. Apply basic browser and navigation skills to find information from the Internet.

Internet Concepts Indicators Grade One

2. Use teacher or librarian selected Web site to find information or learn new things.

The Ohio Department of Education Academic Content Standards are reprinted here with permission from Carol Kuhman, Public Information Officer, Communications.

Information Power Standards and Indicators: 1.3, 1.5, 4.2, 6.1, 6.2, 9.1

Cooperative Teaching Plan:

Library Media Specialist Will:

- Gather a great variety of books about ponds, pond life, pond habitat, and life cycles of pond animals.
- Introduce and discuss the question: What lives in a pond?
- Assist students as they "wander and wonder" through the books provided, getting ideas to help them create questions to answer throughout this unit.
- Invite students to look at books and online resources before supporting them in designing questions.
- With the students, create a KWL (**K**now-**W**ant to Know-**L**earned) chart.
- With the teacher, help students to create thoughtful, detailed questions.
- Support students in small groups as they look through books and pre-selected Web sites in order to begin to think through their research plans.
- Work with students in small groups as they begin research.
- Teach students to locate the section of the library where factual books about pond animals are located.
- Teach students how to use a bookmarked site on the Internet.
- Teach students how to record information about the books they use in their Research Study Guide.
- Assist students as they research their pond animals and plants.
- With the teacher, assess student learning through individual student observation, observation of group cooperation, conversations with individual students, and assessment of the quality/quantity of student work using the Teacher Evaluation Continuum of Understanding.

First Grade Teacher Will:

- Introduce the unit of study: Pond as a Habitat.
- Use student questions gathered in the media center to form a basis for study.

- Guide students as they research and study their chosen animals and plants by introducing the class to the pond life Research Study Guide and by modeling note taking and question answering through language arts mini-lessons and small group instruction.

- Once each student has decided what question he/she will research, hand out and explains the Research Study Guide.

- Encourage student writing as they progress through the unit by regularly conferencing with the students.

- In conversation with students, encourage more thinking and more questions that might need to be answered.

- Accompany students on a field trip to a pond, after preparation and study.

- Create a pond habitat outside the classroom on the wall to showcase student work.

- With the library media specialist, assess student learning through individual student observation, observation of group cooperation, conversations with individual students, and assessment of the quality/quantity of student work using the Teacher Evaluation Continuum of Understanding.

Resources:

Print
Professional Teacher Resources

Kneidel, Sally Stenhouse. *Creepy Crawlies and the Scientific Method: Over 100 Hands-on Science Experiments for Children.* Golden, Colorado: Fulcrum Publishing, 1993.

Kriesberg, Daniel A. *A Sense of Place: Teaching Children about the Environment with Picture Books.* Westport, Connecticut: Teacher Ideas Press, 1999.

Sisson, Edith A. *Nature with Children of All Ages: Activities & Adventures for Exploring, Learning & Enjoying the World around Us.* Englewood Cliffs, New Jersey, 1982. OP

Student Titles

Berger, Melvin. *Look Out for Turtles!* New York: HarperCollins, 1992. OP

Braun Eric. *River, Lakes, and Ponds.* Austin, Texas: Raintree Steck-Vaughn, 2002.

Chermayeff, Ivan. *Fishy Facts.* San Diego: Gulliver Books, 1994. OP

Cooper, Ann. *Around the Pond.* Denver, Colorado: Denver Museum of Natural History Press, 1998. OP

Dewey, Jennifer. *At the Edge of the Pond.* Boston: Little, Brown, 1987. OP

Fowler, Allan. *Life in a Pond.* New York: Children's Press, 1996.

Galko, Francine. *Pond Animals.* Chicago: Heinemann Library, 2003.

Halfmann, Janet. *Life in a Pond.* Mankato, Minnesota: Creative Education, 2000.

Heinz, Brian J. *Butternut Hollow Pond.* Brookfield, Connecticut.: Millbrook Press, 2000.

Hibbert, Adam. *A Freshwater Pond.* New York: Crabtree, 1999.

Morrison, Gordon. *Pond.* Boston: Houghton Mifflin, 2002.

Nadeau, Isaac. *Food Chains in a Pond Habitat.* New York: PowerKids Press, 2002.

Parker, Steve. *Pond & River.* London: DK, 2005.

Pascoe, Elaine. *Pond.* Detroit: Blackbirch Press, 2005.

Sayre, April Pulley. *Lake and Pond.* New York: Twenty-First Century Books, 1996.

Schofield, Jennifer. *Animal Babies in Ponds and Rivers.* Boston: Kingfisher, 2004.

Silver, Donald. M. *Pond.* New York: McGraw-Hill, 1994.

Stewart, David. *Pond Life.* New York: Franklin Watts, 2002.

Electronic Resources

"ExplorA-Pond." *Utah Education Network.* 19 September 2006
    <http://www.ucn.org/utahlink/pond>. [An interactive virtual pond to populate.]
"Exploring Pond Habitats." *Canterbury Environmental Education Center.* 19 September 2006
    <http://www.naturegrid.org.uk/pondexplorer/pond-cross.html>. [Interactive]
"Pond Explorer." *Canterbury Environmental Education Center.* 19 September 2006
    <http://www.naturegrid.org.uk/pondexplorer/pondexplorer.html>. [A good site for teachers
    with activities pages.]
"A Virtual Pond Dip." *Microscopy-UK.* February 2001. 19 September 2006
<http://www.microscopy-uk.org.uk/index.html?http://www.microscopy-uk.org.uk/ponddip/>. [A
    simple guide to microscopic pond life. Interactive.]

Culminating Learning Product: Students will create an illustrated pond habitat on the wall with accompanying research demonstrating what they have learned.

Assessment Overview: Most assessment is informal observation of students at work, but students will also fill out a Research Study Guide which they will evaluate using a Self-Assessment Checklist at the conclusion of the unit. In addition, the teacher and library media specialist will evaluate student work using the Teacher Evaluation Continuum of Understanding.

Adaptations and Extensions:

■ High achieving students might extend their animal study in the areas of interaction with the environment, paying particular attention to plants and habitat. Guided by the library media specialist, they might learn the use of the index in nonfiction books and Internet search strategies.

■ Students not yet developmentally ready for independent work might create a group project, working together with the library media specialist or a parent volunteer to locate informa-tion about a single group animal and how it survives in its habitat. The adult will assist by reading information sources aloud and acting as scribe.

Project Overview

1. Goal: to create awareness of living animals' need to survive and thrive in their habitat and: to inspire students to begin to ask the question "What are my needs and wants?" In order to encourage this to happen, each grade is assigned a habitat to study and to use as a backdrop upon which, and an umbrella under which, to create concrete scientific inquiry. The first grade habitat is fresh water.

2. Because our students know something about ponds, a KWL chart is a good place to begin. This allows us to uncover facts they already know as well as any misconceptions that need to be cleared up.

3. Allowing students to create their own questions with "wandering and wondering" ensures active engagement and helps to keep students interested and motivated.

4. Working with small groups as they are ready to "research" is a great way to introduce the reasons behind library arrangement and to teach students how to give credit to the authors of the sources they use to find their information (bibliography).

5. It is also a good time to begin Internet searching because students have a specific goal in mind.

6. Once students have collected information, we decide how to demonstrate this knowledge. A pond on the hallway wall was our final demonstration of learning.

7. Each student is allowed to add his/her animal and plant to the pond, and around it we place the facts: how it survives, thrives, and adapts to its pond habitat.

8. The evaluation is completed jointly by teacher and media specialist through student observation, recording of the quality/quantity of student work in a research book, observation of group cooperation, and individual discussions to ascertain how much each student has learned.

Research Study Guide

Name_____

I want to answer this question:

_____

- -

_____

_____

_____

- -

_____

Here are more questions I had as I studied:

_____

- -

_____

_____

_____

- -

_____

_____

_____

- -

_____

I looked in these books:

Title _____

_____

Author _____

_____

Title _____

_____

Author _____

_____

I found out these interesting facts:

_____

- -

_____

_____

- -

_____

_____

- -

_____

_____

- -

_____

_____

- -

_____

_____

- -

_____

This is how my animal/plant adapts to the seasons:

_____

- -

_____

- -

_____

- -

_____

Here are some things that threaten pond life:

_____

- -

_____

_____

- -

_____

_____

- -

_____

- -

_____

Here are some new words I learned in my study (and what they mean):

_____

- -

_____

_____

- -

_____

_____

- -

_____

_____

- -

_____

_____

- -

_____

_____

- -

_____

Here is a picture of my animal/plant:

Self Assessment Checklist

Name_____

Did I remember to:

_____ Put my name and the name of my animal on my research?

_____ List the titles and authors of the books I used?

_____ Answer all of my questions about my animal/plant?

_____ Find out something new I want to share with the class?

Teacher Evaluation Continuum of Understanding

Name_____

Did the student exhibit an understanding of the animal/plant chosen for study?
Consider these areas of the study:
    The life span?
    The habitat?
    The external conditions?
    Environmental concerns?

Little/no understanding   **Deep understanding**

Did the student's initial question get answered?
Did the student learn to ask more complex, engaging questions? Did the student begin to understand why we study habitats and how the study relates to humans?

Basic understanding   **Deep understanding**

Was it a naïve/beginning understanding --- or a deeper, more comprehensive understanding?
How can I move this student further along the learning continuum? Does he/she need remediation or more extension?

Needs remediation   **Needs extension strategies**

Did the student participate fully in this project?
(Realizing that each student has a different learning style with different strengths and weaknesses and thus will participate differently . . .) Did the student participate in class discussions? Fill out his/her research guide completely? Include his/her animal/plant on the classroom mural appropriately?

Not yet a contributing member   **Member of learning community**

Unit 5
Superbugs!

Margaret Hale, Media Specialist

Kelly Browder, Second Grade Teacher

James Island Elementary School

1872 Grimball Road, Charleston, South Carolina 29412

843-762-8253

<margaret_hale@charleston.k12.sc.us>

Grade Level: 2

Unit Overview: Let's make SUPERBUGS! Turn a simple independent insect research activity into an engaging group project by stimulating students' natural inquiry processes, using information literacy skills, and creating exciting new creatures. In this project, each student completes independent research (adapted to individual ability levels), shares findings with a group, synthesizes findings into a new group product, creates an eye-popping art product, and shares the product in a group presentation. Students brainstorm questions, use appropriate level library resources and simple Web pages to gather information, and finally put it all together to create something new. This activity is a guaranteed student favorite!

Time Frame: Two Weeks: 4 one-hour library periods with the teacher and the LMS and daily 30-minute science blocks in the classroom with the teacher.

Content Area Standards: South Carolina Curriculum Standards
<http://www.myscschools.com/offices/cso>

Science: Grade 2
I. Inquiry
    A. Process Skills
     2. Classify
      a. Compare, sort, and group concrete objects according to observable properties.
    B. Inquiry
     1. Plan and conduct a simple investigation.
      a. Ask a question about objects, organisms, and events in the environment.
      d. Communicate investigations and explanations.

II. Life Science:
Unit of Study: Animals
    C. Organisms and Their Environments

1. All animals depend on plants. Some animals eat plants for food. Other animals eat animals that eat the plants.
   a. Investigate and describe ways in which animals interact with each other and with the environment.

English/Language Arts: Grade 2

Writing Goal (W) The student will write for different audiences and purposes.

Writing Purposes
W2 The student will write for a variety of **purposes.**
2-W2.1 Demonstrate the ability to use writing to explain and inform.

Communication Goal (C) The student will recognize, demonstrate, and analyze the qualities of effective communication.

Communication: Speaking
C1 The student will use speaking skills to participate in large and small groups in both formal and informal situations.
2-C1.4 Demonstrate the ability to participate in conversations and discussions by responding appropriately.
2-C1.10 Demonstrate the ability to use **visual aids**, props, and technology to support and extend his or her meaning and enhance his or her oral presentations.

Research Goal (RS) The student will access and use information from a variety of appropriately selected sources to extend his or her knowledge.

Selecting a Research Topic
RS1 The student will select a topic for exploration.
2-RS1.2 Demonstrate the ability to ask *how* and *why* questions about a topic of interest.
2-RS1.1 Demonstrate the ability to ask questions to guide his or her topic selection.

Gathering Information and Refining a Topic
RS2 The student will gather information from a variety of sources.
2-RS2.1 Demonstrate the ability to identify pictures, charts, tables of contents, and diagrams as sources of information.
2-RS2.2 Demonstrate the ability to gather information using a variety of resources, including technology, and begin organizing such information.
2-RS2.3 Continue documenting sources by listing titles and authors.
Demonstrate the ability to present his or her research findings in a variety of formats.

The South Carolina English Language Arts Curriculum Standards are reprinted here with permission from Cathy Jones, Interim ELA Coordinator.

Information Power Information Literacy Standards and Indicators: 1.1, 1.3, 2.4, 3.1, 3.2, 3.3, 3.4, 5.2, 5.3, 8.2, 9.1, 9.3, 9.4

Cooperative Teaching Plan:

Library Media Specialist Will:

- Compile resources and Web sites for student research.
- Introduce the research process.
- Model the research process.
- Create a research organizer for recording questions and information.
- Lead group brainstorming session to generate questions students would like to answer about their specific insects.
- Assist students in selecting four guiding questions to include in the Research Planner graphic organizer.
- Assist students in locating and recording information.
- Provide students with research assistance as they use print and electronic resources.
- Assist students to complete the research process and fill out the Research Planner graphic organizer.
- Teach students how to cite sources and assist them as they record information for their sources on the Source Information graphic organizer.
- Model group sharing process for students.
- Assist students as each group shares two physical and two behavioral characteristics of the insect they researched that they would like their group's Superbug to have.
- Assist students, during the group meeting, to complete the Group Organizer (enlarged to 11 by 14 inches to make it easier for students to complete).
- Help groups with focus and tasks.
- Assess student progress throughout project.
- Assess student research process using the Research Checklist.

Teacher Will:

- Introduce the insect unit in the classroom.
- Provide general information about insects.
- Introduce the physical characteristics of insects: legs, abdomen, head, antennae, mouth, and more.
- Introduce the behavioral characteristics of insects: how they move, what they eat, what they do, how they camouflage and more.
- Assign or help students to select insects to research.
- Provide students with research assistance as they use print and electronic resources.
- Assist students to complete the research process and fill out the Research Planner graphic organizer.
- Divide students into collaborative groups of four.
- Assist students as they each share two physical and two behavioral characteristics of the insect they researched that they would like their group's Superbug to have.
- Help groups with focus and tasks.
- Assist students, during the group meeting, to complete the Group Organizer (enlarged to 11 by 14 inches to make it easier for students to complete).

- Assess student progress throughout project.
- Assess student work using the Checklist.

Resources:

Print

Bug Books Series. Chicago, Illinios: Heinemann Library, 1999-2003. (Titles in series include *Ant, Bee, Beetle, Caterpillar, Centipede, Cockraoch, Dragonfly, Earwig, Firefly, Flea, Fly, Grasshopper, Head Louse, Ladybug, Mosquito, Paper Wasp, Pillbug, Snail, Spider, Termite, Tick, Walking Stick.* Authors vary.)

Heinrichs, Ann. *Nature's Friends Series.* Minneapolis, Minnesota: Compass Point Books, 2002. (Titles in series include *Ants, Bees, Butterflies, Fireflies, Grasshoppers,* and *Ladybugs.*)

Kravetz, Jonathan. *Gross Bugs Series.* New York: PowerKids Press, 2006. (Titles in series include: *Boll Weevils, Cockroaches, Locusts, Mosquitoes, Stink Bugs*, and *Ticks.*)

Insects Series. Mankato, Minnesota: Pebble Books/Capstone Press, 1999-2003. (Titles in series include *Ants, Beetles, Bumble Bees, Butterflies, Cicadas, Cockroaches, Crickets, Dragonflies, Fireflies, Flies, Grasshoppers, Honeybees, Ladybugs, Mosquitoes, Moths, Praying Mantises, Termites, Walkingsticks, Wasps* and *Water Bugs.* Authors vary.)

Meister, Cari. *Checkerboard Nature Library Insects Series.* Edina, Minnesota: ABDO Publishing Company, 2001. (Titles in series include *Butterflies, Crickets, Dragonflies, Fireflies, Ladybugs,* and *Mosquitoes.*) *Student Discovery Encyclopedia*: Chicago, Illinois: World Book, Inc. 2005.

Electronic

Col, Jeananda. "Insect Printouts." *Enchanted Learning.* 1999-2006. 20 September 2006 <http://www.enchantedlearning.com/subjects/insects/printouts.shtml>.

Insecta Inspecta. 1 June 2004. 20 September 2006 <http://www.insecta-inspecta.com/>.

Koday, Ed. *Koday's Kids Amazing Insects.* 1998. 20 September 2006. <http://www.ivyhall.district96.k12.il.us/4th/kkhp/1insects/bugmenu.html>.

Audiovisual

Photos and videos accessed via <www.unitedstreaming.com>. (subscription required)

Equipment

Student access computers for Internet searches

Culminating Learning Product: Each group of students creates a large scale drawing of its Superbug on chart paper, bulletin board paper, or large construction paper, diagrams the individual physical characteristics of the Superbug, and writes two sentences about the individual behavioral characteristics of the Superbug. As a final activity, groups introduce their SUPERBUG to the class, sharing the diagramed drawing and sentences.

Assessment Overview: Assessment is conducted in two ways. The teacher uses the simple Checklist to assess whether students have completed all of the required steps. The media specialist uses the Research Checklist, in conjunction with the Research Planner Organizer, to assess how successful a student was with the research component of the project.

Adaptations and Extensions:

- The needs of challenged readers and ELL students can be met by using digital images and videos on the bug they select for independent research.

- Gifted students and those who like an extra challenge may participate in a creative writing component in which they write the story of their Superbug's creation – how all the bugs' characteristics got mixed up!

- Adapt this extension for less motivated writers by requesting it in comic strip format.

- A number of different activities can also extend the unit:

- Students may take a nature walk and observe as many insects as they can find.

- Students can create three-dimensional models of the Superbug.

- Students can also use programs such as Kidspiration® or IHMC Cmap Tools to draw and diagram the Superbug.

- Create an insect observatory by purchasing live insects (including beetles, butterflies, ladybugs, praying mantises, and hissing cockroaches) and viewing habitats from Carolina Biological Supply <http://www.carolina.com>.

Research Planner Organizer

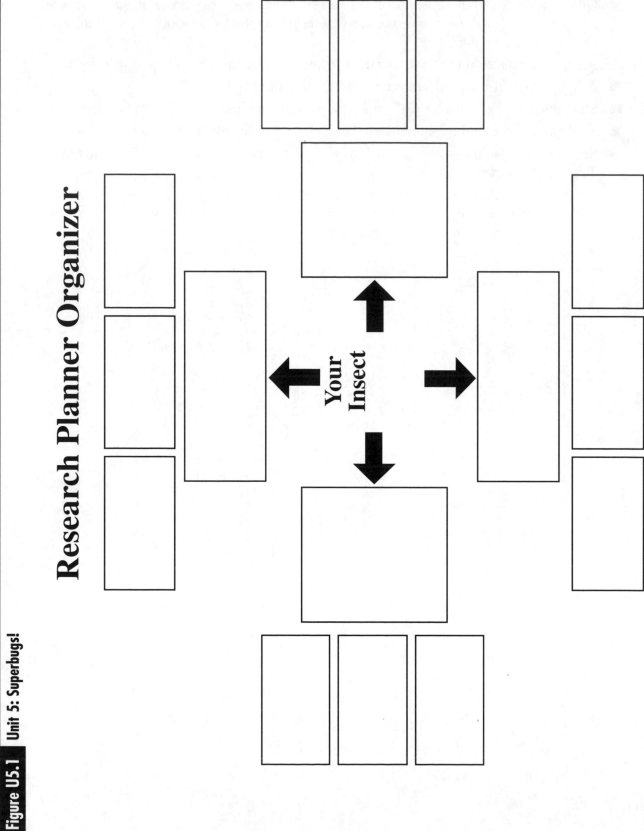

Your Insect

Sample Research Planner Organizer

What does your bug look like?

Your Insect

How does your bug defend itself?

What does your bug eat?

Where does your bug live?

Group Organizer

Physical Characteristics
How will the bug look?

Group Member 1:

Group Member 1:

Group Member 2:

Group Member 2:

Group Member 3:

Group Member 3:

Group Member 4:

Group Member 4:

Superbug!

Directions: Each group member must share 2 physical and 2 behavioral charcteristics of the bug they research. These become characteristics of the Superbug! Write the characteristics in the box for each group member.

Behavioral Characteristics
How will the bug act?

Group Member 1:

Group Member 1:

Group Member 2:

Group Member 2:

Group Member 3:

Group Member 3:

Group Member 4:

Group Member 4:

Source Information

Where I Found My Information

Please use the spaces below to record information about the resources you used to find information about your insect. You must complete a box for every book or Web site you used. You must use at least 2 books and 1 Web site, but feel free to use more!

Book Title: _____

Author's Name: _____

Pages where I found information:

Book Title: _____

Author's Name: _____

Pages where I found information:

Web site Title: _____

Web site Address: _____

Date I looked at the Web site:

Online Database: _____

Database Address: _____

Date I searched the database:

Checklist

Task	Met	Not Yet
1. The student participated in question brainstorming task.		
2. The student used book and Web resources to find information on his or her insect.		
3. The student completed Research Planner Organizer answering questions about his or her insect.		
4. The student shared 2 physical characteristics of his or her insect with group.		
5. The student shared 2 behavioral characteristics of his or her insect with the group.		
6. The student illustrated 2 physical characteristics of his or her insect.		
7. The student labeled 2 physical characteristics of his or her insect.		
8. The student wrote 2 sentences about behavioral characteristics of his or her insect.		
9. The student shared 2 physical characteristics of his or her insect in the group presentation of the Superbug.		
10. The student shared 2 behavioral characteristics of his or her insect in the group presentation of the Superbug.		
11. The student used appropriate voice level, articulation, specific vocabulary, and eye contact during presentation.		
12. The student demonstrated movement and sounds of the Superbug.		
13. The student worked well with all members of the group.		
14. The student shared one thing he or she enjoyed about this project.		

SCORE (Number of Met checks):_____

1-3 = Unsatisfactory   4-6 = Needs Improvement   7-9 = Fair
10-12 = Good   13-14 = Excellent

Research Checklist

Task	Met	Not Yet
1. The student contributed a how or why question during the brainstorming task.		
2. The student successfully located answers to the guiding questions.		
3. The student used at least two print resources to locate information.		
4. The student recorded the title, author, and page number of books used to locate information.		
5. The student used at least one Web site to locate information.		
6. The student recorded the Web site address.		
7. The student identified key words from guiding questions.		
8. The student demonstrated use of the table of contents and index to find information within a book.		
9. The student used pictures in books and Web sites as a source of information.		
10. The student recorded clear notes in the research organizer.		

SCORE (Number of Met checks):_____

1-3 = Unsatisfactory   4-6 = Needs Improvement   7-9 = Fair

10-12 = Good   13-14 = Excellent

Unit 6
The World Beyond Our Neighborhood

Part I: Where I Live

Part II: Children in Other Countries

Martha Taylor, Library Media Specialist

Donna Marzella, Second Grade Teacher

Oakside Elementary School

200 Decatur Avenue, Peekskill, New York 10566

914-737-1591

<metaylor@peekskillcsd.org>

Grade Level: 2

Unit Overview: Many children have little knowledge of the world beyond their own neighborhoods. The initial goals of The World Beyond Our Neighborhood are student understanding of maps, the ability to locate their own community on a map, and an ability to sequence locations from local (city) to global (world). This unit then expands to introduce students to the lives of children in communities in other countries, enabling students to better understand their own lives as well as to embrace and appreciate cultural diversity. As a culminating activity, students present their new knowledge in a PowerPoint® presentation.

Time Frame: Six weeks: Six one-hour library periods with the teacher and the LMS and 12 bi-weekly 45-minute periods in the classroom with the teacher.

Content Area Standards: New York State Learning Standards
<http://www.emsc.nysed.gov/ciai/ls.html>

Social Studies
Standard 3: Geography
Elementary
Students will use a variety of intellectual skills to demonstrate their understanding of the geography of the interdependent world in which we live—local, national, and global—including the distribution of people, places, and environments over the Earth's surface.

1. Geography can be divided into six essential elements which can be used to analyze important historic, geographic, economic, and environmental questions and issues. These six elements include: the world in spatial terms, places and regions, physical settings (including natural resources), human systems, environment and society, and the use of geography. (Adapted from *The National Geography Standards, 1994: Geography for Life*)

Students:

- study about how people live, work, and utilize natural resources
- draw maps and diagrams that serve as representations of places, physical features, and objects; locate places within the local community, State, and nation; locate the Earth's continents in relation to each other and to principal parallels and meridians. (Adapted from *National Geography Standards*, 1994)
- identify and compare the physical, human, and cultural characteristics of different regions and people (Adapted from *National Geography Standards*, 1994)
- investigate how people depend on and modify the physical environment.

English Language Arts
Standard 1: Language for Information and Understanding
Elementary

Students will read, write, listen and speak for information and understanding. As listeners and readers, students will collect data, facts, and ideas; discover relationships, concepts, and generalizations; and use knowledge generated from oral, written, and electronically produced texts. As speakers and writers, they will use oral and written language to acquire, interpret, apply, and transmit information.

1. Listening and reading to acquire information and understanding involves collecting data, facts, and ideas; discovering relationships, concepts, and generalizations; and using knowledge from oral, written, and electronic sources.
   Students:

   - gather and interpret information from children's reference books, magazines, textbooks, electronic bulletin boards, audio and media presentations, oral interviews, and from such forms as charts, graphs, maps and diagrams
   - select information appropriate to the purpose of their investigation and relate ideas from one text to another
   - select and use strategies they have been taught for note taking, organizing, and categorizing information
   - make appropriate and effective use of the strategies to construct meaning from print, such as prior knowledge about a subject, structural and context clues, and an understanding of letter-sound relationships to decode difficult words
   - support inferences about information and ideas with reference to text features, such as vocabulary and organizational patterns.

2. Speaking and writing to acquire and transmit information requires asking probing and clarifying questions, interpreting information in one's own words, applying information from one context to another, and presenting the information and interpretation clearly, concisely, and comprehensibly.
   Students:

   - present information clearly in a variety of oral and written forms such as summaries, paraphrases, brief reports, stories, posters, and charts
   - select a focus, organization, and point of view for oral and written presentations
   - use details, examples, anecdotes, or personal experiences to explain or clarify information

- include relevant information and exclude extraneous material
- use the process of pre-writing, drafting, revising, and proofreading (the "writing process") to produce well-constructed informational texts
- observe basic writing conventions, such as correct spelling, punctuation, and capitalization, as well as sentence and paragraph structures appropriate to written forms.

Standard 3: Language for Critical Analysis and Evaluation
Elementary

Students will read, write, listen, and speak for critical analysis and evaluation. As listeners and readers, students will analyze experiences, ideas, information, and issues presented by others using a variety of established criteria. As speakers and writers, they will present, in oral and written language and from a variety of perspectives, their opinions and judgments on experiences, ideas, information and issues.

2. Speaking and writing for critical analysis and evaluation requires presenting opinions and judgments on experiences, ideas, information, and issues clearly, logically, and persuasively with reference to specific criteria on which the opinion or judgment is based.
   Students:
   - monitor and adjust their own oral and written presentations to meet criteria for competent performance (e.g., in writing, the criteria might include development of position, organization, appropriate vocabulary, mechanics, and neatness. In speaking, the criteria might include good content, effective delivery, diction, posture, poise, and eye contact.)
   - use effective vocabulary and follow the rules of grammar, usage, spelling, and punctuation in persuasive writing.

Standard 4: Language for Social Interaction
Elementary

Students will read, write, listen, and speak for social interaction. Students will use oral and written language for effective social communication with a wide variety of people. As readers and listeners, they will use the social communications of others to enrich their understanding of people and their views.

1. Oral communication in formal and informal settings requires the ability to talk with people of different ages, genders, and cultures, to adapt presentations to different audiences, and to reflect on how talk varies in different situations.
   Students:
   - listen attentively and recognize when it is appropriate for them to speak
   - take turns speaking and respond to others' ideas in conversations on familiar topics
   - recognize the kind of interaction appropriate for different circumstances, such as story hour, group discussions, and one-on-one conversations.

Mathematics, Science, and Technology
Standard 2: Information Systems
Elementary

Students will access, generate, process, and transfer information using appropriate technologies.

1. Information technology is used to retrieve, process, and communicate information and as a tool to enhance learning.

Students:

- use a variety of equipment and software packages to enter, process, display, and communicate information in different forms using text, tables, pictures, and sound.
- access needed information from printed media, electronic databases, and community resources.

2. Knowledge of the impacts and limitations of information systems is essential to its effective and ethical use.
   Students:

   - understand that computers are used to store personal information.

Standard 5: Technology
Elementary

Students will apply technological knowledge and skills to design, construct, use, and evaluate products and systems to satisfy human and environmental needs.

3. Computers, as tools for design, modeling, information processing, communication, and system control, have greatly increased human productivity and knowledge.
   Students:

   - use the computer as a tool for generating and drawing ideas.

The New York State Education Department Standards are reprinted here with permission from William Winchester, Assistant Director Facilities & Business Services.

Information Power Information Literacy Standards and Indicators: 1.1, 1.2, 1.3, 1.4, 1.5, 2.1, 2.4, 3.1, 3.2, 3.4, 6.1, 6.2, 9.1, 9.2

Cooperative Teaching Plan:

Library Media Specialist Will:

- Week One: What is a Map?
  Introduce what is meant by a map.
  Read aloud *As the Crow Flies* and *What is a Map?*
  With the class, examine a map of our school and our city.
  Ask children to find their street on the city map and put a colored dot to indicate where each child lives. Use a key with a list of names and a different color for each child.

- Week Two: Where I Live
  Review the concept that a map is a picture, and examine atlases and globes with students.
  Teach sequencing of locations, from the city where they live (local) to the world (global).
  Read aloud *New York*, *America the Beautiful,* and *This Land is Your Land.*
  With the teacher, help students to create a booklet of maps entitled "Where I Live" in the correct sequence from local to global. Include maps of city, state, the United States, North America, and the world from Web sites listed in the Resources section.

- Week Three: Countries Around the World
  Review the location of the United States on a map of the world.
  Discuss the number of other countries in the world and locate some of the places the

children's families come from.

Read *A Country Far Away* and *Children Just Like Me*.

Introduce the research assignment about what life is like for children living in another country.

■ Weeks Four and Five: Research on Children in Other Countries

Using the Four-Square Graphic Organizer, model research about how children live in one sample country, teaching and modeling proper note-taking using keywords.

Teach and model locating relevant facts limited to the four chosen topics.

Model use of an index and table of contents in a nonfiction book.

Assist students in using a template from Kidspiration® or IHMC Cmap Tools to type notes and take advantage of the software outline assistance.

Model turning notes into complete sentences in Kidspiration® or IHMC Cmap Tools by using a sample page of notes projected onto a large screen for class viewing and participation. With the teacher, demonstrate the required format for the student report which includes six paragraphs: an introduction stating what will be covered, a paragraph for each of the four chosen topics (food, homes, school and free time), and a concluding paragraph.

Teach students how to write a simple bibliographic reference to be included in the report.

■ Week Six: Presentation of Children in Other Countries

Assist children in scanning their reports, flags, and maps into a slide presentation using PowerPoint® software. (Note: Each child will have his or her own slide in the final PowerPoint® presentation).

Direct students to choose a background color, a sound, and a slide transition style to make a creative presentation.

Assess individual student effort on the PowerPoint® Presentation Rubric.

Teacher Will:

■ Week One: What is a Map?

Review what a map is and assign a worksheet similar to "I Spy" to find listed items from the bird's eye view looking down at a map. (Note: A useful worksheet can be found in *Neighborhoods and Communities*, p. 31)

Ask children to draw a map of a room in their home, for homework.

■ Week Two: Where I Live

Read *Me on the Map*.

Teach the children "The Song of the Seven Continents." (Note: Find the words and a sampling of the tune at the *Smithsonian Folkways Recordings* Web site.)

With the library media specialist, help children indicate their street with a colored dot on the city map, locate and color their city on the state map, color their state on the United States map, color the United States on the North America map as well as the world map to complete a booklet entitled "Where I Live."

■ Week Three: Countries Around the World

Elicit questions from students about what they would like to know about children in another country.

Direct them to list the following four topics: food, houses, school and free time.

Assign children to research a specific country, depending upon the available books in the school library.

■ Weeks Four and Five: Research on Children in Other Countries

Set aside time in the classroom for the children to read a country book, take notes, and write their reports.

Assist students in using a template from Kidspiration® or IHMC Cmap Tools to type notes and take advantage of the software outline assistance.

Guide children in evaluating their work critically and revising as needed.

Assist students in assembling a booklet containing their written report, a cover with the country's flag colored by the student and a map of the world with the country colored in.

■ Week Six: Presentation of Children in Other Countries

Assist students in practicing reading their reports aloud.

Assess individual student effort on the Research Report Rubric.

Resources:

Print

Bates, Katharine L. *America the Beautiful.* New York: Aladdin Paperbacks, 2002.

Copsey, Susan Elizabeth. *Children Just Like Me.* New York: Dorling Kindersley, 1995.

DeCapua, Sarah. *New York.* New York: Children's Press, 2002.

Gray, Nigel. *A Country Far Away.* New York: Orchard Books, 1988. OP

Guthrie, Woody. *This Land is Your Land.* Boston: Little, Brown, 1998.

Hartman, Gail. *As the Crow Flies: A First Book of Maps.* New York: Aladdin, 1993.

Reader's Digest Children's Atlas of the World. Pleasantville, New York: Reader's Digest Children's Books, 2000.

Sweeney, Joan. *Me on the Map.* New York: Crown, 1996.

Tamblyn, Catherine, M. *Neighborhoods and Communities.* New York: Scholastic, 2002. [Note: page 31]

We Come From . . . Austin, Texas: Raintree Steck-Vaughn, 1998-2000. (Titles in series include *Brazil, China, France, Germany, India, Jamaica, Kenya, Nigeria, South Africa.* Authors vary.)

Weidenman, Lauren. *What is a Map?* Mankato, Minnesota: Capstone Press, 2001.

Electronic

Col, Jeananda. *Enchanted Learning.* 2001-2006. 20 September 2006 <http://www.enchantedlearning.com>.

"Continents and World." *abcteach.* 2001-2006. 20 September 2006 <http://www.abcteach.com/directory/researchreports/maps/continents_and_world/>.

"Infoplease® Atlas." *Infoplease®.* 2000-2006. 20 September 2006 <http://www.infoplease.com/atlas/>.

Kidspiration® or IHMC Cmap Tools (available for free download at <http://cmap.ihmc.us/>)

"Outline Maps." *Education Place.* 20 September 2006 <http://www.eduplace.com/ss/maps/>.

PowerPoint®

"The Song of the Seven Continents." *Smithsonian Folkways Recordings.* 2004. 20 September 2006 <http://www.folkways.si.edu/search/AlbumDetails.aspx?ID=2998#>.

Equipment

Multi-media projector for full class viewing of the computer screen

Student use computers

Globe

Assorted maps

Culminating Learning Product: Parents and school administrators are invited to attend a culminating celebration where students share their research by reading aloud their reports in conjunction with the PowerPoint® presentation.

Assessment Overview: The teacher assesses the research report using the Research Report Rubric and the library media specialist assesses the final PowerPoint® presentation product using the PowerPoint® Presentation Rubric.

Adaptations and Extensions:

- Explicitly teach vocabulary to struggling learners and ELL students, which enhances comprehension for all learners.
- Promote the use of a bilingual dictionary for ELL students.
- Use a significant number of visuals, pictures or actual items, to help ELL students with understanding.
- Ask ELL students to research their native countries in order to help them relate their own cultures and backgrounds to the reference material and to connect home and school.
- Assign children to work with a partner, pairing proficient readers with struggling learners or ELL students.
- Encourage artistically gifted children to draw, paint, or produce a three-dimensional representation of the country and its culture or to research the art and artists of their country.
- Encourage musically gifted children to play an instrument to accompany the final presentation or investigate the music of their country.
- Provide enrichment for those children who are capable, e.g. research of additional categories for their countries including climate, clothing, dance, art, music, and famous people.

Four-Square Graphic Organizer with Kidspiration®

Children in

Sample Outline Template
with Kidspiration®

FOOD

Seafood

Barbecue meat on sticks

Open markets

HOMES

Cities—apartments
and houses

Villages—wood houses

In villages, people sleep
on hammocks

**Notes for
Children in
Brazil**

SCHOOL

Go to school in morning
or afternoon

Some schools have
computers

Homework

FREE TIME

Karate

Surfing

Many parks and
beaches

Bibliographic Citations

Author's Last Name _____

Author's First Name _____

Title of Book _____

Copyright Date _____

Author's Last Name _____

Author's First Name _____

Title of Book _____

Copyright Date _____

Author's Last Name _____

Author's First Name _____

Title of Book _____

Copyright Date _____

Research Report Rubric

	1 **Does Not Yet Meet Standards**	2 **Meets Standards**	3 **Exceeds Standards**
Researches, Gathers & Organizes Information (Notes)	• Attempts to collect information that relates to the topic • Notes do not yet answer questions	• Collects some information relating to the topic • Information mostly organized in correct categories	• All information collected relates to the topic • Well-organized information always in correct categories
Written Report	• Attempts to transfer notes into well-constructed sentences • Does not yet include details • Not yet able to revise and edit report • Bibliographic information is missing	• Transfers notes into complete sentences with mostly correct punctuation and grammar • Includes good details • An attempt is made to revise report • Includes bibliographic information, but lacks correct format	• Transfers notes into complete sentences with correct paragraphing, punctuation and grammar • Includes explicit details • Self-edits report and makes significant improvements • Report includes a correct, complete bibliography
Cooperation with Partner	• Often wants to have things his/her way	• Usually cooperative and considerate	• Shares work equally and helps partner

PowerPoint® Presentation Rubric

	1 Does Not Yet Meet Standards	2 Meets Standards	3 Exceeds Standards
Process	Not yet cooperative	Usually cooperative and considerate	Works cooperatively with partner
Use of Technology	Not yet able to use scanner and software	Uses scanner and software with assistance	Completes a PowerPoint® slide with minimal guidance
Product	Lacks creativity	Shows from creativity	Shows high creativity

Unit 7
All About Exploring the Internet

Lauren Zucker, Teacher-Librarian

Gerald Aungst, Gifted Support Teacher

Leary Elementary School

157 Henry Avenue, Warminster, Pennsylvania 18974

215-441-6066

<zuckla@centennialsd.org>

Grade Level: 3/4/5

Unit Overview: "I need information for my report. Can I get on the computer?" We hear this request repeatedly from our students. The Internet has become a primary resource for students doing research. But students often equate research with "googling." They produce cut-and-paste reports with little regard for accuracy. In this unit, students go on a treasure hunt to find information at an Internet site about explorers, only to discover that the facts there are wrong. In a quest to set the record straight and fix the site, students learn about searching the Internet critically and effectively.

Time Frame: 5 weeks: five 45-minute weekly sessions in the library with the teacher and librarian and five 45-minute language arts blocks in the classroom or computer lab with classroom teacher.

Content Area Standards: Pennsylvania Department of Education Academic Standards <http://www.pde.state.pa.us/stateboard_ed/cwp/view.asp?a=3&Q=76716>

History
Historical Analysis and Skills Development, Grade 6
8.1.6B Explain and analyze historical sources
8.4 World History, Grade 6
8.4.6A Identify and explain how individuals and groups made significant political and cultural contributions to world history

Reading, Writing, Speaking and Listening
1.2 Reading Critically in All Content Areas, Grade 5
1.2.5B Use and understand a variety of media and evaluate the quality of material produced
1.8 Research, Grade 5
1.8.5B Locate information using appropriate sources and strategies
1.8.5C Organize and present the main ideas from research

Science and Technology
3.7 Technological Devices, Grade 7
3.7.7C Explain and demonstrate basic computer operations and concepts

3.7.7E Explain basic computer communications systems

The Pennsylvania State Academic Standards are quoted with permission of the Pennsylvania State Board of Education.

Information Power Information Literacy Standards and Indicators: 1.2, 1.4, 1.5, 2.1, 2.3, 3.4, 6.1, 9.1, 9.3, 9.4

Cooperative Teaching Plan:

Librarian Will:

■ Prepare library mini-lab for Treasure Hunt activity including worksheets and signs.

■ With teacher, facilitate Treasure Hunt activity and follow-up discussion.

■ Emphasize these key points:
   1. Not everything on the Internet is useful.
   2. Be familiar with your topic by reading books *before* searching.
   3. Check facts with other sources.

■ Demonstrate the publication process of both a book and an Internet site.

■ Instruct students in the "Easy as 1-2-3" strategy for locating information on the Internet:
   1. Subscription Databases
   2. Subject Directories
   3. Search Engines

■ Explain and model how search engines work.

■ Teach students how to get useful results from a search engine query.

■ Teach students how to decode a URL.

■ Teach students how to evaluate a Web site.

■ Review bibliographic information and method for recording references.

■ Collect print resources for students to use during classroom activities.

■ Read and assess student responses to "Now You Try It" activities.

■ Read and respond to student e-mails from culminating activity.

Teacher Will:

■ Introduce topic of world explorers.

■ Complete a KWL activity about students' prior knowledge of the Internet.

■ Organize students into pairs by ability level for differentiation purposes during all activities.

■ With LMS, facilitate Treasure Hunt activity and follow-up discussion.

■ Introduce culminating activity and answer student questions.

■ With students, develop a rubric for evaluation of the culminating activity.

■ Review each prior lesson before the next one.

■ Reinforce the "Easy as 1-2-3" process during follow-up classroom activities.

■ Facilitate the "Now You Try It!" activities following each library lesson.

■ Read and assess student responses to "Now You Try It!" activities.

■ Facilitate the culminating activity.

- Monitor student progress.
- Notify LMS of student special needs or areas needing additional reinforcement during library sessions.
- Read and respond to student e-mails from culminating activity.

Resources:

Print

Fritz, Jean. *Around the World in a Hundred Years: From Henry the Navigator to Magellan*. New York: Putnam & Grosset Group, 1998.

Great Explorations (series). 22 vols. Tarrytown, New York: Marshall Cavendish/Benchmark, 2002-2007.

Goodman, Joan E. *A Long and Uncertain Journey: The 27,000-Mile Voyage of Vasco Da Gama*. New York: Mikaya Press, 2001.

Goodman, Joan E. *Beyond the Sea of Ice: The Voyages of Henry Hudson*. New York: Mikaya Press, 1999.

Kline, Trish. *Discover the Life of an Explorer* (series). 8 vols. Vero Beach, Florida: Rourke Publishing, 2002-03.

Matthews, Rupert. *Explorer*. New York: Dorling Kindersley/Eyewitness Books, 2005.

Meltzer, Milton. *Ferdinand Magellan : First to Sail Around the World*. Tarrytown, New York: Marshall Cavendish/Benchmark Books, 2001.

Molzahn, Arlene Bourgeois. *Explorers!* (series). 8 vols. Berkeley Heights, New Jersey: Enslow Publishers, 2004-2005.

Moore, Christopher. *Champlain*. Plattsburgh, NY: Tundra Books, 2004.

Parker, Nancy Winslow. *Land Ho! Fifty Glorious Years in the Age of Exploration*. New York: Harper Collins Publishers, 2001. OP

St. George, Judith. *So You Want to Be an Explorer?* New York: Philomel Books, 2005.

Starkey, Dinah. *Scholastic Atlas of Exploration*. New York: Scholastic, 1993. OP

Wolinsky, Art. *Internet Power Research Using the Big6 Approach, Revised Edition*. Berkeley Heights, New Jersey: Enslow Publishers, 2005.

Electronic

Abilock, Debbie. "Curriculum Collaboration Toolkit." *NoodleTools*. 2000-2005. 24 October 2006 <http://www.noodletools.com/debbie/consult/collab/cctool.html>

"Age of Exploration." *The Mariner's Museum*. 2004. 23 October 2006 <http://www.mariner.org//educationalad/ageofex/>.

All About Explorers. 28 February 2005. 23 October 2006 <http://www.allaboutexplorers.com>.

Col, Jeananda. "Zoom Explorers." *Enchanted Learning*. 1996-2006. 23 October 2006 <http://www.enchantedlearning.com/explorers/>.

Engels, Andre. "Discoverer's Web." *Andre Engels Homepage*. 2002. 23 October 2006 <http://www.win.tue.nl/~engels/discovery/>.

Media Awareness Network. 2006. 23 October 2006 <http://www.media-awareness.ca/english/>

November, Alan. "Resources." *November Learning*. 24 October 2006 <http://www.alannovember.com/Default.aspx?tabid=159>.

Ricketts, Karen. "The Dawn of Discovery." *Cobb County School District*. 23 October 2006 <http://www.cobbk12.org/~thinklinks/Grade4/Exploration/>.

Audiovisual

Library Skills for Children: Using the Internet. DVD. Schlessinger Media, 2003.

Equipment

Interactive Presentation Manager™ (digital white board, used for full class presentations and demonstration of Web sites during library sessions throughout the unit)
Computer lab or mini-lab

Culminating Learning Product: "How Could They Be So Wrong?" After an initial Treasure Hunt activity in which students discover that the All About Explorers Web site contains faulty information, students work in pairs to review one biography from the site. They use the skills they have learned about locating useful information in books and on the Internet to identify three important facts about the explorer's life and accomplishments that are incorrect at the AAE Web site. The teams then draft an e-mail to the webmaster of the site, which asks him or her to correct the errors, citing their reliable sources of information as reference to support their claim.

Assessment Overview: Students are informally assessed on their class discussions as well as their responses to classroom activities and "Now You Try It!" activities. The classroom teacher and LMS review student responses and performance to determine whether re-teaching needs to take place. Students are formally assessed on their understanding of research principles and writing skills on the culminating activity using a student-and-teacher-designed rubric. Students also complete a Student Self Assessment of the unit to provide feedback to the teacher.

Adaptations and Extensions: Biographies and lesson activities at the All About Explorers Web site are differentiated by difficulty and lend themselves to various adaptations.
See <http://www.allaboutexplorers.com/teachers/> for details. Web Treasure Hunts available at <http://www.allaboutexplorers.com/webquest/> are also coded by ability level:

- ■ Basic level: These hunts contain fact-oriented questions. The answers are relatively easy to locate on the page.

- ■ Moderate level: These hunts contain fact-oriented questions which require some additional searching or deeper reading to answer.

- ■ Advanced level: Advanced hunts are more challenging and may require students to use inference and logic to determine answers.

Note: This unit and the All About Explorers Web site were developed by the authors. See <http://www.allaboutexplorers.com/about.html> for more information about the purpose of the site and its development. Additional information and lesson plans are also available there. Depending on the technology available to teachers and students, e-mail created during the culminating activity can be sent, as the webmaster's e-mail address <webmaster@allaboutexplorers.com> is live. The authors will read and respond to any e-mails sent to that address.

Explorer Treasure Hunt

Names: _____

Explorer: _____

Your mission: Find the answers to the three questions from the Web site about your famous explorer. Use the two links on the Web page to find the information you need. *Be careful!* Be good researchers and check both pages for each question so you get all the information you need. Write your answers below.

1. _____
2. _____
3. _____
The Big Question: What are the similarities and differences in the information you found at the two sites?   _____   _____   _____   _____

Now You Try It: Easy As 1-2-3

Names: _____

Explorer: _____

Your mission: Select one basic fact about your explorer from the last lesson (such as birth date) that was wrong at the All About Explorers Web site. Locate that fact in three other sources: a book, a subscription database, and a subject directory. Record the fact and your sources here:

Fact: _____

Book:

    Author: _____

    Title: _____

    Publisher: _____

    Copyright date: _____

Subscription Database:

    Author: _____

    Title of article: _____

    Web site URL: _____

    Copyright date: _____

Subject Directory:

    Author: _____

    Title of article: _____

    Web site URL: _____

    Copyright date: _____

Now compare what you found with the information at All About Explorers. On the back, explain how you know that the fact there is incorrect.

Student-and-Teacher-Designed Rubric (Sample)

Below Basic	Basic	Proficient	Advanced
No incorrect facts are identified *or* no facts are accurately corrected.	Only one or two incorrect facts are identified. At least one is corrected.	Three incorrect facts are identified. Two of the three are corrected accurately.	Three incorrect facts are accurately identified and corrected.
E-mail cites no sources for corrected information *or* the sources given are inaccurate.	E-mail cites only one source for corrections or the sources given are questionable.	E-mail cites two sources for the corrections given.	E-mail cites at least three independent sources for the corrections given.
E-mail has many errors throughout.	E-mail has several obvious errors in spelling, punctuation, grammar, and mechanics.	E-mail has few minor errors in spelling, punctuation, grammar, and mechanics.	E-mail has no errors in spelling, punctuation, grammar, and mechanics.
Writing is difficult or impossible to understand. The writer's tone is rude or disrespectful.	Writing is unclear. The writer's tone is bland or impolite.	Writing is clear but simple. The writer's tone is respectful but not entirely persuasive.	Writing is clear, detailed, and polished. The writer's tone is persuasive and engaging.

Student Self Assessment

Names: _____

Something I learned about information on the Internet...
The process I would follow to find out information about a topic would be...
Something I learned about URLs...
Two things I would like to learn more about...
One thing I liked best about the Internet lessons...
One thing I would change about the Internet lessons...

Unit 8
Biography Bash: A Study of Heroes

Dorcas Hand, Director of Libraries

Amy Williams, Fourth Grade Team Leader

**Jeri Lodato, Educational Technology Coordinator
and former Fourth Grade Teacher**

Alisa Eng, Academic Support Coordinator; Kelley Elliott, Computer Lab Teacher

Annunciation Orthodox School

3600 Yoakum Blvd., Houston, Texas 77006

713-620-3622 (Library)

<dhand@aoshouston.org>

Grade Level: 4

Unit Overview: Biography Bash: A Study of Heroes teaches critical thinking, research process, and biographical research as well as creative presentation skills. In the fall, students begin to study heroic traits as listed by Martha Kaufeldt in *Begin with the Brain: Orchestrating the Learner-Centered Classroom*; they apply this list to characters from literature and history throughout the year until it is time for the Biography Bash. Students then choose a person whose heroic qualities they admire; the project facilitates an in-depth study of this person. During a field trip to the public library, students begin individual research, which continues back in the library media center and culminates in an individual book, a 3-slide PowerPoint® presentation, and a Hero Award presentation ceremony for each hero. Topics are invisibly differentiated. Basic-Average-Challenge (B-A-C) are applied by the reading level of available biographies in the school library. Choice elements in the project encourage students to work with their strengths to reach to new heights of understanding and presentation.

Time Frame: 8 weeks or more
Preteaching: Two hours of study skills in the classroom with academic support coordinator.
One hour of reading in the classroom with classroom teacher.
One hour in the library with LMS and classroom teacher.
One hour in the computer lab with the computer teacher.
Project: One 3-hour session at the public library with LMS, classroom teacher, and academic support coordinator.
One hour in library with LMS and classroom teacher.
One hour of study skills in the classroom with academic support coordinator.
Thirteen to fifteen hours in the classroom (reading, language arts, social studies combined) with the classroom teacher.

Thirteen 45-minute classes in the computer lab with the computer teacher.
Additional Time: 2-4 hours homework.
Three hours of presentation in the multipurpose room with all teachers of this project, third grade classes, and parents.
Additional time in any area as needed for individual students to complete assignments. Almost all work is done on campus.

Content Area Standards: Texas Essential Knowledge and Skills (TEKS)
<http://www.tea.state.tx.us/teks/index.html>

§110.6. English Language Arts and Reading, Grade 4

(10) Reading/comprehension. The student comprehends selections using a variety of strategies. The student is expected to:

- (E) use the text's structure or progression of ideas such as cause and effect or chronology to locate and recall information;
- (G) paraphrase and summarize text to recall, inform, or organize ideas.
- (H) draw inferences such as conclusions or generalizations and support them with text evidence [and experience] ; and
- (J) distinguish fact and opinion in various texts.
- (L) represent text information in different ways such as in outline, timeline, or graphic organizer.

(11) Reading/literary response. The student expresses and supports responses to various types of texts. The student is expected to:

- (C) support responses by referring to relevant aspects of text [and his/her own experiences].

(12) Reading/text structures/literary concepts. The student analyzes the characteristics of various types of texts (genres). The student is expected to:

- (B) recognize that authors organize information in specific ways.

(15) Writing/purposes. The student writes for a variety of audiences and purposes and in a variety of forms. The student is expected to:

- (C) write to inform such as to explain, describe, [report,] and narrate;
- (E) exhibit an identifiable voice in personal narratives and in stories.

(16) Writing/penmanship/capitalization/punctuation. The student composes original texts, applying the conventions of written language such as capitalization, punctuation, and penmanship to communicate clearly. The student is expected to:

- (A) write legibly by selecting cursive or manuscript as appropriate.

(17) Writing/spelling. The student spells proficiently. The student is expected to:

- (D) spell accurately in final drafts.

(18) Writing/grammar/usage. The student applies standard grammar and usage to communicate clearly and effectively in writing. The student is expected to:

(C) employ standard English usage in writing for audiences, including subject-verb agreement, pronoun referents, and parts of speech.

(19) Writing/writing processes. The student selects and uses writing processes for self initiated and assigned writing. The student is expected to:

(C) revise selected drafts by adding, elaborating, deleting, combining, and rearranging text;

(D) revise drafts for coherence, progression, and logical support of ideas.

(H) proofread his/her own writing and that of others.

§113.6. Social Studies, Grade 4

(22) Social studies skills. The student applies critical-thinking skills to organize and use information acquired from a variety of sources including electronic technology. The student is expected to:

(A) differentiate between, locate, and use primary and secondary sources such as computer software; interviews; biographies; oral, print, and visual material; and artifacts to acquire information about the United States and Texas;

(B) analyze information by sequencing, categorizing, identifying cause-and-effect relationships, comparing, contrasting, finding the main idea, summarizing, making generalizations and predictions, and drawing inferences and conclusions;

(C) organize and interpret information in outlines, reports, databases, and visuals including graphs, charts, timelines, and maps;

(E) identify the elements of frame of reference that influenced the participants in an event; and

(F) use appropriate mathematical skills to interpret social studies information such as maps and graphs.

(23) Social studies skills. The student communicates in written, oral, and visual forms. The student is expected to:

(B) incorporate main and supporting ideas in verbal and written communication;

(D) create written and visual material such as journal entries, reports, graphic organizers, outlines, and bibliographies; and

(E) use standard grammar, spelling, sentence structure, and punctuation.

§126.3. Technology Applications, Grades 3-5

(2) Foundations. The student uses data input skills appropriate to the task. The student is expected to:

(D) produce documents at the keyboard, proofread, and correct errors;

(E) use language skills including capitalization, punctuation, spelling, word division, and use of numbers and symbols as grade-level appropriate;

(3) Foundations. The student complies with the laws and examines the issues regarding the use of technology in society. The student is expected to:

(B) model respect of intellectual property by not illegally copying software or another individual's electronic work.

(5) Information acquisition. The student acquires electronic information in a variety of formats, with appropriate supervision. The student is expected to:

(A) acquire information including text, audio, video, and graphics;

(6) Information acquisition. The student evaluates the acquired electronic information. The student is expected to:

(A) apply critical analysis to resolve information conflicts and validate information;
(B) determine the success of strategies used to acquire electronic information; and
(C) determine the usefulness and appropriateness of digital information.

(7) Solving problems. The student uses appropriate computer-based productivity tools to create and modify solutions to problems. The student is expected to:

(B) use appropriate software to express ideas and solve problems including the use of word processing, graphics, databases, spreadsheets, simulations, and multimedia; and
(C) use a variety of data types including text, graphics, digital audio, and video.

(9) Solving problems. The student uses technology applications to facilitate evaluation of work, both process and product. The student is expected to:

(B) use software features, such as slide show previews, to evaluate final product.

(10) Communication. The student formats digital information for appropriate and effective communication. The student is expected to:

(A) use font attributes, color, white space, and graphics to ensure that products are appropriate for the defined audience;
(B) use font attributes, color, white space, and graphics to ensure that products are appropriate for the communication media including multimedia screen displays, Internet documents, and printed materials;

(11) **Communication.** The student delivers the product electronically in a variety of media, with appropriate supervision. The student is expected to:

(A) publish information in a variety of media including, but not limited to, printed copy, monitor display, Internet documents, and video; and
(B) use presentation software to communicate with specific audiences.

(12) **Communication.** The student uses technology applications to facilitate evaluation of communication, both process and product. The student is expected to:

(B) evaluate the product for relevance to the assignment or task;

Information Power Information Literacy Standards and Indicators: 1.1, 1.2, 1.3, 1.4, 1.5, 2.1, 2.2, 2.3, 2.4, 3.1, 3.2, 3.3, 3.4, 4.2, 5.3, 6.2, 8.2, 8.3

Cooperative Teaching Plan:

Library Media Specialist Will:

- With teachers, design the unit, including rubrics and all student handouts.
- Compile the list of available biographies by reading level and assist in the differentiation of topics by level of difficulty, as well as designing choices by interest or skill.
- Arrange the trip to the public library.
- Lead trip to the public library and provide orientation during the visit.
- Supervise library research in print resources.
- Work with students in the adult stacks at the public library to find appropriate materials.
- Supervise individual students in locating periodicals by using indices.
- Continue to guide student research in the school's library media center.
- Assist in computer lab to teach database search methods and NoodleBib application.
- Assist in assessment of notes, notes organization, and bibliography.

Classroom Teachers Will:

- With library media specialist, design the unit, including rubrics and all student handouts.
- Implement the advance preparation in character education, teaching heroic qualities. (Note: Students study an admirable person from whom he or she can learn positive lessons.)
- Accompany students to the public library and work with them there as needed to locate and read appropriate biographical resources.
- Provide class time for research, writing, and organizing as all unit work is done at school.
- Provide class time to complete the various pieces of the project according to the timeline.
- Plan, schedule, and facilitate the awards ceremony.
- Lead assessment of all final products.

Academic Support Coordinator Will (in the context of the fourth grade study skills class):

- Introduce the process of researching a biography.
- Teach students how to extract the needed information from a biographical piece. (Using a newspaper on Texas history and a biography of Sam Houston, tie the skills to other curriculum topics).
- Teach the IIM (Independent Investigative Method) of note taking and organization of notes from several sources, a visual method which helps children to keep up with the various threads of learning.
- Teach bibliography skills using NoodleBib and assist students to begin research by recording the bibliographic data on a NoodleBib template.

- Teach mind mapping as a graphic way to illustrate information in specific biographical information.
- Assist in assessment of notes, notes organization, and bibliography.

Computer Teacher Will:

- Pre-teach PowerPoint®: font and color formatting, Word Art, and text boxes.
- Teach access and use of online subscription sources, including *Facts on File, EBSCO Searchasaurus* and *World Book Online*.
- Provide limited access to the Internet for additional information to any students who need more.
- Provide computer class time to continue research online, as appropriate, or to type project.
- Provide class time and teaching support for creation of the PowerPoint® slides.
- Provide class time to support location of a map of the place determined by the students to be most important in each hero's life.
- Provide class time and support for typing various written products.
- Provide time and adult support in computer class to use NoodleBib to complete the bibliography.
- Facilitate the final presentation of the compiled PowerPoint® including all students from each class.
- Assess all PowerPoint® slide products; assist in assessment of other typed products.

Resources:

Curriculum

"Independent Investigative Method." *Active Learning Systems*. 2005-2006. 24 November 2006. <www.iimresearch.com>.

Kaufeldt, Martha. "Life Skills for Success." (Chart p. 201) *Begin with the Brain: Orchestrating the Learner-Centered Classroom*. Tucson: Zephyr Press, 1999.

Margulies, Nancy and Nusa Maal. *Mapping Inner Space: Learning and Teaching Visual Mapping*. Second Edition. Tucson: Zephyr Press, 2001.

Print

A broad collection of leveled biographies written at third grade to high school reading levels.

Current Biography series. New York: H.W. Wilson, 1940-.

Junior Book of Authors and Illustrators series. New York: H.W. Wilson, 1934-.

The Lincoln Library of Sports Champions. 14 vols. Cleveland: Lincoln Library, 2004.

Something about the Author series. Detroit: Gale Research, 1971-.

World Book Encyclopedia. Chicago: World Book, Inc., 2006.

Electronic

"NoodleBib." *NoodleTools*. 1999-2006. 24 November 2006 <http://www.noodletools.com/>. (requires subscription)

"Biography." *InfoPlease*. 2000-2006. 24 November 2006 <http://www.infoplease.com/people.html>.

Biography.com. 24 November 2006 <http://www.biography.com/>.

EBSCO Searchasaurus. 10 October 2006 <www.ebsco.com>. (requires subscription)

Facts on File Online Databases (*American History Online*, *World History Online*, and *Science Online*) 24 November 2006 < http://www.fofweb.com/>. (requires subscription)
PowerPoint®
World Book Online. 24 November 2006 <http://www.worldbookonline.com>. (requires subscription)

Culminating Learning Product:

- A memory book with required configuration of pages that demonstrates student assimilation of information.

- An autobiographical essay.

- A memory box containing visual and/or three-dimensional symbols for various aspects of the hero's life.

- Three PowerPoint® slides including a title slide, a brief biography, and a life map.

- The hero award oral presentation (think Nobel Prize for heroic qualities) to parents and other classes.

Assessment Overview: Students receive a series of assessment rubrics to cover all aspects of the project. Teachers use these rubrics formatively to assist students to improve their products through several drafts by indicating specific areas for improvement of each product. (Note: A student can be in the NO category for one item but the WOW category for another aspect of the same product.) Students also use the rubrics formatively as they progress through the total project. Student copies of the rubric are annotated with many teacher comments. (Note: A student in the BASIC group can score WOW, and a CHALLENGE student can score only OK.)

Adaptations and Extensions:

This unit meets the educational and developmental needs of every student in several ways.

- Topics are differentiated by difficulty (see Cooperative Teaching Plan under librarian responsibilities and the Unit Overview for details). Students are each offered a list of level-appropriate topics from which they choose three that interest them; the teachers assign one of the three, checking that no other student in the class has the same topic.

- Two other pieces of the unit are level-differentiated: the letters written "by" the hero studied and the autobiographical questions.

- Students may choose to weight more heavily the written autobiography or the visual memory box, which allows them to play to their own strengths; all students must complete both pieces, but one is larger and one smaller according to student option.

- Throughout the project, the librarian, the computer teacher, the classroom teachers and the academic support coordinator remain available to all students as needed.

Overview

Choosing a Hero: Select a person you would like to study from the color list you are given.* The person can be living or dead but may not be a current sports figure or movie star. You must look up at least five different people who interest you to see if there is information available.

You will write a preliminary paragraph about three choices explaining why these people interest you and what heroic characteristics you think each demonstrates. These people should be people you admire. You will be making a memory book about this person's life.

It is very important that you seriously and thoroughly follow the research and note-taking steps at the beginning of this project. The more time and effort a student spends at the beginning of the project, the easier and more interesting the process becomes.

Your teacher will show you models for each element, and some assignments will also be part of a PowerPoint® presentation. Most of the activities will be completed at school. If any work is assigned for homework, remember that this is YOUR project. Do not work ahead, but do stay aware of the due dates. All of the pieces will be compiled into a memory book of your person's life.

1) **Note-taking.** You have practiced note-taking. Use the IIM pages provided and follow instructions to take notes about your person's life. Major topics might include Birth and Death, Childhood and Early Life, Later Life--Family, Career, Travels, etc. **Remember: you want to find ways your person exhibited hero skills and made an impact on the world.** These notes will be used for every element of your project. Remember, if you take time and put in more effort at the beginning, the process will be easier and more interesting as you go along.

2) **Color Coding the Notes.** Use instructions on the IIM Color Coding sheet to sort your notes by the major topic areas (Birth and Death, Childhood and Early Life, Later Life--Family, Career, Travels, etc.)

3) **Title Slide.** Create a Title Slide for your person using PowerPoint® using the PowerPoint® Slide Instructions sheet.

4) **Map and Map Label.** Complete two Map Label Cards listing your hero's name, field, birth and death dates, main heroic quality or reason for importance, the place in the world you think is most important to his/her life, and why it is important. Locate and print a map of the important place. One label and the printed map will become part of your final memory book, and one label will be used to create a bulletin board timeline.

These labels will surround a world map in the hall and be connected to the correct world location by yarn. You will be expected to string the yarn from your label to the correct place on the map.

These labels will be numbered in chronological order by birth so that a timeline can also be posted in the hall.

5) **Hero Slide.** Create a Hero Slide using PowerPoint® for your person. Include a photograph or illustration of your hero and list basic facts as instructed on the PowerPoint® Slide Instructions sheet.

6) **CHOICE – Friendly Letter OR Business Letter.** In the voice of your person, write:

Friendly Letter *(Orange Level)* Write a friendly letter to your parent. You may describe your personal accomplishments or some hardship you may have experienced. Your letter should reflect something personal about you. (Write on only one side of your paper.)

(Yellow Level) Write a friendly letter to another famous person who lived during your time. You may describe your personal accomplishments or some hardship you may have experienced. Your letter should reflect something personal about you. (Write on only one side of your paper.)

(Blue Level) Write an imaginary friendly letter to another famous person in your field who lived in a different time than you. You may describe your personal accomplishments or some hardship you may have experienced. Your letter should reflect something personal about you. (Write on only one side of your paper.)

Business Letter *(Orange Level)* Write a business letter to a person in your field to ask for a job. Your letter will need to explain what your qualifications are for the job you are seeking. (Write on only one side of your paper.)

(Yellow Level) Write a business letter to a person in your field to offer a product you have invented or would like to develop. You could offer a service you can provide. Your letter will need to explain specifics about the invention or service you are offering. (Write on only one side of your paper.)

(Blue Level) Write a business letter to a person in your field to request a service you need to further your professional goals (your inventions or knowledge). Your letter will need to explain why you need the services you are requesting. (Write on only one side of your paper.)

7) **Autobiography Questions.** Answer the 14 questions on the autobiography or memory box sheet. With the information, you will create two products – a typed autobiography in paragraph form and a memory box.

Answer all of the questions but choose how you demonstrate your understanding of the answers.

Choice A: Emphasize the written autobiography and make a small visual or three-dimensional memory box. Include **nine** answers in the written autobiography and **five** symbols in the memory box.
Choice B: Emphasize the memory box of visual or three-dimensional symbols and write a shorter autobiography. Include **nine** symbols in the memory box and **five** answers in the written autobiography.

The memory box can be a shoebox or a container your hero might use (e.g. saddlebag, purse, measuring cup). The maximum size is a standard shoebox: 15" x 10" x 6". The box or container will be on display so the items should be visible. Think of symbols to represent answers to the questions for the memory box. You can draw, find clipart, make, find, or purchase inexpensive small items for your box. Type and attach labels to all items in the memory box; the labels should explain in several sentences the meaning of each item/symbol and credit the source of the image. You should not use any clip art images or symbols here that duplicate images for your Life Map Slide.

8) **Life Map Slide.** Begin by making a draft of a timeline including mind mapping symbols to represent your hero's life. Your final Life Map will be a PowerPoint® slide beginning with your person's birth and including at least seven more dates in sequential order, each with a visual symbol as instructed on the PowerPoint® Slide Instructions sheet.

9) **Hero Skills Award.** Using the Nobel Prize as your model, invent an award to present to your person. This award should have a title that reflects the hero skills this person demonstrated most completely throughout his/her life (e.g. responsibility, persistence, generosity). Create a 3-D symbol to use in your presentation. The symbol should reflect your understanding of your person's hero skills and accomplishments and may combine more than one object or image. The final award can be a combination of two to three symbols but must be a single unit when you pick it up. It can be created from found objects or handmade by you; it may not be a purchased trophy.

10) **Hero Award Acceptance Speech.** Write a "Hero Acceptance Speech" including a brief explanation of the award and why your person has won it as instructed on the Hero Award Acceptance Speech sheet.

11) **Bibliography.** Record the bibliographic information about your sources on your bibliography forms. Note exactly where you found your information. Remember to use your IIM skills. Then use NoodleBib to make your final bibliography.
   - ■ You must use at least three sources and no more than one basic encyclopedia.
   - ■ Only one of the three required sources may be an electronic source.
   - ■ If you use more than three sources, you may use more than one electronic source.

12) **Heroes Award Presentation Day.** Dress like your person to present your hero's acceptance speech for the Hero Award before an audience of your parents and students from other grades. Your Hero PowerPoint® Slides will be shown while you are speaking. Your memory box and completed memory book will be on display.

The Librarian compiles the leveled topic lists by examining the existing biography collection for Basic, Average, and Challenge level biographies. Classroom teachers review the list considering other factors, including the complexity of the person's contributions to the world and the relative availability of other information. Too much information (Shakespeare) can be as problematic as too little (your great uncle the biologist) for this first foray into researching from multiple sources. A very few topics appear on two level lists, but none on three.

Each level list is printed on a single color (Orange for Basic, Yellow for Average, Blue for Challenge). The colors are maintained as constants throughout the assignment wherever there are leveled assignments, to help the teachers as much as the students. The CHOICE option is offered to all levels, as a way to inspire deeper interest and personal investment in the project as recommended by several books on the brain-compatible classroom, including Martha Kaufeldt's.

Topic Selection

After reviewing a variety of people to study for Biography Bash, select three people you would be interested in studying. Complete the following:

Person to study: _____

Why I want to study this person? _____

_____

_____

_____

_____

Person to study: _____

Why I want to study this person? _____

_____

_____

_____

_____

Person to study: _____

Why I want to study this person? _____

_____

_____

_____

Research—IIM Color Coding

- Keep the broad topics listed below in mind while you research.

- Take your notes on IIM sheets. Complete the "top" section for each reference you use. Remember to use a different line for each note and use your own words.

- You will categorize your notes according to these topics later using the colors in parentheses for each topic. (Depending on the person you are studying, you may have many notes or few notes for individual sections.)

- There are two categories with asterisks *. These categories are very important and you should focus on taking notes that relate to each. Keep in mind, your reference will not say, "The hero skill used by _____ was _____." or "His contribution affected the world by _____."

- You must determine what to include using the information you are learning.

TOPICS

Birth and Death (brown)

Childhood and Early Life (blue)
    (school, family)

Later Life (Family, Career, Travels, etc.) (green)
    (family, career, travels, etc.)

*Hero Skills/Character Traits (red)
    (includes personality)

*Contributions to the World; How the Contribution(s) Affected the World (orange)
    (important facts including honors, awards, accomplishments)

Other/Tidbits (black)
    (These are the least important, the extra bits beyond the required information. These are not the focus of your research.)

Bibliography

Map Label Cards

Hero's Name _____	**Hero's Name** _____
Field _____	**Field** _____
Birth & Death Dates _____	**Birth & Death Dates** _____
Place of Importance _____ _____	**Place of Importance** _____ _____
Why _____	**Why** _____
Student Name	**Student Name**

Choice—Autobiography or Memory Box *(Orange Level)*

Answer all of the questions but choose how you demonstrate your understanding of the answers.

Choice A: Emphasize the written autobiography and make a small visual or three-dimensional memory box. Include **nine** answers in the written autobiography and **five** symbols in the memory box.

Choice B: Emphasize the memory box of visual or three-dimensional symbols and write a shorter autobiography. Include **nine** symbols in the memory box and **five** answers in the written autobiography.

Note: In both choices, the autobiography must be typed using paragraph form.

Years
What years did your life span?

Fame
For what are you most famous? Did your fame come while you were alive?

Problem
What is a problem you solved?

Daily Life
How did you spend a typical day (besides working)? Did you have a hobby?

Daily Work
How did you spend a typical day (working in your field)?

Skills
What skills were needed to perform your duty?

Education/Training
What education (schooling) did you receive for your job/field?

Clothes
What clothing did you wear? Did you have a particular uniform or clothing for your job?

Tools
What tool(s) did you use?

Life Around You
What was happening in your city and country during your lifetime?

Family
Who were your parents and siblings? Your wife/husband and children?

Friends
Who were your friends? (include at least 2)

Influence
Who is a person who influenced you and how? (parent or spouse OK)

Impact
What positive impact did your life's work have on others?

Field
What is your field of work?

Choice—Autobiography or Memory Box (*Yellow Level*)

Answer all of the questions but choose how you demonstrate your understanding of the answers.

Choice A: Emphasize the written autobiography and make a small visual or three-dimensional memory box. Include **nine** answers in the written autobiography and **five** symbols in the memory box.

Choice B: Emphasize the memory box of visual or three-dimensional symbols and write a shorter autobiography. Include **nine** symbols in the memory box and **five** answers in the written autobiography.

Note: In both choices, the autobiography must be typed using paragraph form.

Years
  Who is another famous person who lived during your lifetime?
Fame
  Did your fame come while you were alive?
Problem
  What is a problem you solved and how did you solve it?
Daily Life
  What was the daily process of participating in your hobby?
Daily Work
  How many hours might you spend working? Did the work result in a particular product?
Skills
  How did you receive practice in your skills?
Education/Training
  Has the education (amount/type) changed over the years?
Clothes
  What clothing did someone of the opposite sex in your field wear?
Tools
  Did the tool(s) change over the course of your lifetime? Why?
Life Around You
  What was happening in a different country during your lifetime?
Family
  Who are some extended family members you knew well? (grandparents, uncles and aunts, cousins)
Friends
  Who were your friends/colleagues at work?
Influence
  Who is a person who influenced you and how? (beyond a parent or spouse)
Impact
  Did your life's work have a negative impact on anyone?
Field
  What are some other jobs in your field?

Choice—Autobiography or Memory Box *(Blue Level)*

Answer all of the questions but choose how you demonstrate your understanding of the answers.

Choice A: Emphasize the written autobiography and make a small visual or three-dimensional memory box. Include **nine** answers in the written autobiography and **five** symbols in the memory box.

Choice B: Emphasize the memory box of visual or three-dimensional symbols and write a shorter autobiography. Include **nine** symbols in the memory box and **five** answers in the written autobiography.

Note: In both choices, the autobiography must be typed using paragraph form.

Years
> Who is another famous person in your field who lived during your lifetime?

Fame
> What effect did your fame have on your field, your life, your family?

Problem
> What effect did your problem and solution have on your field?

Daily Life
> What effect did your hobby have on your field?

Daily Work
> What was the daily process of working in your field?

Skills
> How did you pass your skills on to younger practitioners of your work?

Education/Training
> What education (amount/type) would someone currently in your field need?

Clothes
> What clothing did someone working in your field in a different country wear?

Tools
> What tool(s) did someone working in your field in a different country use? Why?

Life Around You
> What was happening in two different countries during your lifetime? How did these world events affect your life?

Family
> To whom in your family were you closest? Why?

Friends
> What did your friends/colleagues do for a living?

Influence
> Who is a person (or group) outside your family whom you directly influenced by your work and how?

Impact
> Is there any negative impact of your work? Could it be avoided now? How? Could it be rectified now? How?

Field
> What changes have happened in your field? Why?

PowerPoint® Slide Instructions

Title Page

■ Title page should include the Hero's full name in the Title Box and should also include the student's full name in the Subtitle box.

■ Font formatting is encouraged if time allows.

Hero Slide

■ Hero Slide should include the Hero's full name centered in the Title Box at the top of the slide.

■ A picture of the hero (saved from the Internet) should be included on either side of the slide. The picture should be a clear image.

■ There should be a total of **five** bullets opposite the image: first bullet should be the birth and death dates of the Hero with parenthesis around the dates {i.e. (1914-1975)}, the remaining four bullets should be important information from the Hero's life in phrases beginning with strong verbs.

■ Font formatting, Word Art, Text Boxes, and color are encouraged if time allows.

Life Map Slide

■ Life Map Slide should include at least **eight** text boxes including the dates of and the corresponding important event in the Hero's life.

■ The text boxes should be connected using Auto Shapes-Connectors with arrows creating a mapping of the events.

■ Each text box should have a corresponding clip art image next to it relating to the content of that text box. (Internet images may also be used and you will cite them briefly.)

■ Font and connector formatting, as well as Word Art, Text Boxes and color are encouraged if time allows.

Hero Award Acceptance Speech

Think of this presentation as an acceptance speech for your award. Remember, your award reflects a hero skill (perseverance, bravery, humor, etc.). You may use any character sheets you have received throughout the year, if desired. Written below is a basic structure for you to **adapt** for your hero. Rewrite it to match the information about your hero.

Award for _____

Thank you for this _____ award. You will notice the award is

_____ *(the actual award you are going to make)* that represents

_____.

I showed _____ when I _____

_____.

(*include several additional sentences. *This is important!)

I also want to thank _____ for his/her assistance/support. He/she

_____.

I am most proud of _____.

*I made a difference in the world by _____

_____. (and /or) *I

affected the lives of others by _____

_____.

Without my accomplishments, imagine how the world would be different. (*include additional sentence explaining)

Thank you again.

The * represents very important parts of your speech and <u>must</u> be included.
You will type your acceptance speech. It is due at the end of the day on
_____. (If it is complete sooner, please submit early.)
The actual award will be designed/built by you outside of class, and it is also due on _____.
(Recall the symbols we discussed in class as you consider your award.)
The presentations are the very next week on_____!

Classroom Rubric 1

	WOW	GOOD	OK	NO
Research & Notes	All completed. Notes are included from one book, one encyclopedia, one electronic resource, and at least one additional source. Notes reflect student understanding of information and are not copied word for word.	All completed. Notes are included from one book, one encyclopedia, and one electronic resource. Notes are not copied word for word.	Mostly completed. Notes are included from one book, one encyclopedia, and one electronic resource.	Not completed. Notes from fewer than three resources. Notes incomplete. OR Notes not useful because the student can't understand them. OR Notes mostly copied word for word.
Notes Organization	Color coding used correctly. All required topics covered well. Includes childhood, education, family and marriage, character traits, importance to the world. Very detailed.	Color coding used. Most required topics covered adequately. Includes childhood, education, family and marriage, character traits, importance to the world. Fairly detailed.	Color coding incomplete. Required topics covered minimally. Random additional information. Includes mention of childhood, education, family and marriage, character traits, importance to the world. Very brief.	Minimal color coding. Not all required topics covered. No additional information. Does not include all topic areas. Those areas included are very brief.
Map and Map Label	Includes a thoughtful answer to the heroic quality and main reason for importance. Neatly, correctly and completely filled in.	Heroic quality and main reason for importance adequately answered. Neatly, mostly correctly and completely filled in.	Heroic quality and main reason for importance barely answered. Mostly correctly and completely filled in.	Randomly filled in.

Classroom Rubric 2

	WOW	GOOD	OK	NO
Friendly or Business Letter	Letter demonstrates strong understanding of the request. Letter shows creative application of the hero's voice and point of view in making this request.	Letter demonstrates understanding of the request. Letter indicates effort to apply the hero's voice and point of view in making this request.	Letter shows minimal understanding of the request. Letter indicates little effort to understand the hero's perspective.	Letter shows no understanding of the request. Letter indicates no understanding of the hero's perspective.
Autobiography Questions	Questions completely answered. Additional information (when it is available) included in the answer.	Questions mostly answered. Little additional information is included.	Questions mostly answered.	Many questions not answered.
Student will select one Emphasized and one Small of the following two assignments				
Autobiography (Emphasized or Small)	Demonstrates thorough understanding of the hero's perspective on his own life. **Emphasized** includes nine topics. OR **Small** includes five topics. May include additional information.	Indicates some understanding of the hero's perspective on his own life. **Emphasized** includes nine topics. OR **Small** includes five topics.	Indicates an understanding of the facts, but not the hero's perspective on his own life. **Emphasized** includes seven to eight topics. OR **Small** includes fewer than five topics.	Indicates minimal understanding of the facts or the hero's perspective. **Emphasized** includes five to seven topics. OR **Small** includes two to three topics.
Memory Box (Emphasized or Small)	Images and objects included indicate creative approach to visually representing aspects of the hero's life. **Emphasized** includes nine topics. OR **Small** includes five topics. May include additional symbols.	Images and objects indicate factual understanding of aspects of the hero's life. **Emphasized** includes nine topics. OR **Small** includes five topics.	Images and objects indicate incomplete understanding of aspects of the hero's life. **Emphasized** includes seven to eight topics. OR **Small** includes fewer than five topics.	Images and objects indicate minimal understanding of the assignment. **Emphasized** includes five to seven topics. OR **Small** includes two to three topics.

Classroom Rubric 3

	WOW	GOOD	OK	NO
Hero Skills Award	The Award demonstrates thought and deep understanding of multiple aspects of the hero's life. The chosen symbols lead viewers to deeper understanding of the heroic aspects of the person's life.	The Award demonstrates thought and understanding of important aspects of the hero's life. The chosen symbol(s) leads viewers to understand the hero beyond the obvious.	The Award demonstrates basic understanding of the hero's life. The Award is an obvious symbol of an important aspect of the hero's life.	The Award demonstrates some knowledge of the hero's life. The Award is somewhat related to the hero.
Hero Skills Speech	Completion of the speech template indicates deep understanding of this person's importance to the world, especially the heroic qualities demonstrated during his life.	Completion of the speech template indicates understanding of this person's importance to the world, especially the heroic qualities demonstrated during his life.	Completion of the speech template indicates some understanding of this person's importance to the world, especially the heroic qualities demonstrated during his life.	Completion of the speech template indicates little understanding of this person's importance to the world, especially the heroic qualities demonstrated during his life.
Bibliography	List includes one encyclopedia, one book, one electronic source and at least one additional resource. All sources consulted are included. All sources consulted are correctly cited by using NoodleBib.	List includes one encyclopedia, one book, one electronic source. Most sources consulted are included. Most sources consulted are correctly cited by using NoodleBib.	Two or three required types of resources are included. Some resources consulted are included. Some resources consulted are correctly cited by using NoodleBib.	Only one type of resource is included. Few sources consulted are included. Few sources consulted are correctly cited by using NoodleBib.

Overall Rubric

	WOW	GOOD	OK	NO
Timeliness	All products are completed and delivered on time. (Note: early completion is not an advantage.)	Most products are completed and delivered on time. No products were more than one day late.	Some products are completed and delivered on time. Only one to two products were more than one day late.	Few products are completed and delivered on time. Several products were more than one day late.
Spelling (for each product)	All places, people, and words spelled correctly.	Only one to two spelling errors.	Only three to five spelling errors.	Many spelling errors.
Neatness	Every page is neat and easy to read. Pages are in correct order, well labeled, and attractive.	Most pages are neat and easy to read. Most pages are in correct order, well labeled, and attractive.	Many pages are neat and easy to read. Many pages are in correct order, well labeled, and attractive.	Some pages are neither neat nor easy to read. Many pages are not in correct order or well labeled.

Computer Rubric 1

	WOW	GOOD	OK	NO
Title Slide	First and last name of both student and hero included. Font has been formatted. Word Art, Text Boxes, and Color have been added.	First and last name of both student and hero included. Font has been formatted.	First and last name of both student and hero included. Font has not been formatted.	First names only of both student and/or hero. Font has not been formatted.
Hero Slide	Hero's first and last name appears centered at the top of the page. Birth and death dates of hero is the first bullet with parentheses around the dates. Events are in correct sequence. Strong verbs are used for each hero accomplishment. Bullets are lined up correctly. Two clear images are used: one of the hero and one related to the hero's field. Font has been formatted. Word Art, Text Boxes, and Color have been added.	Hero's first and last name appears centered at the top of the page. Birth and death dates of hero is the first bullet with parentheses around the dates. Events are in correct sequence. Active verbs are used for each hero accomplishment. Bullets are lined up correctly. Image of the hero is clear. Font has been formatted. Word Art, Text Boxes, or Color has been added.	Hero's first and last name appears centered at the top of the page. Birth and death dates of hero is the first bullet with no parentheses around the dates. Events are in correct sequence. Basic verbs are used for each hero accomplishment. Bullets are lined up correctly. Image of the hero is clear. Font has not been formatted.	Hero's first name only appears uncentered at the top of the page. Birth and death dates of hero is the first bullet with no parentheses around the dates. Events are not in correct sequence. Verbs are used for each hero accomplishment. Bullets are lined up incorrectly or no bullets are used at all. Image of the hero is grainy and unclear. Font has not been formatted.

Computer Rubric 2

	WOW	GOOD	OK	NO
Life Map Slide	Seven dates are included, each with a clip art. Exact dates are included at the beginning of the text boxes. Connectors are used to link the text boxes in a manner that logically flows. Clip art is used that directly relates to each text box and no clip art is duplicated from elsewhere in the total project. Internet images also used. Information is presented in creative and interesting phrases beginning with strong verbs. All text boxes are evenly spaced throughout the page. Font has been formatted. Color has been added to connectors and text boxes.	Seven dates are included, each with a clip art. Dates (year only) are included at the beginning of the text boxes. Connectors are used to link the text boxes in a manner that logically flows. Clip art is used that directly relates to each text box and no clip art is duplicated from elsewhere in the total project. Information is presented in creative phrases beginning with active verbs. All text boxes are evenly spaced throughout the page.	Seven dates are included, each with a clip art. Dates (year only) are included in the text boxes. Connectors are used to link the text boxes but in a confusing manner. Clip art is used but some images are repeated or some are omitted totally or incorrectly placed. Information is presented in phrases beginning with verbs. All text boxes are evenly spaced throughout the page.	Fewer than seven dates are included in the text boxes. Incomplete dates are included. Only some connectors are used to link the text boxes. Only some clip art is used. Information is not presented in phrases. Text boxes are not evenly spaced throughout the page.

Unit 9
Cultures of the Sun:
Exploring the Aztec and Inca Cultures

Laurie Dunlap, Library Media Specialist

Toni Buzzeo, Children's Author, Library Media Specialist

Mary Semons and Dolores White, Multiage Grade 4/5 Teachers

Carole Thompson, Computer Teacher

Hanson/Jewett Elementary Schools

932 Long Plains Road, Buxton, Maine 04093

<ldunlap@sad6.k12.me.us>

Grade Level: 4/5

Unit Overview: The Aztec and Inca cultures are powerful learning tools for multiage students engaged in a multi-disciplinary unit involving language arts, social studies, information literacy, visual and performing arts, and technology. Students research either the Aztec or Inca culture in order to create an illustrated journal from the point of view of a selected member of that society. The journal reveals students' understanding of their research findings and their ability to apply complex thinking skills such as abstracting and comparison and contrast. The book is assessed using the Self-Assessment Journal Rubric (both formative and summative). Finally, students contribute the cover and three scanned pages of their journals, read aloud, as well as a reflection on their learning process to an online slideshow created in iMovie.

Time Frame: 9 weeks: Four one-hour sessions in the library media center for research with the LMS and classroom teachers; daily one-hour language arts blocks with the classroom teachers (LMS in attendance during one weekly classroom block); four forty-five minute sessions with the computer teacher in the computer lab to record readings and reflections.

Content Area Standards: State of Maine Learning Results
<http://www.state.me.us/education/lres/lres.htm>

Social Studies: History

Standard A. CHRONOLOGY
Students will use the chronology of history and major eras to demonstrate the relationships of events and people. Students will be able to:
Social Studies - Elementary Grades 5-8
HA1. Describe the effects of historical changes on daily life.

HA2. Identify the sequence of major events and people in the history of Maine, the United States, and selected world civilizations.

Standard B. HISTORICAL KNOWLEDGE, CONCEPTS, AND PATTERNS
Students will develop historical knowledge of major events, people, and enduring themes in the United States, in Maine, and throughout world history. Students will be able to:
Social Studies - Elementary Grades 5-8
HB2. Demonstrate an understanding of selected themes in Maine, United States, and world history (e.g., revolution, technological innovation, migration).
HB3. Demonstrate an understanding of selected turning points in ancient and medieval world history and the continuing influence of major civilizations of the past.

Social Studies: Geography

Standard A. SKILLS AND TOOLS
Students will know how to construct and interpret maps and use globes and other geographic tools to locate and derive information about people, places, regions, and environments. Students will be able to:
Social Studies - Elementary Grades 3-4
HA1. Construct and compare maps of Maine, the United States, and regions of the world to interpret geographical features and draw conclusions about physical patterns.

Standard B. HUMAN INTERACTION WITH ENVIRONMENTS
Students will understand and analyze the relationships among people and their physical environment. Students will be able to:
Social Studies - Elementary Grades 3-4
HB3. Use a variety of materials and geographic tools to explain how the physical environment supports and constrains human activities.

English Language Arts

Standard A. PROCESS OF READING
Students will use the skills and strategies of the reading process to comprehend, interpret, evaluate, and appreciate what they have read. Students will be able to:
English Language Arts - Elementary Grades 3-4
A5. Read a variety of narrative and informational texts independently and fluently.
English Language Arts – Elementary Grades 5-8
A2. Reflect on what has been discovered and learned while reading, and formulate additional questions.
A4. Use specific strategies (e.g., rereading, consultation) to clear up confusing parts of a text.
A11. Generate and evaluate the notes they have taken from course-related reading, listening, and viewing.

B. LITERATURE AND CULTURE
Students will use reading, listening, and viewing strategies to experience, understand, and appreciate literature and culture. Students will be able to:
English Language Arts – Elementary Grades 3-4
B1. Demonstrate awareness of the culture and geography pertinent to the texts they read.

B11. Apply effective strategies to the reading and use of nonfiction (e.g., reference sources, articles, histories, biographies, autobiographies, diaries, and letters) using texts with an appropriate complexity of content and sophistication of style.
English Language Arts – Elementary Grades 5-8
B11. Read literature and view films which illustrate distinct cultures in various types of works and formulate and defend opinions gathered from the experience.

D. INFORMATIONAL TEXTS
Students will apply reading, listening, and viewing strategies to informational texts across all areas of curriculum. Students will be able to:
English Language Arts – Elementary Grades 3-4
D1. Use information contained in chapter and section headings, topic sentences, and summary sentences to construct the main ideas.
D2. Use various informational parts of a text (e.g., index, table of contents, glossary, appendices).
D3. Read for a variety of purposes (e.g., to answer specific questions, to form an opinion, to skim for information).
D4. Summarize informational texts (e.g., identify the main idea or concept and the supporting detail).
D7. Recognize when and how new information in a text connects to prior knowledge.
English Language Arts – Elementary Grades 5-8
D6. Describe new knowledge presented in informational texts and how it can be used.

Standard E. PROCESSES OF WRITING AND SPEAKING
Students will demonstrate the ability to use the skills and strategies of the writing process. Students will be able to:
English Language Arts - Elementary Grades 3-4
E1. Identify strengths and weaknesses in their own writing and seek effective help from others.
E2. Improve their finished product by revising content from draft to final piece.
E3. Use planning, drafting, and revising to produce, on-demand, a well-developed, organized piece that demonstrates effective language use, voice, and command of mechanics.
E4. Report orally and summarize personal discoveries they have made as a result of reading and viewing.

Standard F. STANDARD ENGLISH CONVENTIONS
Students will write and speak correctly, using conventions of standard written and spoken English. Students will be able to:
English Language Arts - Elementary Grades 3-4
F1. Edit written work for standard English spelling and usage, evidenced by pieces that show and contain:

- few significant errors in the use of pronouns and adjectives.
- attention to the proper use of adverbial forms and conjunctions.
- few significant errors in the spelling of frequently used words.
- no significant errors in the capitalization of words that begin sentences and few significant errors in the capitalization of proper nouns and titles.
- no significant errors in the use of ending punctuation marks and an understanding of how to use commas.

Standard G. STYLISTIC AND RHETORICAL ASPECTS OF WRITING AND SPEAKING

Students will use stylistic and rhetorical aspects of writing and speaking to explore ideas, to present lines of thought, to represent and reflect on human experience, and to communicate feelings, knowledge, and opinions. Students will be able to:

English Language Arts - Elementary Grades 3-4

G3. Write essays and make remarks that clearly state or suggest a central idea and provide supporting detail.

Standard H. RESEARCH-RELATED WRITING AND SPEAKING

Students will work, write, and speak effectively when doing research in all content areas. Students will be able to:

English Language Arts - Elementary Grades 3-4

H1. Ask and seek answers to questions.

H2. Use print and non-print resources (e.g., encyclopedias, dictionaries, people, indexes) to gather information on research topics.

English Language Arts — Elementary Grades 5-8

H3. Create bibliographies.

H6. Use magazines, newspapers, dictionaries, journals, and other print sources to gather information for research topics.

The State of Maine Learning Results are reprinted here with permission from Susan Gendron, Commissioner of Education.

National Educational Technology Standards

<http://cnets.iste.org/students/s_stands.html>

Please refer to the Web site for text of the standards and indicators.

Standard 3. Technology Productivity Standards

First Indicator

Standard 4. Technology Communication Tools

Second Indicator

Standard 5. Technology Research Tools

First and second indicators

Information Power Information Literacy Standards and Indicators: 1.1, 1.3, 1.4, 1.5, 2.4, 3.1, 3.2, 3.3, 3.4, 5.2, 5.3, 8.2, 8.3

Cooperative Teaching Plan

Library Media Specialist Will:

- Teach note taking skills during previous semester in a first research project.
- Review location of resources in the library.
- Provide instruction on using library sources to locate information.
- Review use of nonfiction and reference resources (indexes, tables of contents, keywords)
- Assist students in locating facts about each culture and taking notes.
- Teach bibliography skills using the Bibliography Format sheet.

- Guide students in their search for information on their individual cultures.
- Participate as a group leader on cultural craft-making day.
- Support students in choosing a role in their culture's society.
- Support students in developing a character using the Character Study sheet.
- Support students in creating a Storyboard for presentation of journal entries in book form.
- Contribute to design of rubrics and checklists.
- Support students in assessing note-taking and bibliography using the Self-Assessment Writing Rubric.

Classroom Teachers Will:

- Clear all walls in classrooms at start of trimester and decorate doorway with sign saying: "Welcome to the 15th Century" for first day of the unit.
- Guide students in decorating and creating the culture assigned to each classroom (one classroom is Aztec culture and one classroom is Inca culture) during the first two weeks of the trimester.
- Support students in research in the library media center.
- Offer students multiple opportunities to compare and contrast the two cultures.
- Provide resources and materials and organize volunteers for a cultural craft-making day.
- Support students in choosing a role in their culture's society.
- Support students in developing a character using the Character Study sheet.
- Support students in using the Journal Planning Sheet to organize and synthesize information found during research.
- Support students in creating a Storyboard for presentation of journal entries in book form.
- Guide students in writing journal entries based on researched facts from the point of view of their chosen character.
- Guide students in using the Self-Assessment Writing Rubric as a formative assessment.
- Support students in revising journal entries using the Journal Checklist and Self-Assessment Writing Rubric.
- Support students in creating a Proof Book (final rough draft) with final copy of journal entries and an illustration for each (to be copy editing for final production).
- Guide students in using the Self-Assessment Writing Rubric as a summative assessment.
- Contribute to design of rubric and checklists.
- Guide students in preparing a performance piece and developing their individual contributions using the Performance Checklist.

Computer Teacher Will:

[Note: In the absence of a computer teacher, the LMS and classroom teacher share these responsibilities.]

- Provide instruction on using the Internet to locate information.
- Guide students in online search for information on their individual cultures.
- Contribute to design of rubric.
- Support students in contributing three digitally photographed pages of their journals (read aloud), and a reflection on their learning process to an online slideshow created in iMovie and loaded on the district Web site. (Note: Alternatively, scan pages.)

Resources:

Print
Nonfiction for Research
"Aztecs," *Kids Discover* 12:3 (March 2002).
"Incas," *Kids Discover* 10:3 (March 2000).
Shuter, Jane. *The Incas*. Chicago: Heinemann, 2002.
Shuter, Jane. *The Aztecs*. Chicago: Heinemann, 2002.
Santella, Andrew. *The Aztec*. New York: Children's Press, 2003.
Takacs, Stephanie. *The Inca*. New York: Children's Press, 2003.

Fiction for Pleasure
Clark, Ann Nolan. *Secret of the Andes*. New York: Puffin, 1980.
Morpurgo, Michael. *The Nine Lives of Montezuma*. London: Egmont, 2002.

Electronic
"The Ancient Aztec." *ThinkQuest*. August 1999. 21 September 2006
    <http://library.thinkquest.org/27981/>.
"Conquistadors." *Oregon Public Broadcasting*. 2000. 21 September 2006
    <http://www.pbs.org/opb/conquistadors/>.
"Daily Life in the Inca Empire." *MrDonn.org*. 1999-2006. 21 September 2006
    <http://incas.mrdonn.org/empire.html>.
Ogburn, Dennis E. "The Empire of the Inca." *Milleville Public Schools*. 27 October 1997. 21
    September 2006 <http://www.millville.org/workshops_f/Acker_Inca/inca.htm>.
"Teacher's Guide: Aztecs." *Kids Discover*. 21 September 2006
    <http://www.kidsdiscoverteachers.com/>. Requires purchase.
"Teacher's Guide: Incas." *Kids Discover*. 21 September 2006
    <http://www.kidsdiscoverteachers.com/>. Requires purchase.
"Welcome to Mexico." *Snaith Primary School*. 21 September 2006
    <http://home.freeuk.net/elloughton13/mexico.htm>.
World Book Online. <http://www.worldbookonline.com/>. Requires subscription.

Audiovisuals
Ancient Aztec Empire. DVD. Schlessinger Media, 2004.
Ancient Aztec: The Fall of the Empire. DVD. Schlessinger Media, 2004.
Ancient Inca. DVD. Schlessinger Media, 1998.

Equipment
Television/DVD player
Laptop computers
Computer lab
Data projector
Binding machine
Various art supplies

Culminating Learning Product: Students write and illustrate a journal from the perspective of a selected community member in the Aztec or Inca culture. The cover and three pages of each student's journal (read aloud by the student) are mounted on the school Web site along with a written reflection on the project as a whole.

Assessment Overview: Students complete the Self-Assessment Journal Rubric twice: once prior to final revisions (formative); once after completion of the written product (summative).

Adaptations and Extensions:

- Able learners create a story arc (rising narrative action) in their journals and may complete additional journal pages.

- Able learners are encouraged to delve more deeply into the complexities of the culture and reflect those complexities in the lives of their characters, their problems, and their solutions.

- Challenged readers and ELL students access resources written at their levels.

- Challenged readers and ELL students are given additional support in their research groups in the library.

- Academically challenged students are provided with additional adult input and support from Resource Room teachers when completing their journals.

Bibliography Format

Name_____

For a book with one author, follow this format.
Shuter, Jane. *The Incas.* Chicago: Heinemann, 2002.

Note: If you use a second line, you must indent five spaces.

First Book

1. _____, _____. _____ .
   Author's last name, first name .   Title of book. (underlined)

   _____: _____, _____ .
   City of publication: Publisher,   Date of publication .

Second book

2. _____, _____. _____ .
   Author's last name, first name .   Title of book. (underlined)

   _____: _____, _____ .
   City of publication: Publisher,   Date of publication .

For an unsigned magazine article, follow this format.
Smith, Michael E. "Who Were the Aztecs?" *Calliope.* December 2005: 4-7.

Note: If you use a second line, you must indent five spaces.

3. _____, _____. "_____."
   Author's last name, first name .   Title of article (in quotation marks).

   _____ . _____: _____ .
   Title of magazine (underlined).   Date of magazine : Page numbers .

Bibliography Format (continued)

For a Web Site:

Ogburn, Dennis E. "The Empire of the Inca." *Milleville Public Schools*. 27 October 1997. 21
     September 2006 <http://www.millville.org/workshops_f/Acker_Inca/inca.htm>.

Note: If you use a second line, you must indent five spaces.

First Web site

4.   _____, _____ .   "_____."
       Author's last name, first name .   Title of page. (in quotes)

       _____ .   _____.   _____.
       Title of Web site (underlined)   Copyright date of Web site.   Today's date.

       < _____ > .
       Web site address (in angle brackets) .

Second Web site

5.   _____, _____ .   "_____."
       Author's last name, first name .   Title of page. (in quotes)

       _____ .   _____.   _____.
       Title of Web site (underlined)   Copyright date of Web site.   Today's date.

       < _____ > .
       Web site address (in angle brackets) .

Third Web site

6.   _____, _____ .   "_____."
       Author's last name, first name .   Title of page. (in quotes)

       _____ .   _____.   _____.
       Title of Web site (underlined)   Copyright date of Web site.   Today's date.

       < _____ > .
       Web site address (in angle brackets) .

Character Study

Directions: *Think about the character you have developed for your journal. List his or her role in society and name. Then, choose two different problems or situations he or she would encounter. Describe the problem and your character's response to the problem. Then, decide what this response tells you about your character. What character trait does it show?*

Name_____

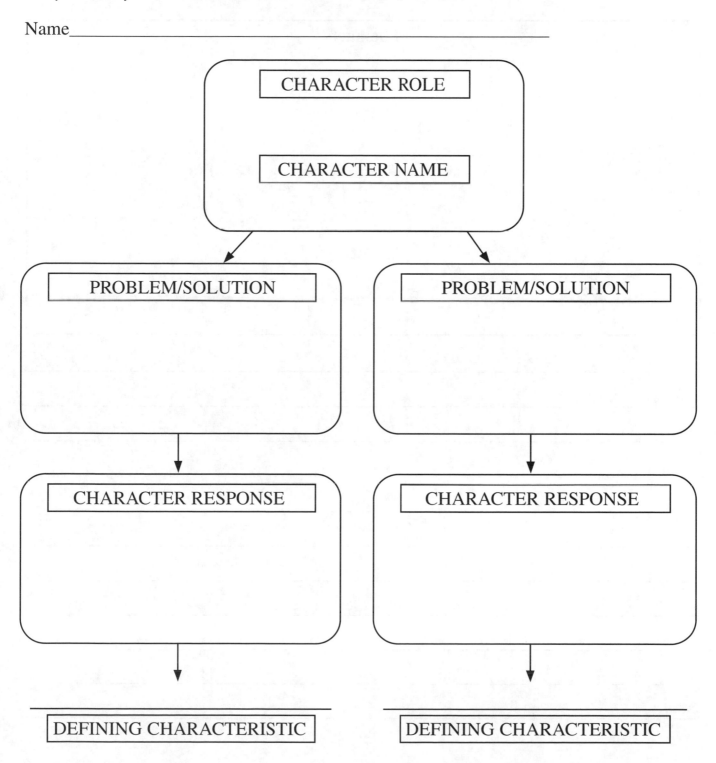

CHARACTER ROLE

CHARACTER NAME

PROBLEM/SOLUTION

PROBLEM/SOLUTION

CHARACTER RESPONSE

CHARACTER RESPONSE

DEFINING CHARACTERISTIC

DEFINING CHARACTERISTIC

Journal Planning Sheet

Name_____ Entry #_____

Directions: *Use this sheet to plan each of your journal entries: list the facts you will use in the box at the top and write a draft of your journal entry incorporating them below.*

The Facts

_____

_____

_____

_____

_____

_____

_____

_____

_____

_____

Storyboard

Name_____

Directions: *In each square represent the main scene you will be writing about and illustrating on that page of your journal.*

Journal Checklist

Name_____

Directions: *Please be sure that you include a check for each item. To assess the quality of the journal, also complete the Self Assessment Journal Rubric.*

RESEARCH

_____ Notecards: In your own words
                One fact on a card

_____ Fact Sheet

_____ Bibliography

WRITING

_____ Text Storyboard

_____ Draft Pages (a minimum of six)

_____ Completed Proof Book

_____ Author Blurb

ILLUSTRATION/DESIGN

_____ Art Storyboard

_____ Map

_____ Cover (Title, Author/Illustrator, and Illustration)

_____ Illustrations for each journal entry

_____ Title Page (includes Title, Author/Illustrator)

Self Assessment Journal Rubric

Directions: *As you reflect on your journal, please put a check in the appropriate column for each item.*

	PARTIALLY MEETS	MEETS	EXCEEDS
SOCIAL STUDIES			
I included the religion, government/history, achievements, and people of my culture in my journal entries			
LANGUAGE ARTS			
I planned and drafted my journal as evidenced by my completed checklist.			
I wrote, revised, and edited my journal.			
All of my journal entries are written in the voice of my chosen character.			
My journal entries reflect the information my classmates and I located during our research.			
My journal entries show strong voice.			
I wrote and recorded a carefully written, thoughtful reflection on my experiences to accompany my slide in the iMovie slideshow.			
TECHNOLOGY			
I located information about my culture from selected Web sites.			
I cited all picture and information sources on the bibliography page in my journal.			
I contributed (and read aloud) a page in my journal to the online iMovie slideshow.			
ART			
My final illustrations show craftsmanship/quality work, various uses of pencil and colored pencil, balanced compositions, variety in color value and line/texture.			
INFORMATION LITERACY			
I created a complete set of note cards with facts from at least four sources. Each note follows the two rules of note-taking.			
I used the information on my note cards to create an interesting journal based on TRUE information.			
I properly cited each source I used in creating my book.			

Unit 10
History Fair

Abigail Garthwait, Library Media Specialist

Dian Jordan, Fifth Grade Teacher

Asa Adams Elementary School

10 Goodridge Drive, Orono, Maine 04473

207-581-2487

<abigail@umit.maine.edu>

Grade Level: 5

Unit Overview: The History Fair kick-off takes place when the library media specialist presents an historical fiction booktalk in which students are introduced to a wide array of high-quality books with short and enticing teasers. As students devour their selections, they jot down questions or topics about which they want to know more regarding the historical time period. Students then analyze and categorize these notes into two or three complex "burning questions" which they exhaustively research before creating a project that conveys the essence of their results. A history fair, attended by classes of younger students during the school day and open to parents and community members in the evening, is the exciting culminating activity.

Time Frame: 8 weeks: Four 45-minute periods in the library media center with the teacher and LMS. Approximately 4 weeks of independent research assistance by SLMS. At least three writing periods per week for eight weeks and 12 activity blocks in the classroom, supervised by the teacher. Writing and activity blocks vary in length from 30 to 60 minutes. One evening history fair.

Content Area Standards: State of Maine Learning Results
<http://www.state.me.us/education/lres/lres.htm>

Social Studies: History, Middle Grades 5-8

Standard B Historical Knowledge, Concepts and Patterns
Students will develop historical knowledge of major events, people and enduring themes in the United States, in Maine and throughout world history.
B.1 Demonstrate an understanding of the causes and effects of major events in United States history and the connections to Maine history with an emphasis on events up to 1877, including but not limited to: Declaration of Independence; The Constitution; Westward Expansion; Industrialization; Civil War.

English Language Arts, Middle Grades 5-8

Standard A. Process of Reading
Students will use the skills and strategies of the reading process to comprehend, interpret, evaluate and appreciate what they have read.
A.1 Formulate questions to be answered while reading.
A.5 Understand stories and expository texts from the perspective of the social and cultural context in which they were created.
A.9 Explain orally and defend opinions formed while reading and viewing.

Standard F. Standard English Conventions.
Students will write and speak correctly, using conventions of standard written and spoken English.
F.1. Edit written work for standard English spelling and usage.
F.2 Demonstrate command of the conventions necessary to make an informal speech or presentation, effectively engaging peers and fielding responses.

The State of Maine Learning Results are reprinted here with permission from Susan Gendron, Commissioner of Education.

National Educational Technology Standards
<http://cnets.iste.org/students/s_stands.html>

Please refer to the Web site for text of the standards and indicators.

Standard 5. Technology Research Tools
First indicator

Information Power Information Literacy Standards and Indicators: 1.3, 1.5, 2.1, 2.4, 3.4, 9.1

Cooperative Teaching Plan:

Library Media Specialist Will:
- Present a booktalk on high-quality historical fiction of the United States.
- Develop an appropriate *PortaPortal* <http://www.portaportal.com/> or Web page of resources for historical research.
- With the teacher, approve student selection of an historical novel.
- Help students to revise burning questions of personal interest about the time period.
- Present resources and research strategies relevant to this assignment.
- Teach full group lessons on Internet searching and electronic periodical index use.
- Review strategies for utilization of resources.
- Verify students' ability to use efficient search strategies by assessing student progress as reflected on the History Fair Research Planner.
- Assist in the classroom during the student creation of visual projects.
- With teacher, prepare for, supervise, and participate in the history fair.

Teacher Will:

- Introduce project in the classroom, with goals and expectations.
- With library media specialist, approve student selection of an historical novel.
- Evaluate student "book report" which includes a summary and reflection, using the Book Report Rubric.
- Supervise student compilation of four or five burning questions of personal interest about the time period.
- Orchestrate student writing of a research report and creation of a visual project related to what they have learned.
- Assess student research report using the Research Paper Product Descriptor.
- With library media specialist prepare for and supervise the history fair.

Resources:

Print

An abundant supply of quality historical fiction and nonfiction history books, including:

Fiction authors such as Avi, the Collier brothers, Pam Conrad, Christopher Paul Curtis, Paula Fox, Kathryn Lasky, Lois Lowry, Scott O'Dell, Ann Rinaldi, Elizabeth George Speare, Rosemary Sutcliff, Mildred Taylor, Theodore Taylor, Anne Turner, Yoshiko Uchida, Yoko Watkins, and Jane Yolen,
Nonfiction authors such as Rhoda Blumberg, Leonard Everett Fisher, Russell Freedman, Jean Fritz, Milton Meltzer, Jim Murphy, Diane Stanley, and Jerry Stanley.

Adamson, Lynda G. *American Historical Fiction: An Annotated Guide to Novels for Adults and Young Adults*. Phoenix: Oryx Press, 1999.

Adamson, Lynda G. *Recreating the Past: A Guide to American and World Historical Fiction for Children and Young Adults*. Westport, Connecticut: Greenwood Press, 1994.

Book Report. Libraries Unlimited.

McCutcheon, Marc. *Everyday Life in the 1800's*. Cincinnati: Writers Digest Books, 2001.

Moulton, Candy Vyvey. *The Writer's Guide to Everyday Life in the Wild West*. Cincinnati: Writers Digest Books, 1999. OP

Taylor, Dale. *Writer's Guide to Everyday Life in Colonial America*. Cincinnati: Writers Digest Books, 1999. OP

Varhola, Michael J. *The Writer's Guide to Everyday Life during the Civil War*. Cincinnati: Writer's Digest Books, 1999. OP

World Book Encyclopedia. Chicago: World Book, Inc., 2006.

Electronic

American Memory. Library of Congress. 10 September 2006 <http://memory.loc.gov/>.

Ben's Guide to the United States Government. 8 March 2004. 10 September 2006 <http://bensguide.gpo.gov/>

EyeWitness to History: History Through the Eyes of Those Who Lived It. 10 September 2006. <http://www.eyewitnesstohistory.com/>.

The National Archives: Educators and Students. 10 September 2006. <http://www.archives.gov/education/>.

PortaPortal. 10 September 2006. <http://www.portaportal.com/>.

Equipment
Student use computers

Culminating Learning Product: A history fair is the culminating activity. Students dress in period costumes and display their projects on tables arranged in chronological order around the gym. Cardboard backdrops contain artwork, creative writing and other artifacts. The excitement is palpable as students scurry hither and yon putting the last minute touches on their costumes or projects. Their excited voices carry across the gym as they quiz each other about their time period – no one wants to be asked questions they can't answer! During the day, classes of younger students tour the fair. This provides an opportunity for fifth graders to hone their skills at answering questions about their time period. They hone their ability to articulate concise answers to broad questioning. An evening open house allows students to share their new understandings with both parents and community members. At the end of a long day, students say they are very tired, but the glow in their cheeks and the sparkle in their eyes indicate what a thrilling event it has been.

Assessment Overview: The classroom teacher assesses student products using the Book Report Rubric and the Research Paper Product Descriptor. No summative information literacy assessment is given other than what is implicitly embedded in their research. However, the primary focus of the library media specialist is on formative assessment as it is essential that each student learn how to organize his or her searches independently. The History Fair Research Planner provides students with a "framework" for the research process and allows the LMS and teacher to see at a glance what problems might arise.

Adaptations and Extensions:

- For students who do not have sufficient historical background before beginning to read their fiction books, supply students with a nonfiction book to read first.

- Assist challenged readers and ELL students to find historical fiction at the appropriate independent reading level. [Note: Interlibrary loan is recommended if the library collection lacks depth.]

- Computer printouts of students' writing make the final product look professional especially when a student's handwriting is difficult to read.

Research Planner

Name_____

Historical Fiction Title_____

Time Period_____

Major Events:

Your Questions:

Initial Keywords:	New Keywords

Places that you have checked (Use keywords above; add new ones as you discover them):

_____ Card catalog/online library catalog.

_____ Noted OTHER keywords from the subject headings on the entry.

_____ Located books found with catalog search

    _____ used book index   _____ used book's table of contents

_____ World Book Encyclopedia   _____ Print or _____ Electronic

_____ Historical encyclopedia(s)   OR   _____ Chronology books

_____ Magazine Index(es) (which ones?) _____ _____

    _____ Located articles found with index search

_____ Vertical File (what headings did you check?) _____

_____ Internet research

    _____ Used LMC 's PortaPortal (Web-based bookmarks/favorites)

    _____ Began search with Google

        _____ Too many "hits?' Try narrowing your search terms

        _____ Too few "hits?" Try making your search term broader

        _____ Developed and implemented plan to improve search

_____ Local historical society

_____ Individual who lived during this time period or who is an expert on the time period

Book Report Rubric

	Poor	Fair	Good	Excellent
Paragraph ■ main idea ■ characters ■ time period ■ location ■ story evaluation				
Four things learned about time period / details				
Grammar ■ good sentences ■ paragraphs ■ punctuation ■ spelling ■ time period				
Appearance ■ neatly done ■ easy for others to read				

Research Paper Product Descriptor

Parts	Points		Attributes
	Self Assessment	Teacher Assessment	
Title Page	_____	_____	**Elements** ■ Illustration depicting topic ■ Title of paper in bold ■ Name / Date ■ Teacher's name
Note Cards	_____	_____	**Complete** ■ Organized and labeled
Body of Paper	_____	_____	**Explains information in own words** ■ Accurate ■ Factual ■ Describes important areas ■ Organized into paragraphs ■ Complete ■ Includes a CONCLUSION explaining what you learned from this assignment
Mechanics	_____	_____	**Organized paragraphs** ■ Correct grammar, spelling capitals, & punctuation ■ Complete and interesting sentences ■ Margins ■ Indented
Bibliography	_____	_____	**Followed guidelines** ■ Sources in ABC order
Other	_____	_____	
		_____	**Your Average Score**

Student Comments	Teacher Comments

Unit 11
Canyons by Gary Paulsen:
An Archaeological Study

Bernie Tomasso, Library Media Specialist

Cathy Wood, Grade 6 Teacher

Leslie B. Lehn Middle School

30 Maple Avenue, Port Byron, New York 13140-9647

315-776-8939

<btomasso@twcny.rr.com>

Grade Level: 6

Unit Overview: *Canyons* by Gary Paulsen: An Archaeological Study introduces archaeology to sixth graders who spend a year studying various world cultures, with an emphasis on ancient and medieval civilizations. Students read the novel and complete activities related to archaeological themes and Southwest United States. In addition, students explore what constitutes a civilization and what leads to its downfall. This first research project sets the stage for five research projects completed in the sixth grade and for the research process used in subsequent years.

Time Frame: Fourteen 42-minute class periods with the teacher in the classroom and six 42-minute periods in the library media center with library media specialist and teacher.

Content Area Standards: New York State Learning Standards
<http://www.emsc.nysed.gov/top/learning.html>

Social Studies, Intermediate

Standard 1: History of the United States and New York. Students will use a variety of intellectual skills to demonstrate their understanding of major ideas, eras, themes, developments, and turning points in the history of the United States and New York.

Key Idea 2: Important ideas, social and cultural values, beliefs, and traditions from New York State and United States history illustrate the connections and interactions of people and events across time and from a variety of perspectives.

Students will:

■ Understand the relationship between the relative importance of United States domestic and foreign policies over time.

Key Idea 3: Study about the major social, political, economic, cultural, and religious developments in New York State and United States history involves learning about the important roles and contributions of individuals and groups.

Students will:

- Complete well-documented and historically accurate case studies about individuals and groups who represent different ethnic, national, and religious, groups, including Native American Indians, in New York State and the United States at different times and in different locations.

- Gather and organize information about the important achievements and contributions of individuals and groups living in New York State and the United States.

- Classify major developments into categories such as social, political, economic, geographic, technological, scientific, cultural, or religious.

Standard 3: Geography. Students will use a variety of intellectual skills to demonstrate their understanding of the geography of the interdependent world in which we live—local, national, and global—including the distribution of people, places, and environments over the Earth's surface.

Key Idea 1: Geography can be divided into six essential elements which can be used to analyze important historic, geographic, economic, and environmental questions and issues. These six elements include: the world in spatial terms, places and regions, physical settings (including natural resources), human systems, environment and society, and the use of geography. (Adapted from *The National Geography Standards*, 1994: Geography for Life)

Students will:

- Map information about people, places, and environments.

- Describe the relationships between people and environments and the connections between people and places.

Math, Science, and Technology, Intermediate

Standard 2: Information Systems Students will access, generate, process, and transfer information using appropriate technologies.

Key Idea 1. Information technology is used to retrieve, process, and communicate information and as a tool to enhance learning.

Students:

- use a range of equipment and software to integrate several forms of information in order to create good quality audio, video, graphic, and text-based presentations.

- systematically obtain accurate and relevant information pertaining to a particular topic from a range of sources, including local and national media, libraries, museums, governmental agencies, industries, and individuals.

Key Idea 2. Knowledge of the impacts and limitations of information systems is essential to its effective and ethical use.

Students:

- understand the need to question the accuracy of information displayed on a computer because the results produced by a computer may be affected by incorrect data entry.

English Language Arts, Intermediate

Standard 1: Students will read, write, listen, and speak for information and understanding.
1. Listening and reading to acquire information and understanding involves collecting data, facts, and ideas; discovering relationships, concepts, and generalizations; and using knowledge from oral, written, and electronic sources.

Students:

- Interpret and analyze information from textbooks and nonfiction books for young adults, as well as reference materials, audio and media presentations, oral interviews, graphs, charts, diagrams, and electronic databases intended for a general audience.

- Compare and synthesize information from different sources.

- Use a wide variety of strategies for selecting, organizing, and categorizing information.

- Relate new information to prior knowledge and experience.

2. Speaking and writing to acquire and transmit information requires asking probing and clarifying questions, interpreting information in one's own words, applying information from one context to another, and presenting the information and interpretation clearly, concisely, and comprehensibly.

Students:

- Produce oral and written reports on topics related to all school subjects.

- Establish an authoritative stance on the subject and provide references to establish the validity and verifiability of the information presented.

- Use the process of pre-writing, drafting, revising, and proofreading ("the writing process") to produce well-constructed informational texts.

- Use standard English for formal presentation of information and vocabulary, selecting appropriate grammatical constructions and vocabulary, using a variety of sentence structures, and observing the rules of punctuation, capitalization, and spelling.

Standard 2: Students will read, write, listen, and speak for literary response and expression.
1. Listening and reading for literary response involves comprehending, interpreting, and critiquing imaginative texts in every medium, drawing on personal experiences and knowledge to understand the text, and recognizing the social, historical and cultural features of the text.

Students:

- Recognize different levels of meaning.

2. Speaking and writing for literary response involves presenting interpretations, analyses, and reactions to the content and language of a text. Speaking and writing for literary expression involves producing imaginative texts that use language and text structures that are inventive and often multilayered.

Students:

- Present responses to and interpretations of literature, making references to the literary elements found in the text and connections with their personal knowledge and experience.

- Use standard English effectively.

Standard 3: Students will read, write, listen, and speak for critical analysis and evaluation.
1. Listening and reading to analyze and evaluate experiences, ideas, information, and issues requires using evaluative criteria from a variety of perspectives and recognizing the difference in evaluations based on different sets of criteria.

Students:

- Evaluate their own and others' work based on a variety of criteria (e.g., logic, clarity, comprehensiveness, conciseness, originality, conventionality) and recognize the varying effectiveness of different approaches.

Information Power Information Literacy Standards and Indicators: 1.4, 1.5, 2.1, 2.3, 2.4, 3.1, 3.3, 3.4, 5.3

Cooperative Teaching Plan:

Library Media Specialist Will:

- Provide background materials on archaeology and Texas for the classroom.
- Cooperatively develop culminating activities.
- Discuss dynamics of group work using the Finding Good Teammates handout.
- Discuss choosing a topic that interests the student and also is at an appropriate level of difficulty using the Preparing an Exhibition handout.
- Provide overview of topics and timeline for completion of project using the *Canyon* Projects Overview handout.
- Provide bibliographic instruction.
- Provide feedback on project according to previous discussion on what constitutes an exemplary project, referring to Preparing an Exhibition handout as a guideline.
- Assess research process using the Library Media Center Assessment Rubric.

Teacher Will:

- Cooperatively develop culminating activities.
- Introduce unit and Social Studies vocabulary on archaeology.
- Conduct Archaeological Dig activity.
- Read *Canyons* with students.
- Discuss novel and assign journal activities.
  Journal Activity: Each time that we read *Canyons*, you are to record your thoughts and feelings about what you've just read. They do not have to be in complete sentences—words or phrases are fine—but they must show that you are becoming involved in the story.
- Provide examples of projects while reading the novel so students have an awareness of culminating activities.
- Grade projects using the Teacher Scoring Guide and oral presentations using the Oral Presentation Rubric.

Resources:

Print

Eastman, Charles A. *Indian Boyhood*. Scituate, Massachusetts: Digital Scanning, Inc., 2001. (Available at http://www.ebooks.com)

Heinrich, Ann. *America the Beautiful. Texas*. Chicago: Childrens Press, 1999.

Jackson, Helen Hunt. *A Century of Dishonor: A Sketch of the United States Government's Dealings with Some of the Indian Tribes*. Scituate, Massachusetts: Digital Scanning, Inc., 2001. (Available at http://www.ebooks.com)

Paulsen, Gary. *Canyons*. New York: Laurel Leaf, 1991.

Travel Brochures and Maps available from Texas Department of Transportation 1-800-452-9292
and El Paso Convention & Visitors Bureau 1-800-351-6024.
World Book Encyclopedia. Chicago: World Book, Inc., 2006.

Electronic

"Battle With The Apache, 1872." *Eye Witness to History.* 1999. 17 November 2006
<http://www.eyewitnesstohistory.com/pfapache.htm>.

Carlisle, Jeffrey D. "Apache Indians." *The Handbook of Texas Online.* 6 June 2001. 17 November
2006 <http://www.tsha.utexas.edu/handbook/online/articles/view/AA/bma33.html>.

City of El Paso, Texas. 2006. 17 November 2006 <http://www.ci.el-paso.tx.us/>.

Curtis, E.S. *Notes from "The North American Indian": Volume 1-The Apache.* 17 November
2006 <http://www.curtis-collection.com/tribe%20data/apache.html>.

Dog Canyon Hiking, Sacramento Mountains, Alamogordo NM. 17 November 2006
<http://www.rozylowicz.com/retirement/dogcanyon/dogcanyon.html#history>.

"Gary Paulsen." *Random House, Inc.* 2003. 14 November 2006
<http://www.randomhouse.com/features/garypaulsen/>.

"Guadalupe Mountains." *National Park Service.* 19 November 2006. 25 November 2006
<http://www.nps.gov/gumo/>.

"The Plains Indians of Texas." *El Centro College History Department.* 14 November 2006
<http://www.angelfire.com/tx2/ecc/plains.html>.

"Ribbons of Time." *Douglas Preston and Lincoln Child.* 17 November 2006
<http://www.prestonchild.com/solonovels/preston/ribbons/index.html>.

TexasOnline. 1999-2006. 14 November 2006 <http://www.state.tx.us/>.

TravelTex. 2006. 17 November 2006. <http://www.traveltex.com/travelguide/Order.aspx>.

Audiovisual

The Apache. VHS. Schlessinger Media, 1993.
The West. DVD. Turner Home Entertainment and PBS, 1996.

Equipment

Television
DVD/VHS player

Culminating Learning Product: Oral presentations and a selected product.

Assessment Overview: Teacher and peer assessment of products using teacher-developed rubric. Self-assessment and teacher assessment of oral presentations using Oral Presentation Rubric. Library media specialist critique of oral presentation graphic based on previous discussion of traits of an exemplary project and the Preparing an Exhibition handout. Library media specialist assessment of the research process using the Library Media Center Assessment Rubric.

Adaptations and Extensions:
To meet the needs of gifted/exceptional learners, students may:

■ Design their own project (much as an Eagle Scout might) with librarian or technology teacher.

■ Search for poetry that correlates with *Canyons* topics or write their own poetry.

■ Write and illustrate a children's book about a related topic.

■ Read an additional book after *Canyons* to use as a comparison/contrast.

- Participate in a debate on a related topic such as forced relocation or lack of respect for Native culture.

To meet the needs of challenged learners, teachers may:

- Provide books on tape or e-books.
- Collaborate with the special education teacher to identify areas of strength and design a suitable project.
- Include specific goals from each student's IEP.

To extend the unit, these expansions may be pursued:

- Assist students in developing a connection with a local sixth grade class which has a large Native population. Students read *Canyons* and meet for a discussion of related topics. Questions are prepared ahead of time and approved by the teacher.
- Visit a cultural fair.
- Invite a Native American speaker.
- Study and prepare Native foods.

Canyons **Project Overview**

Students may work with a partner with teacher permission. Please be aware that you will share the same grade. Both partners must demonstrate their participation in the project.

Topics may be chosen from the following list:

1. Create a newspaper using historical events referred to in the novel *Canyons* by Gary Paulsen. This will require research about the time period between 1860 and 1890.

2 Research and develop a timeline that shows changes between the 1800's and the present. Research changes in technology, military weapons, life styles of Apache Indians, etc.

3. Research and develop a timeline of other events that occurred between 1860 and 1890. You may choose United States or world events or a special topic such as sports or technology.

4. Build a learning center about the book *Canyons*. Your center will look like a science fair display board with information about the author, characters, setting, plot, etc.

5. Conduct a research project about the Apache Indians. This will include information about their culture, history, beliefs, traditions, government, folk tales, and present day life.

6. Research American soldiers in the 1800's. This will include finding information about their duties, uniforms, weapons, training, life in a fort, etc.

7. Write two one page letters to the editor. First, express your support of the military action at Dog Canyon. Then, oppose the military action at Dog Canyon. Include facts from the book.

8. Prepare a storyboard. Include characters, setting, plot, author, and themes.

9. Develop and perform a skit showing one or more important scenes approved by the teacher.

10. Conduct an author study including information about Paulsen and other works he has written.

11. Report on desert life. Include desert plants as well as animals that live in the desert.

12. Prepare a music report. Research what a symphony or other piece of classical music includes. Locate a recording of *Mahler's Resurrection Symphony* or an example of similar classical music from the same period. Write a report about the composer. Include details about the piece and why the composer chose to name it as he or she did.

13. Undertake a geography project. Draw and provide a legend for a map, which includes the El Paso, Texas area, the natural resources that are found there, as well as manufactured products. Describe the climate of the area also.

Finding Good Teammates

You can save yourself much trouble in a team project by being careful when forming teams. Please find teammates who are compatible with you in the following areas:

■ **Schedule:** If you can't find time when the whole team can meet, you will be miserable.

■ **Interests:** If you can't get all teammates interested in the same topics, you won't build a quality piece.

■ **Attitudes:** If all of you want to be the boss, you'll eat each other alive.

■ **Work Habits:** If highly organized people try to work with "whenever" people, everyone goes nuts.

■ **Goals for This Course:** If you want to take a C and run, don't team up with perfectionists.

■ **Final Note:** It is better to have a mix of talents on your team than for all teammates to have similar strengths and weaknesses.

Guidelines for Preparing an Exhibition

1. In an exhibition, you are asked to demonstrate:

    KNOWLEDGE
    ■ What you know and what you've learned.

    SKILLS
    ■ How you communicate your knowledge to others.
    ■ How you work with others.

2. In an exhibition, you must make sure:

    ■ To clearly state your major ideas. Say simply and directly what a person should learn from your exhibit.

    ■ To use examples to fully develop your ideas. Once you've decided what you're saying, then give examples to prove it.

    ■ To check your exhibit for grammar, spelling, and neatness. **TAKE PRIDE IN YOUR WORK; IT SAYS WHO YOU ARE.**

    ■ To include graphic illustrations that provide information about your exhibit. Create visuals that help people understand your major ideas.

    ■ To check your exhibit for accuracy of information. (Make sure you have the facts to support your ideas.)

3. In a cooperative exhibition, make sure that everyone knows what is expected of him or her, that the work is evenly divided, and that a schedule is developed to complete the task.

Oral Presentation Rubric

EXEMPLARY	SATISFACTORY	NOT YET
The talk reflects a thorough understanding of the project and relates it to *Canyons*.	The talk reflects a good understanding of the project and relates it to *Canyons*.	The talk reflects little understanding of the project and does not relate to *Canyons*.
Audience questions are answered thoroughly and accurately.	Audience questions are answered, but leave some ambiguity or need for clarification.	Audience questions are not all addressed or are confusing. Leaves audience with too many questions.
The talk is well prepared as evidenced through a smooth performance.	The talk is prepared but not completely smooth. Speaker depends too much on notes or notes are unorganized.	The talk is not well prepared or smooth. Speaker is obviously lacking notes and/or information.
Voice level and eye contact are appropriate.	Voice level is low and/or little eye contact with audience. Talks too slowly or quickly.	Voice level is too low. No eye contact with audience

Archaeological Dig Notes

Leader_____

Scribe_____

Artist _____

Presenter _____

What type of society lived at your site:	**List evidence of economic activity.**
Hunters and Gatherers?	
Fishermen?	
Farmers and Herders?	
Traders?	**List evidence of culture or social structure.**

Scribe: Describe artifacts here	**Artist: Describe artifacts here.**
1.	1.
2.	2.
3.	3.
4.	4.

Presenter Notes:

Self Assessment Criteria

COMPLETENESS

- Have you completed all task requirements?

CLARITY

- Does your exhibition demonstrate a logical and understandable plan of organization?
- Are your major ideas clearly stated?
- Are your major ideas fully developed through the use of appropriate examples?
- Has attention been given to grammar, spelling and neatness?

RESEARCH AND INFORMATION

- Is your information accurate and relevant?
- Does it cover the basic facts and important concepts?
- Have you included appropriate documentation?
- Have you used reliable and varied sources?

GRAPHIC REPRESENTATION

- Are your graphic illustrations useful rather than merely decorative?
- Do your graphics provide information about your exhibition?
- Do your graphics help people understand your major ideas?

STUDENT REFLECTION

- What did you personally learn?
- What did your class learn?
- What skills did you learn or improve upon?
- What did you do well?
- What would you have done differently?

TEACHER SCORING GUIDE

Quality	Possible Points	Score
a. Project is done on time	20 pts.	_____
b. Project is neat and in an acceptable form	20 pts.	_____
c. Project shows an understanding of the book	20 pts.	_____
d. Project shows understanding of the assignment	20 pts.	_____
e. Project shows effort	20 pts.	_____
	Total	_____

Library Media Center Assessment Rubric

Requirements	Insufficient	Basic	Proficient	Advanced
The student: ■ *Clearly states the focused topic.* **(6 Points Possible)**	Topic has an imprecise or unclear focus. The focus needs to be narrowed or clarified. **(Points 2.5)**	Topic has a discernable focus but lacks preciseness. **(Points 4.0)**	Topic has a clear focus and is adequately precise. **(Points 5.0)**	Topic has a very clear focus that is precise, appropriately narrow, and well articulated. **(Points 6.0)**
The student: ■ *Clearly articulates the process used to identify and locate resources.* ■ *Uses search techniques appropriate for the topic.* ■ *Uses specific and effective search techniques.* **(6 Points Possible)**	Research process does not adequately take account of the topic focus and is much too broad in application. Consistent mistakes are made in applying basic search techniques. Student demonstrates confusion related to application of search terms and search techniques. **(Points 2.5)**	Research process is articulated but needs more focus and clarity. Basic search techniques are adequately applied but student demonstrates few or no advanced search strategies. Errors are made in the application of search techniques. **(Points 4.0)**	Research process adequately takes account of the issues related to the topic. Clear use of basic and advanced search techniques. **(Points 5.0)**	Research process is clear, concise, and well focused. Uses basic and advanced search techniques very well and applies search techniques consistently well across all library resources. **(Points 6.0)**
The student: ■ *Selected resources that were appropriate for the topic.* ■ *Demonstrated how each resource supported the thesis statement and research topic.* **(6 Points Possible)**	Most resources selected are not appropriate for supporting the topic focus. Little or no demonstration of the appropriateness of resources for topic relevance, or confusion related to resource relevance. **(Points 2.5)**	Most of the resources selected are appropriate for the topic. Demonstration of the appropriateness of resources for topic relevance is adequate for most resources. **(Points 4.0)**	All of the resources selected are appropriate for the topic. Demonstration of the appropriateness of resources is well documented and clearly stated. **(Points 5.0)**	All of the resources selected are very well focused on the topic or specific sub-aspects. Demonstration of the appropriateness of resources is very well documented with in-depth analysis of each resource. **(Points 6.0)**

Unit 12
Food for the Community and You

Faith A. Delaney, Library Media Specialist

Lauren Buchmann, Sixth Grade Teacher

Mary Shawkey, Family & Consumer Science Teacher;

Tom Bechtel, Tech Ed Teacher

Wheatland Middle School

919 Hamilton Park Drive, Lancaster, Pennsylvania 17603

717- 291-6125

<Fdelaney@comcast.net>

Grade Level: 6

Unit Overview: Food for the Community and You addresses two issues of current concern: world hunger and obesity. It offers students a chance to understand and alleviate hunger in their own community and to learn about healthy food choices for themselves as they organize and implement a food drive to benefit an area of their community. Beginning in the library media center, students research hunger in the world and in their community, then study food groups and healthy diets with the family and consumer science teacher. Next, students advertise their food drive and collect donations. The collection site includes a physical model of the new food guide pyramid designed and built by the students in their tech ed class. Finally, food is collected and displayed in the new food guide pyramid prior to distribution.

Time Frame: Five weeks: Six 90-minute periods in the family and consumer science (FCS) room with the FCS teacher, six 90-minute periods in the tech ed room with the tech ed teacher, three 45-minute periods in the library media center with the LMS and the classroom teacher, periodic classroom visits by the LMS to the classroom to check progress, and work in the classroom as needed with the classroom teacher.

Content Area Standards:
Pennsylvania Department of Education Academic Standards
<http://www.pde.state.pa.us/stateboard_ed/cwp/view.asp?a=3&Q=76716>

Civics and Government
5.2.6 Rights and Responsibilities of Citizenship, Grade 6
A. Compare rights and responsibilities of citizenship
- Personal responsibility of the individual to society.

D. Describe the importance of political leadership and public service.

Health, Safety and Physical Education
10.1.6 Concepts of Health Grade 6
C. Analyze nutritional concepts that impact health.
- caloric content of foods
- relationship of food intake and physical activity (energy output)
- nutrient requirements
- label reading
- healthful food selection

Science and Technology
3.7.4 Technological Devices, Grade 4
A. Explore the use of basic tools, simple materials and techniques to safely solve problems.

B. Select appropriate instruments to study materials.

Family and Consumer Sciences
Food Science and Nutrition, Grade 6
C. Analyze factors that effect food choices.

D. Describe a well-balanced daily menu using the dietary guidelines and the food guide pyramid.

The Pennsylvania State Academic Standards are quoted with permission of the Pennsylvania State Board of Education.

Information Power Information Literacy Standards and Indicators: 4.1, 4.2, 9.1, 9.2, 9.3, 9.4

Cooperative Teaching Plan:

Library Media Specialist Will:
- With the classroom, FCS, and tech ed teachers, draw up a time frame for the unit.
- Collect print and non-print resources to implement the unit.
- With the classroom, FCS, and tech ed teachers, introduce the food bank project.
- Schedule classes in the media center.
- Assist students in developing appropriate search strategies.
- Assist students in searching for information in print and electronic sources.
- With classroom and FCS teacher, guide students and conference with them individually during the research process.
- Contact a local speaker to address classes.
- Contact local food bank selected for donations and arrange for pickup or delivery.
- Contact local newspaper or television station to publicize the students' achievement.
- With the classroom teacher, collaboratively assess the research portion of the unit formatively using the Instructional Rubric: Research and Food Drive.
- Assess the research portion of the unit summatively using the Performance Activity Assessment Rubric: Research.

Classroom Teacher Will:

■ With the LMS and FCS and tech ed teachers, draw up a time frame for the unit.

■ With the LMS and the FCS and tech ed teachers, introduce the food bank project.

■ Discuss what students know and would like to know about hunger in the community.

■ Discuss the problem of hunger both nationally and locally.

■ Assist students in locating several food donation sites in the community.

■ Schedule a speaker for a class period.

■ Encourage students to choose/vote on the site they will use for their food donations.

■ Assist students in planning and implementing an advertising campaign for the food drive (Note: consider working with the art teacher on the advertising campaign).

■ With the LMS, collaboratively assess the research portion of the unit formatively using the Instructional Rubric: Research and Food Drive and summatively assign a report card grade.

Family & Consumer Science Teacher Will:

■ With the LMS and the classroom and tech ed teachers, draw up a time frame for the unit.

■ With the LMS and the classroom and tech ed teachers, introduce the food bank project.

■ With the classroom teacher, schedule classes for students to learn about food and nutrition.

■ Instruct students about the *New Food Guide Pyramid* and dietary guidelines for good health.

■ With the classroom teacher, discuss each day's food collection and help students choose where to place the items on the physical model of the pyramid.

■ Display each day's donated food in appropriate spaces on the model of the food pyramid.

■ Remove foods on the model and box for pickup at the end of the day.

■ Assess student knowledge of nutrition formatively using the Instructional Rubric: Personal Nutrition and summatively using the Performance Activity Assessment Rubric: Personal Nutrition.

Tech Ed Teacher Will:

■ With the LMS and the classroom and FCS teachers, draw up a time frame for the unit.

■ With the LMS and the classroom and FCS teachers, introduce the food bank project.

■ With the classroom teacher, schedule classes for students to plan and build the New Food Pyramid Model.

■ Assist students in planning and designing a transportable physical model of the food pyramid that includes shelves for each food group.

■ Help students generate a list of materials needed to build the model.

■ Purchase materials needed.

■ Instruct students in safety and use of tools.

■ Oversee the building of the model by students.

■ Assess student learning formatively using the Instructional Rubric: Visual Representation of the Food Guide Pyramid and summatively using the Performance Activity Assessment Rubric: Safety Procedures and the Performance Activity Assessment Rubric: Visual Representation of the Food Guide Pyramid.

Resources:

Print

d'Elgin, Tershia. *What Should I Eat? A Complete Guide to the New Food Pyramid.* New York: Ballantine Books, 2005.

Evers, Connie. *How to Teach Nutrition to Kids.* Portland, Oregon: 24 Carrot Press, 2003.

Faiella, Graham. *Food Pyramid and Basic Nutrition: Assembling the Building Blocks of a Healthy Diet.* New York: Rosen, 2005.

Miller, Edward. *The Monster Health Book.* New York: Holiday House, 2006.

Local telephone book (look under Human Service Agencies/Food Resources to find a guest speaker and to select the site the students want to receive donations.)

Electronic

Levine, Larry and Jane Finn Levine. "Program Description." *Kids Can Make a Difference.* 27 September 2006 <http://www.kidscanmakeadifference.org/prog.htm>.
Summary: an educational program focusing on the root causes of hunger and poverty. Major goal is to stimulate students to take follow-up actions to make a difference.

USDA. *Steps to a Healthier You.* 27 September 2006. <http://www.mypyramid.gov>
Summary: Excellent Web site full of resources and information for use in developing education materials to assist in understanding Federal food guidance. Includes video game, animations, tips on personal diet.

Audiovisuals

Fantastic Food Pyramid. DVD. Teacher's Video Company, 2003.
New Food Guide Pyramid. DVD. Educational Video Network, 2004.
Film footage on community needs reported by local TV station(s).

Guest Speaker

Representative from local food bank or similar community organization visits school to talk about hunger in the community.

Poster

Anatomy of My Pyramid. Agriculture Dept., Center for Nutrition Policy and Promotion. Washington, D.C., 2005. Summary: 9x11". Sold in pkg. of 50 for $24.00.

Equipment

Television and DVD player
Student use computers

Culminating Learning Product: Students make a visual representation of the Food Guide Pyramid and advertise and collect food for a food drive. Students donate the food to their chosen group.

Assessment Overview: Assessments for this unit are shared by all teachers involved.

The library media specialist and the sixth grade teacher collaboratively assess the research portion of the unit formatively using the Instructional Rubric: Research and Food Drive, the teacher focusing on the content and the library media specialist focusing on the quality and quantity of the sources located.

The library media specialist assesses the research portion of the unit summatively using the Performance Activity Assessment Rubric: Research.

The family and consumer science teacher assesses the student's knowledge of nutrition formatively using the Instructional Rubric: Personal Nutrition and summatively using the Performance Activity Assessment Rubric: Personal Nutrition.

The tech ed teacher formatively assesses the physical model of the food pyramid using the Instructional Rubric: Visual Representation of the Food Guide Pyramid and summatively using the Performance Activity Assessment Rubric: Safety Procedures and the Performance Activity Assessment Rubric: Visual Representation of the Food Guide Pyramid.

Adaptations and Extensions: Working in cooperative groups, students find needed adaptations for varying ability levels.

In tech ed, differentiated instruction allows some students to plan the model of the food pyramid while others build and paint the model from the plans.

In FCS, differentiated instruction includes written reports for on-grade level learners and drawn and cut pictures of food groups and diets for challenged learners and ELL students.

To extend the unit, students design posters to advertise the food drive using non-English languages spoken in the community.

To extend the unit, students work for a day at a local food bank packaging a nutritionally balanced box of food for distribution.

Instructional Rubric: Research and Food Drive

	SELF		PEER		TEACHER	
	Met	Not Yet	Met	Not Yet	Met	Not Yet
I have located and read information from three sources on hunger in our community.						
I have written an action plan that could impact on the issue.						
I have completed a cause-and-effect chart for each action plan.						
I have listed local organizations that provide for people in need in our community.						
I have listed organizations and groups that need food in ourcommunity.						
I have helped to select a group to receive food.						
I have helped to choose the date(s) for the food drive.						
We have determined the extent of our food drive campaign.						
We have developed appropriate publicity for our target audience.						
We have advertised to our target group.						
We have collected and displayed the food in our pyramid model.						
We have donated the food to our chosen group.						

STUDENT: _____   PEER: _____

COMMENTS:

Instructional Rubric: Personal Nutrition

	SELF		PEER		TEACHER	
	Met	Not Yet	Met	Not Yet	Met	Not Yet
I have found 2 food labels illustrating the New Food Guide Pyramid.						
I have read an article discussing the New Food Guide Pyramid.						
I have made a visual representation of the New Food Guide Pyramid.						
We have chosen one of the Dietary Guidelines for Good Health and presented this guideline to the class.						
I have defined the six food guidelines.						
I have planned a one day personal diet that reflects my understanding of the New Food Guide Pyramid and the Dietary Guidelines for Good Health.						

STUDENT: _____   PEER: _____

COMMENTS:

Instructional Rubric: Visual Representation of the Food Guide Pyramid

	SELF		PEER		TEACHER	
	Met	Not Yet	Met	Not Yet	Met	Not Yet
We have selected a design of a scaled model of the New Food Guide Pyramid.						
We have selected the appropriate materials with which to build the model.						
I have been observed following safety rules at my station.						
I have been observed exhibiting on-task behavior at my station.						
I have participated in the building of the model. We have completed and submitted our model for approval.						

STUDENT: _____   PEER: _____

COMMENTS:

Performance Activity Assessment Rubric: Research

Performance Activity: You will research information on hunger in your community, organize and implement a food drive, and choose a group to receive the food donation.

Exceptional	Identifies community problems and locates and reads information from more than three sources including a variety of media	Describes two or more courses of action that impact on a community issue using examples	Identifies more than one positive effect and more than one negative effect of a course of action with supporting rationale
Commendable	Identifies community problems and locates and reads information from three sources independently	Describes two or more courses of action that impact on a community issue	Identifies more than one positive effect and more than one negative effect of a course of action
Satisfactory	Identifies community problems and locates and reads information from three sources with guidance	Describes one course of action that impacts on a community issue	Identifies one positive and one negative effect of a course of action
Unsatisfactory	Does not identify community problems or locate and read information from three sources	Does not describe a course of action that impacts on a community issue	Does not identify a positive or negative effect of a course of action

Performance Activity Assessment Rubric: Personal Nutrition

Performance Activity: Study food groups and healthy diets. Demonstrate an understanding of the New Food Guide Pyramid and Dietary Guidelines for good health and plan a healthy personal diet.

Exceptional	Names the six food groups, explains the concept of a the food pyramid and compares it to one other food guide	Identifies the Dietary Guidelines for Good Health, explains their relationship to good health, and elaborates on the consequences of ignoring them	Plans a personal diet for one day which reflects the pyramid and guidelines and describes the impact following that diet would have on their health
Commendable	Names the six food groups and explains the concept of the food pyramid	Identifies the Dietary Guidelines for Good Health and explains their relationship to good health	Plans a personal diet for one day which reflects the pyramid and guidelines and names the lifestyles changes needed
Satisfactory	Names the six food groups and categorizes food into each group	Identifies the Dietary Guidelines for Good Health	Plans a personal diet for one day which reflects the pyramid and guidelines
Unsatisfactory	Does not name the six food groups or categorize food into each group	Does not identify the Dietary Guidelines for Good Health	Does not plan a personal diet for one day which reflects the pyramid and guidelines

Performance Activity Assessment Rubric: Visual Representation of the New Food Guide Pyramid

Performance Activity: Organize and implement a food drive to benefit your community. The collection site will include a physical model of the Food Guide Pyramid you designed and built.

Exceptional	Created a visually pleasing model of the Food Guide Pyramid	Provided accompanying materials for publicity to increase scope of food drive	Food collected outside of the school to represent all food groups	Chose a community group to receive the food donation
Commendable	Created a visually pleasing model of the Food Guide Pyramid	Model labeled with additional nutritional information	Food collected school-wide to represent all food groups	Chose a community group to receive the food donation
Satisfactory	Labeled a physical model of the Food Guide Pyramid	Model labeled	Food collected from the class to represent all food groups	Chose a community group to receive the food donation

Performance Activity Assessment Rubric: Safety Procedures

Performance Activity: Design and build a physical model of the New Food Guide Pyramid for the collection site with attention to proper use of tools and materials and safety procedures.

Exceptional	Consistently follows prescribed safety procedures and suggests improved safety measures	Consistently focuses attention on task/activity and monitors the area to minimize distractions
Commendable	Consistently follows prescribed safety procedures and reminds others to work safely	Consistently focuses attention on task/activity and avoids distracting others
Satisfactory	Consistently follows prescribed safety procedures	Consistently focuses attention on task/activity
Unsatisfactory	Does not follow prescribed safety procedures	Does not consistently focus attention on task/activity

Unit 13
PQI (Personal Quest for Information)

Linda D. Sherouse, Library Media Specialist

**Sherry Hoffman, Wendy Crowley, Noreen Forbes, and
Brenda Tharp: Grade 6 Teachers**

North Hampton School (PreK-8)

201 Atlantic Ave., North Hampton, New Hampshire 03862

603-964-5501

<lsherouse@sau21.k12.nh.us>

Grade Level: 6

Unit Overview: PQI is a personalized research unit that capitalizes on students' natural curiosity. It is designed to teach students how to find the information they seek, utilize it in an ethical and effective manner, and present it in a self-selected format. PQI is one step in a PreK through eighth grade information skills progression leading toward a culminating oratorical speech in the final years. Students suggest three topics of personal interest. The library media specialist and teachers then determine those topics best suited for each student with attention to abilities and special needs, information accessibility, and audience. Then the process of their Personal Quest for Information begins.

Time Frame: 30-35 school days:
Weeks 1 and 2: six library periods (42-minutes) with LMS and classroom teacher; three computer lab periods (42-minutes) with computer teacher, classroom teacher, and LMS; 10 classroom periods (42-minutes) with classroom teacher.
Weeks 3-6: four to six library periods (42-minutes)—all one-on-one student assistance with the LMS; 20 classroom periods (42-minutes) with classroom teacher (LMS in the classroom approximately three periods during presentations and reflection circle).

Content Area Standards: New England Common Assessment Program (NECAP) Grade-Level Expectations and Test Specifications in Mathematics, Reading, and Writing
<http://www.ed.state.nh.us/Education/doe/organization/curriculum/NECAP/GLEs.htm>

Uncopyrighted material available online from the New Hampshire Department of Education, Concord, New Hampshire.

Written and Oral Communication

W-6-2: In response to literary or informational text, students show understanding of plot/ideas/concepts by...
W-6-2.2 Summarizing key ideas
W-6-2.3 Connecting what has been read (plot/ideas/concepts) to prior knowledge or other texts, by referring to relevant ideas

W-6-3: In response to literary or informational text, students make and support analytical judgments about text by...
W-6-3.1 Stating and maintaining a focus (purpose), a firm judgment, or point of view when responding to a given question
W-6-3.4 Organizing ideas, using transition words/phrases and writing a conclusion that provides closure

W-6-6: In informational writing, students organize ideas/concepts by...
W-6-6.1 Using an organizational text structure appropriate to focus/controlling idea
W-6-6.2 Selecting appropriate information to set context, which may include a lead/hook

W-6-7: In informational writing, students effectively convey purpose by...
W-6-7.2 Stating and maintaining a focus/controlling idea on a topic

W-6-8: In informational writing, students demonstrate use of a range of elaboration strategies by...
W-6-8.1 Including facts and details relevant to focus/controlling idea, and excluding extraneous information
W-6-8.2 Including sufficient details or facts for appropriate depth of information: naming, describing, explaining, comparing, use of visual images

Reading

R-6-16: Generates a personal response to what is read through a variety of means and through . . .
R-6-16.1 Comparing stories or other texts to related personal experience, prior knowledge, or to other books
R-6-16.2 Providing relevant details to support the connections made or judgments (interpretive, analytical, evaluative, or reflective)

R-6-7 Demonstrate initial understanding of informational texts (expository and practical texts) by . . .
R-6-7.1a Obtaining information from text features (e.g., table of contents, glossary, index, transition words/phrases, bold or italicized text, headings, subheadings, graphic organizers, charts, graphs, or illustrations)
R-6-7.1b Obtaining information from text features (e.g., maps, diagrams, tables, captions, timelines, citations, or transitional devices)
R-6-7.2 Using information from the text to answer questions related to main/central ideas or key details
R-6-7.3 Organizing information to show understanding (e.g., representing main/central ideas or details within text through charting, mapping, paraphrasing, summarizing, or comparing/ contrasting)
R-6-7.4 Generating questions before, during, and after reading to enhance understanding and recall; expand understanding and/or gain new information.

R-6-8: Analyze and interpret informational text, citing evidence as appropriate by . . .
R-6-8.1 Connecting information *within* a text or *across* texts

R-6-8.2 Synthesizing information within or across text(s)(e.g., constructing appropriate titles; or formulating assertions or controlling ideas)

R-6-15: Research by reading multiple sources (including print and non-print texts) to report information, to solve a problem, or to make a decision, or to formulate a judgment by . . .
R-6-15.1 Identifying potential sources of information
R-6-15.2 Evaluating information presented, in terms of relevance
R-6-15.3 Gathering, organizing, and interpreting the information
R-6-15.4 Using evidence to support conclusions

Information Power Information Literacy Standards and Indicators:
1.1, 1.2, 1.3, 1.4, 1.5, 2.2, 2.3, 2.4, 3.1, 3.2, 3.3, 3.4, 4.1, 4.2, 5.1, 5.2, 5.3, 6.1, 6.2, 8.2, 8.3

Cooperative Teaching Plan:

Library Media Specialist Will:

■ Provide pathfinders which guide students in researching through the online tools listed below as well as through the library media center's automation system.
Prior to the start of the unit, schedule lab time for students to review subscription online sources:
> "Biography Resource Center" by *Thomson Gale*
> *CultureGrams*™
> "Curriculum Resource" by *NewsBank*
> *EBSCO*
> *Grolier Online*
> "KidsPage" by *NewsBank*
> *MarcoPolo*
> *netTrekker*
> *unitedstreaming*

■ Teach a lesson using the computer projector in the library to look at the pathfinders as a group and differentiate between sources and tools:
> The Internet is a tool—not a source.
> *Grolier Online* is a tool for accessing the *New Book of Knowledge*, which is an encyclopedia source.
> *Curriculum Resource* and *KidsPage* are tools for accessing newspaper or magazine articles from a variety of sources.

■ Demonstrate the need to verify the validity of Web sites by comparing two sites about the city of Mankato <http://www.ci.mankato.mn.us/> and <http://city-mankato.us/>.

■ Demonstrate how bias can be hidden in an Internet site and why one needs to follow the URL back to the source to avoid adopting the opinion of one group or person.

■ Teach students the differences between book publication and Internet dissemination of information, demonstrating why they should use predetermined sources only rather than open searching.

■ Discuss validation of resources not found through tools provided.

■ Lead a discussion of plagiarism and ownership of information.

■ Present the interview as a resource and examine the varying expertise of those adults with whom they have daily contact.

- Provide one-on-one assistance with topic definition and initial direction for research, as requested by teacher.
- Assist students during research phase of the project.
- Support students in formative and summative self-assessment.

Teachers Will:

- Introduce students to the "PQI Challenge."
- Teach double-column note taking skills in which students differentiate between the main idea and its supporting details in articles of varying length, ordered by difficulty.
- Provide all process checklists and documentation.
- Check individual progress at checkpoints.
- Provide students with a calendar of the expected timetable for the unit.
- Provide students with rubrics and quality standards.
- Provide assistance to students or seek assistance of the LMS when inadequate information has been found.
- Instruct students in the construction of a bibliography.
- Provide a non-judgmental environment where students feel safe to share in front of peers.
- Support students in formative and summative self-assessment.

Resources:

Print

Used only when specific books are available on the student's topic; many of these print items are interlibrary loaned.

Electronic

Farnsworth, R. Bruce. *Mankato MN Home Page*. 1995-2006. 27 October 2006 <http://city-mankato.us/>.

Greater Mankato. 27 October 2006 <http://www.ci.mankato.mn.us/>.

"Knowing What's What and What's Not: The Five W's (and One "H") of Cyberspace." *Media Awareness Network*. 2006. 10 October 2006 <http://www.media-awareness.ca/english/resources/special_initiatives/wa_ resources/ wa_shared/tipsheets/5Ws_of_cyberspace.cfm>.

Online Databases and encyclopedias (requiring subscription):

"Biography Resource Center." ThomsonGale. 10 October 2006 <http://www.gale.com/BiographyRC/>.

CultureGrams™. 10 October 2006 <www.culturegrams.com>.

"Curriculum Resources." *NewsBank*. 10 October 2006 <http://www.newsbank.com/>.

EBSCO. 10 October 2006 <www.ebsco.com>.

Grolier Online. 10 October 2006 <http://auth.grolier.com/cgi-bin/authV2?bffs=N>.

"Kidspage." *NewsBank*. 10 October 2006 <http://www.newsbank.com/>.

MarcoPolo. 10 October 2006 <http://www.marcopolo-education.org/>.

NetTrekker. 10 October 2006 <www.nettrekker.com>.

unitedstreaming. 10 October 2006 <www.unitedstreaming.com>.

Human

A wide range of community members with an interest in or knowledge of topics under study.

Culminating Learning Product: Students choose from a varied list of possible presentation formats (video, PowerPoint®, enactment, news interview, map, model, mural, illustration, report, musical or dance presentation, skit) based on Howard Gardner's theory of multiple intelligences.

Assessment Overview: Assessment is an ongoing part of the process. Each of the five sections of the PQI project has its own rubric for evaluation by the student in conjunction with their group leader, with a total of 100 points possible for the project as a whole.

Adaptations and Extensions:

This unit meets the educational and developmental needs of every student through their choice of research topic. A team of teachers, educational associates, special education instructors, and library media center personnel addresses each student's progress or difficulties as soon as they arise. The LMS is available to the students at all times. The LMS and her assistant agree to exchange places in instances where the LMS is teaching and a sixth grader has a research need. The sixth graders' needs are the highest priority during this unit.

Students whose verbal abilities are challenged, whether special education or ELL students, are encouraged to use digital video or a digital camera and a PowerPoint® to present instead of depending on their speaking abilities.

Extensions to this unit are minimal as each student is encouraged to reach beyond the mundane knowledge level of the taxonomy to synthesis of new ideas and new information gleaned from the research process and presented through an area of intelligence.

Pathfinder: Infocenter™

My Topic_____   My Name_____

Infocenter™
<http://nhslmc.sau21.k12.nh.us/InfoCentre>

I tried these key words: _____   _____

_____   _____   _____

_____   _____   _____

_____ I used advance search.

_____ I used a Boolean operator.

_____ I used the Browser to check my spelling and see if that was why I came up with no hits.

Other libraries to search:
        <http://nhplib.org/>
        <http://www.nhu-pac.library.state.nh.us/>.

Be sure to make a list of what you find and wish to borrow from this list. We can interlibrary loan these resources for you. (Caution: Plan ahead. This type of loan can take 1-2 weeks for us to receive the resources.)

Pathfinder: netTrekker℠

My Topic_____   My Name_____

netTrekker℠
<www.nettrekker.com>

I tried these key words: _____   _____

_____   _____   _____

_____   _____   _____

I found and used these subject words: _____

_____   _____   _____

I tried Level(s): Circle the ones you tried.

Elementary   Middle School   High School

Pathfinder: EBSCO

My Topic_____   My Name_____

EBSCO

_____ I used EBSCO Student Resources as my first search.

      _____ I checked off all resources.
      _____ I used Advanced Search.

_____ I restricted my search to Full Text
_____ I did not restrict my search to Full Text. (Note: When not searching Full Text, you will have to give your librarian a list of the articles you need.

I tried these key words: _____   _____

_____   _____   _____

_____   _____   _____

My best resource was_____

because _____

_____

_____

_____

_____

_____

Challenge

This challenge is made up of five sections, each with a special purpose. You will receive a separate page for each step with specific directions and expectations. The final grade will be based on the total points earned throughout the challenge.

The five sections and possible points for each are as follows:

1. MY QUESTIONS (10)

This will include what you want to know about your topic at the start and what you hope to learn.

2. MY SEARCH PROCESS (10)

This will be an overview of the steps, problems, and successes in your search for information. It will also include:

PATHFINDER CHECKLIST (5)

on which you will keep track of places you have searched

BIBLIOGRAPHY FORMS (5)

which you must fill out as you utilize each resource

3. WHAT I HAVE LEARNED. . .

THE NOTES (10)

THE PRESENTATION (30)

This is where you will share what you have learned with your class. YOU will select how you want to accomplish this.

4. WHAT THIS MEANS TO ME

This is where you will tell what you have learned about research and yourself as a researcher.　(15)

5. BIBLIOGRAPHY (15)

This will be an accurate list of all materials used. You MUST use three different sources of information. Examples below:

newspaper	periodical (magazine)	personal interview
book	valid Internet sites	what else?

POSSIBLE TOTAL POINTS** (100)

**All points will be based on QUALITY of work. Written work MUST be carefully edited and follow quality paper standards which includes presentation in ink or typed.

Project Points

Name_____

Project	Part	My Score
#1	My Questions (10 points)	_____
#2	My Search Process (10 points) Pathfinder (10 points)	_____ _____
#3	What I Have Learned	
	Notes (10 points) The Presentation (30 points)	_____ _____
#4	What This Means to Me (15 points)	_____
#5	Bibliography (15 points)	_____
	MY TOTAL	_____

Weekly Reflection Sheet

Name_____

Directions: *Complete this sheet and meet with your teacher or librarian.*

How has your search been going for you this week?

_____

_____

_____

_____

_____

_____

_____

How can a teacher or librarian help you?

_____

_____

_____

_____

_____

_____

_____

Teacher/Librarian Initials:

_____

#1 My Questions

Name_____

(10 points)

My PQI topic is _____

Some things I already know are:

Some QUESTIONS I would like to answer about my topic are:

I selected this topic because:

MY QUESTION: 10 POINT RUBRIC

Quality	Possible Points	Score
1. Things I know (3 or more facts).	3	_____
2. Questions (4 or more questions).	3	_____
3. Reason topic selected (explains your interest).	2	_____
4. Follows quality paper standards.	2	_____
	TOTAL	_____

#2 My Search Process

Name_____

(20 points): (5) Pathfinder checklist (5) Bibliography forms (10) Search Process questions

A. Pathfinder checklist :
Check off each resource that you explored for information.

B. Bibliography forms:
Fill out a bibliography form for each source you will use for any notes. You must use three different sources. (Hint: Staple a form to any articles you have printed or to any notes that you have taken.)

C. My Search Process: Answer each question below carefully and completely.
    1. What steps did you take to find information? (What did you do first, second, etc.)

    2. What problems did you have in finding information and how did you solve them?

    3. What were your best sources of information?

    4. How did other people (friends, teachers, parents, etc.) help you? Be specific.

MY SEARCH PROCESS: 20 POINT RUBRIC

Quality	Possible Points	Score
1. Pathfinder checklist shows good effort.	5	_____
2. Showed teacher completed bibliography forms from three different sources.	5	_____
3. MY SEARCH PROCESS questions follow quality paper standards (edited and written in complete sentences)	2	_____
4. Each question is answered with specific information.	2 (each question)	_____
	TOTAL	_____

#3 What I Have Learned

Name_____

(40 points)

A. NOTES (10)
1. Notes must be passed in on the day of your presentation.
2. All notes will be taken in two-column form.
3. The number of notes should reflect two weeks worth of research work.

B. THE PRESENTATION (30): YOU BECOME THE TEACHER!
Now it is time to share what you have learned. You must include the major findings or main ideas from your research. Share this in an interesting way to help your audience understand what you have learned. Presentation time must be 3-5 minutes.

Consider your own style and consider your audience. Some possible ideas are:

*Make a video.   *Become the person you researched.
*Conduct a news interview.   *Create a map.
*Construct a model   *Create a mural.
*Illustrate your findings.   *Write a report (with cover & title page).
*Share information with music or dance.   *Write/perform a skit.

WHAT I HAVE LEARNED: NOTES 10 POINT RUBRIC

Quality	Possible Points	Score
1. Notes passed in on day of presentation.	2	_____
2. All notes are in two-column form.	2	_____
3. Number of notes equal to two weeks worth of research and work.	6	_____
	TOTAL	_____

WHAT I HAVE LEARNED: PRESENTATION 30 POINT RUBRIC

Quality	Possible Points	Score
Points will be earned based on your presentation rubrics. The 3-5 minute time limit must also be considered.		
	TOTAL	_____

Presentation Rubric for a Shadow Box/Diorama

SHADOW BOX/DIORAMA
___neatly made
___sturdy construction
___eye appeal/colorful
___has to do with topic
___separate paragraph, carefully written & edited
___explanation with required information
___eye contact with audience
___voice loud and clear
___follows time limits
___completed when due
*If shared as a group:
___all participated equally

Name _____
Comments:

_____

_____

_____

_____

Total Points   Grade

_____   _____

0=not at all   1=somewhat   2=satisfactory   3=excellent

Presentation Rubric for a Model

MODEL
___looks like what it represents
___big enough to see details
___parts clearly labeled
___sturdy/tough construction
___neatly done
___has to do with topic
___separate paragraph, carefully written & edited
___explanation with required information
___eye contact with audience
___voice loud and clear
___follows time limits
___completed when due
*If shared as a group:
___all participated equally

Name _____
Comments:

_____

_____

_____

_____

Total Points   Grade

_____   _____

0=not at all   1=somewhat   2=satisfactory   3=excellent

Presentation Rubric for a Video

VIDEO
___interesting to audience
___loud, clear voices
___appropriately done (rated G!)
___includes required information
___knew lines and stayed in role
___good use of costume and props
___good background & lighting
___camera held steady, not jumpy
___follows time limits
___completed when due
*If shared as a group:
___all participated equally

Name _____
Comments:

_____

_____

_____

_____

Total Points   Grade

_____   _____

0=not at all   1=somewhat   2=satisfactory   3=excellent

Presentation Rubric for a Written Piece

WRITTEN PIECE
___neatly done/quality paper standards
___carefully edited
___ink or typed
___eye-catching cover with title, author & visual
___includes required information
___stays on topic
___flows well
___follows the RECIPE!
___completed when due

Name _____
Comments:

_____
_____
_____
_____

Total Points _____   Grade _____

_____   _____
0=not at all   1=somewhat   2=satisfactory   3=excellent

Presentation Rubric for a Song/Interpretive Dance

SONG/INTERPRETIVE DANCE
___words (actions) clearly understood
___includes required information
___words (actions) clearly connected to topic
___makes sense
___good tempo for material presented
___holds audience attention
___knew lines (dance)
___long enough to present all information
___completed when due
*If shared as a group:
___all participated equally

Name _____
Comments:

_____
_____
_____
_____

Total Points _____   Grade _____

_____   _____
0=not at all   1=somewhat   2=satisfactory   3=excellent

Presentation Rubric for a Game

GAME
___neatly done
___creative/eye appeal
___directions clearly stated on separate paper,
   in ink or typed
___directions carefully edited
___includes required information
___sticks to topic being taught/shared
___makes sense/works!
___fun & informative for the audience
___whole class participates
___not too hard but challenging
___follows time limits
___completed when due
*If shared as a group:
___all participated equally

Name _____
Comments:

_____
_____
_____

Total Points _____   Grade _____

_____   _____
0=not at all   1=somewhat   2=satisfactory   3=excellent

Presentation Rubric for an Oral Piece

ORAL PIECE

___voice is loud and clear (no monotone)
___makes eye contact with audience
___interesting to audience
___familiar with text (can pronounce all words)
___includes all required information
___includes a quality visual connected to topic
___specific and on topic
___follows time limits
___completed when due

Name _____
Comments:

_____

_____

_____

_____

Total Points   Grade

_____   _____

0=not at all   1=somewhat   2=satisfactory   3=excellent

Presentation Rubric for a Skit

SKIT

___creative/interesting to audience
___face audience/speak clearly
___includes costumes and props
___players know parts well
___required information included
___sticks to topic (appropriate)
___clearly well planned
___follows time limits
___completed when due
*If shared as a group:
___all participated equally

Name _____
Comments:

_____

_____

_____

_____

Total Points   Grade

_____   _____

0=not at all   1=somewhat   2=satisfactory   3=excellent

Presentation Rubric for a Poster/Mural

POSTER/MURAL

___neatly done
___has eye appeal/creatively organized
___clearly shows what you are trying to teach/share
___labeled/quality paper standards
___letters/pictures large enough to be seen
___explanation with required information
___eye contact with audience
___voice loud and clear
___follows time limits
___completed when due
*If shared as a group:
___all participated equally

Name _____
Comments:

_____

_____

_____

_____

Total Points   Grade

_____   _____

0=not at all   1=somewhat   2=satisfactory   3=excellent

Presentation Rubric for Overheads/Slides

OVERHEADS/SLIDES

___neatly done
___clear writing/carefully edited
___creatively designed with eye appeal
___color used if possible
___includes required information
___clear explanation given
___holds audience interest
___eye contact with audience
___voice loud and clear
___follows time limits
___completed when due
*If shared as a group:
___all participated equally

Name _____

Comments:

_____

_____

_____

_____

Total Points   Grade

_____   _____

0=not at all   1=somewhat   2=satisfactory   3=excellent

Presentation Rubric for a Puppet Show

PUPPET SHOW

___puppets match what you are sharing/teaching
___puppets have eye appeal
___puppets are visible to all
___puppeteers out of sight
___knows lines well
___voices can be heard clearly (good expression)
___sticks to topic
___includes required information
___creative/entertaining for audience
___follows time limits
___completed when due
*If shared as a group:
___all participated equally

Name _____

Comments:

_____

_____

_____

_____

Total Points   Grade

_____   _____

0=not at all   1=somewhat   2=satisfactory   3=excellent

#4 What This Means to Me

Name_____

(15 points)

Answer the following questions about this project and yourself as a researcher. Be specific!

1. What was easiest for you in this whole process?

2. What did you find most difficult?

3. What will you do differently the next time you do research?

4. What things would make you "pat yourself on the back?"

5. What advice do you have for teachers in guiding students with research?

MY SEARCH PROCESS: 15 POINT RUBRIC

Quality	Possible Points	Score
1. Follows quality paper standards. (includes editing, paragraphs, complete sentences)	5	_____
2. Each answer includes specific information or reasons.	2 each	_____
	TOTAL	_____

#5 The Bibliography

Name_____

(15 points)

1. You must list all references used in your project.

2. Each bibliography entry must follow correct format. (Follow sample guide sheet carefully.)

3. Entries must be listed in alphabetical order by the author's last name. If the author is not given use the first MAIN word in the title.

4. Bibliography must be passed in on the day of your presentation.

THE BIBLIOGRAPHY: 15 POINT RUBRIC

Quality	Possible Points	Score
1. Follows quality paper standards.	5	_____
2. Follows correct bibliography format.	5	_____
3. Entries listed in alphabetical order by author's last name.	5	_____
	TOTAL	_____

Unit 14
If These Walls Could Speak

Ronda Hassig, Library Media Specialist

Kathy Hill, Communication Arts and Reading Teacher

Harmony Middle School

10101 West 141st St., Overland Park, Kansas 66221

913-239-5210

<rhassig@bluevalleyk12.org> and *<khill@bluevalleyk12.org>*

Grade Level: 6

Unit Overview: We live in a world full of walls. Some we build around our hearts, others we build to keep the world in or out. If These Walls Could Speak integrates social studies, communication arts, and reading as students learn about physical and emotional walls from multiple perspectives. The Great Wall of China as well as the prison walls of Guantanamo Bay offer students the opportunity to learn about ancient and current events that may impact their lives. The unit is built upon selected stories in *Talking Walls* and *Talking Walls, the Story Continues* by Margy Burns Knight as well as easy books about bias. After listening, mapping, and charting, students research their favorite wall using print sources and online data bases and produce a variety of learning products.

Time Frame: Six and one half hours in the library media center: 90 minutes for charting, mapping and directions for research; two hours for research; three one-hour blocks for reading bias books. The library media specialist teaches the social studies portion on one side of the library and directs the research. The classroom teacher facilitates the reading of bias books.
 (Note: It is best to have the library set up in three areas: bias books on four long tables on one side; pictures of walls on four tables plus an easel for charting and possibly a projector for the *Talking Walls* CD's; a third area for research.)

Content Area Standards: Blue Valley School District Standards, Overland Park, Kansas
<http://curriculum.bluevalleyk12.org/blue_valley/gen/blue_valley_generated_pages/Home_p54.html>

6th Grade Communication Arts Content Area Standards

Standard 1 - Reading: Student reads and comprehends text across the curriculum.
Benchmark 4: The student comprehends a variety of texts (narrative, expository, technical & persuasive).
 Student will know:
 A. Dictionaries, thesauri, Internet, atlases, encyclopedias

Student will be able to:

11. understand and use the references available in the classroom, school, and public libraries that are appropriate to the task.

14. generate and respond logically to literal, inferential, evaluative, and critical thinking questions before, during, and after reading the text.

Student will know:

A. Inferences and conclusions

Student will be able to:

15. use information from the text to make inferences and draw conclusions.

Student will know:

A. Paraphrasing, organization, summary, stated and implied main ideas, main events, important details

Student will be able to:

19. use paraphrasing and organizational skills to summarize information (stated and implied main ideas, main events, important details) from appropriate-level narrative, expository, persuasive, and technical texts in logical order.

Student will know:

A. Purpose for reading: to be informed, to follow directions, to be entertained, to solve problems

Student will be able to:

23. establish purposes for both assigned and self-selected reading.

Student will know:

A. Fact and opinion, propaganda (e.g., advertising, media, politics, warfare), bias, and stereotypes

Student will be able to:

26. distinguish between fact and opinion, and recognize propaganda (e.g., advertising, media, politics, warfare), bias, and stereotypes in various types of appropriate-level texts.

Standard 3 - Writing: The student writes effectively for a variety of audiences, purposes, and contexts.

Benchmark 1: The student uses writing as a tool for learning throughout the curriculum.

The student will know:

A. Writing process

The student will be able to:

1. process in various formats such as notes, outlines, lab reports, journal entries, research reports, speeches, business letters, poems, advertisements, procedures and steps to various projects in the content areas.

Benchmark 7: The student uses clear and fluent sentences.

The student will know:

A. Sentence fluency

The student will be able to:

10. write complete sentences (simple and compound) that flow and sound natural.

Benchmark 8: The student uses standard American English conventions.

The student will know:

A. Capitalization

The student will be able to:

11. use correct capitalization.

Benchmark 9: The student uses a variety of modes of writing for different purposes and audiences.

The student will be able to:

18. write for a specific purpose and audience (to inform, entertain, persuade) in the fol-

lowing modes—expository pieces, e.g., lab reports, math projects, social studies reports, and summaries.

Standard 4 - Research: The student applies reading and writing skills to demonstrate learning.
Benchmark 1: The student uses effective research practices.
> The student will be able to:
> 2. locate and use a variety of appropriate print and non-print resources to gather information.

Benchmark 2: The student uses ethical research practices.
> The student will be able to:
> 8. express information in own words using evidence and examples. (
> 10. construct a bibliography or works cited page with author, title, publisher, year, website, and copyright date to cite references for all information used or reproduced from any source.

6th Grade Social Studies Content Area Standards

Standard 5 (Concept): People, Places, Environments—the student uses a working knowledge and understanding of the concepts of people, places, and environments.
Benchmark 5 (Enduring Understandings): Geographic factors cause humans to adapt, interact with, and modify their environment.
> The student will know:
> 6. and describes how places and regions may be identified by cultural symbols (e.g., Acropolis in Athens, Muslim minaret, Indian sari, Parthenon, Coliseum, Great Wall, and pyramids).

Standard 7 (Concept): Individual Development and Identity—the student uses a working knowledge and understanding of the concepts of individual development and identity.
Benchmark 7 (Enduring Understandings): History represents the story of human diversity and the development of individual and national identity over time.
> The student will know:
> 6. and describes key accomplishments of ancient China (e.g., Great Wall of China, Shi Huangdi, dynastic cycle, Mandate of Heaven, Taoism, Confucianism, civil service, and the Silk Road).

Standards reprinted with permission from the Blue Valley School District.

Information Power Information Literacy Standards and Indicators: 1.1, 1.4, 1.5, 2.1, 2.4, 3.1, 3.2, 3.3, 3.4, 5.1, 5.2, 6.2, 7.2, 8.2, 9.1, 9.2

Cooperative Teaching Plan:

Library Media Specialist Will:
- Arrange the library media center in three areas.
  - One side houses tables containing the bias books that students Read and Chart, Read and Respond to, and Just Read.
  - The other side houses four tables, each with three pictures of different physical walls and four cards with one fact about one of the walls, for a total of 12 cards at each table. Four

students sit at each table. (Note: adjust numbers for larger groups or time limitations. Works best with 16 students.)

- Assist students at each table as they match the four facts with the corresponding wall.
- Direct students in their creation of a Wall chart while reading or playing CDs of *Talking Walls* and *Talking Walls, the Story Continues.*
- Help table groups to locate walls in atlases and mark them on large blank world maps.
- Advise individual students as they locate all countries on personal-size world maps.
- Assist individual students as they choose a wall and answer questions about its location using an atlas, *CultureGrams™*, *Lands and Peoples*, and the *World Almanac* in either print form or from online subscription databases.
- Help students as they complete the KWL activity on their wall, writing five facts they know, five facts they want to know, and 10 facts they learned.
- Assist students in answering their essential questions and completing their bibliography.
- Assess the walls chart, world map, physical walls research questions, and KWL with bibliography using the Assessment Rubric.

The Teacher Will:

- Teach atlas skills in preparation for table activity.
- Teach bibliographic citation skills for the sources used in individual wall research.
- Teach students the meaning of bias.
- Supervise students in reading the bias books and recording them in their literature logs.
- Assess the literature logs.
- Engage students in a study of the novel *Randall's Wall* by Carol Fenner.
- Support students in completion of the title pages assignment.
- Read and assess title pages assignment, *Randall's Wall* activities and literature logs using the Communication Arts Assessment Rubric.

Resources:

Print

Allan, Nicholas. *The Hefty Fairy*. New York: Arrow, 1990. OP

Allen, Judy. *What is a Wall, After All?* Cambridge, Massachusetts: Candlewick, 1993. OP

Cohen, Barbara. *Molly's Pilgrim*. New York: Lothrop, Lee & Shepard, 1983.

Cohen, Miriam. *No Good in Art*. New York: Morrow, 1980.

DePaola, Tomie. *Oliver Button is a Sissy*. New York: Harcourt, 1979.

Dugan, Barbara. *Loop the Loop*. New York: Greenwillow, 1992.

Ernst, Lisa Campbell. *Sam Johnson and the Blue Ribbon Quilt*. New York: HarperCollins, 1985.

Fenner, Carol. *Randall's Wall*. New York: Simon and Schuster, 1991.

Haggerty, Mary Elizabeth. *A Crack in the Wall*. New York: Lee & Low, 1993. OP

Henkes, Kevin. *Chrysanthemum*. New York: HarperCollins, 1991.

I Dream of Peace; Images of War by Children of Former Yugoslavia. New York: HarperCollins, 1994 OP

Innocenti, Roberto. *Rose Blanche*. San Diego: Harcourt, 1996.

Knight, Margy Burns. *Talking Walls*. Gardiner, Maine: Tilbury House, 1992.

Knight, Margy Burns. *Talking Walls: The Story Continues*. Gardiner, Maine: Tilbury House, 1997.

Lasker, Joe. *Nick Joins In*. Chicago: Whitman, 1980. OP

Lee, Milly. *Landed.* New York: Farrar Strauss Giroux, 2006.

Lionni, Leo. *Tillie and the Wall.* New York: Knopf, 1989. OP

Mills, Lauren. *The Rag Coat.* Boston: Little, Brown & Company, 1991.

Mochizuki, Ken. *Baseball Saved Us.* New York: Lee & Low, 1993.

Monk, Lorraine. *Photographs that Changed the World.* New York: Doubleday, 1989. OP

Maruki, Toshi. *Hiroshima No Pika.* New York: Lothrop, Lee and Shepard Books, 1980

Rappapport, Doreen. *The School is Not White! A True Story of the Civil Rights Movement.* New York: Jump at the Sun, 2005

Schotter, Roni. *Captain Snap and the Children of Vinegar Lane.* New York: Orchard, 1989.

Uchida, Yoshiko. *The Bracelet.* New York: Philomel, 1993.

Electronic

CultureGrams™. 10 October 2006 <www.culturegrams.com>. (subscription required)

Infoplease. 2000-2006. 27 October 2006 <http://www.infoplease.com/>.

"Lands and Peoples." *Grolier Online.* 10 October 2006 <http://auth.grolier.com/cgi-bin/authV2?bffs=N>.

Warlick, David. "Citation Machine™." *The Landmark Project.* 2006. 10 October 2006 <http://citationmachine.net/>.

Internet Sites for additional walls not in *Talking Walls* books:
Guantanamo Bay

U.S. Naval Station Guantanamo Bay, Cuba. 27 October 2006 <http://www.nsgtmo.navy.mil/>.

Beckett, Brad. *Photos from Guantanamo Bay, Cuba.* 27 October 2006 <http://www.bradbeckett.com/gbay/>.

"Detainees at Guantanamo Bay." *NPR.* 2006. 27 October 2006 <http://www.npr.org/templates/story/story.php?storyId=4711397>.

Israeli Separation Wall

"The Wall." *P4PD.* 27 October 2006 <http://www.p4pd.org/wall.html>.

"Military: The Fence/Security Barrier/Separation Barrier." *GlobalSecurity.* 2000-2006. 27 October 2006 < http://www.globalsecurity.org/military/world/israel/fence-imagery.htm>.

"Saving Lives - Israel's Security Fence." *Israel Ministry of Foreign Affairs.* 2004. 27 October 2006 <http://www.mfa.gov.il/MFA/MFAArchive/2000_2009/2003/11/Saving%20Lives-%20Israel-s%20Security%20Fence>.

"The Separation Wall." *American Task Force on Palestine.* 2005. 27 October 2006 <http://www.americantaskforce.org/the_wall.htm>.

Demilitarized Zone (DMZ), Korea

"DMZ - The Demilitarized Zone." *Granite School District.* 27 October 2006 <http://media.graniteschools.org/Curriculum/korea/dmz.htm>.

"Demilitarized Zone - South Korea." *World Photo Gallery.* 27 October 2006 <http://www.globalphotos.org/sk-dmz.htm>.

"North Korea: Nuclear Standoff." *PBS.* 27 October 2006 <http://www.pbs.org/new-shour/indepth_coverage/asia/northkorea/dmz.html>.

Audiovisual

Talking Walls. CD-Rom. Redmond, Washington: Edmark Corporation, 1999.
Talking Walls: The Story Continued. CD-Rom. Redmond, Washington: Edmark Corporation, 2000.

Supplies

Laminated pictures of each physical wall
Four facts on large index cards on each wall
Large laminated world maps without country names
Small individual world maps without country names
Large, clear plastic bags to hold easy books and response cards
Construction paper (11x17") for student folders to hold work

Culminating Learning Product: Students produce a wall chart, wall map, physical walls research worksheet, and KWL for the social studies component. They also answer their essential question. They log all of their easy reading and bias work for the communication arts component in addition to reading *Randall's Wall* by Carol Fenner for the communication arts component.

Assessment Overview:

Using the Assessment Rubric, the library media specialist assesses students on:

- map skills as they use an atlas to correctly place a wall's location on a world map;
- spelling and legibility on all written work;
- accuracy of information and citation of sources for the research portion of the KWL;
- answer to the essential question drawn from their research and answered in complete sentences.

The communication arts teacher assesses students on:

- the title pages assignment;
- literature logs for the bias books;
- *Randall's Wall* activities.

Adaptations and Extensions:

This unit can be adapted in many ways:

- Require fewer or more walls. Additional walls may include:
    - Tower of London—England
    - Nelson Mandela Prison Walls—South Africa
    - Krah des Chevaliers—Syria
    - Great Zimbabwe—Zimbabwe
    - Laseaux Cave—France
    - Forbidden City—China
    - Vatican—Vatican City
    - Inca Ruins—Peru
- Extend the requirements for research for gifted students (for example, ask them to discuss whether their wall was successful in its purpose or to compare their wall with an ancient or modern wall while considering its success. One pairing might be the Great Wall of China and the Wall in Gaza between the Israelis and Palestinians).

- Add math components (for example, students might learn about positive and negative space).

- Add science components (for example, students might build dams).

- Promote the use of a bilingual dictionary for ELL students.

- Allow challenged readers and ELL students to use the CDs on which both books are read aloud.

- Employ visuals and pictures to help ELL and academically challenged students.

- Invite ELL students to research a wall from their home country.

- Assign students to work with a partner, pairing proficient readers with struggling learners and ELL students.

- Employ the CDs which have multiple resources for information on each wall read aloud.

- Encourage artistically talented students to draw, paint, or produce a three-dimensional sculpture of their walls.

This unit can also be extended:

- Read other novels instead of/in addition to *Randall's Wall*. Possibilities include: *Journey Home* by Yoshiko Uchida, *December Stillness* by Mary Downing Hahn, *Daphne's Book* by Mary Downing Hahn, *Foxman* by Gary Paulsen, *Afternoon of the Elves* by Janet Lisle, and *Among the Hidden* by Margaret Peterson Haddix.

- Share video footage of the Berlin Wall falling or pieces of the actual wall for students to touch.

- Invite students to create a graffiti wall outside the library in the hallway with facts they learned about their individual physical walls or comments on emotional walls.

- Share Pink Floyd's "The Wall" or Michael Jackson and Paul McCartney's "Ebony and Ivory" and invite student discussion.

- Ask students to add appropriate graffiti to their wall folders.

- Share lines 32-36 from "Mending Wall" by Robert Frost <http://www.bartleby.com/118/2.html> with students to guide their thinking about walls.

Easy Reading List

Read and Chart – Choose three of the following titles and read and chart them.
Refer to the poster to see how to chart.

_____ Allan, Nicholas. *The Hefty Fairy.*

_____ DePaola, Tomie. *Oliver Button is a Sissy.*

_____ Cohen, Barbara. *Molly's Pilgrim.*

_____ Henkes, Kevin. *Chrysanthemum.*

_____ Ernst, Lisa Campbell. *Sam Johnson and the Blue Ribbon Quilt.*

_____ Masuki, Toshi. *Hiroshima no Pika.*

Read and Respond – Choose three of the following titles in the bags and read and respond to the cards.

_____ Allen, Judy. *What is a Wall, After All?*

_____ Uchida, Yoshiko. *The Bracelet* and Mochizuki, Ken. *Baseball Saved Us.*

_____ Lionni, Leo. *Tillie and the Wall.*

_____ Innocenti, Roberto. *Rose Blanche.*

_____ Mills, Lauren. *The Rag Coat.*

_____ Rappapport, Doreen. *The School is not White!*

Read

_____ Lasker, Joe. *Nick Joins In.*

_____ Dugan, Barbara. *Loop the Loop.*

_____ *I Dream of Peace, Images of War by Children of Former Yugoslavia.*

_____ Cohen, Miriam. *No Good in Art.*

_____ Haggerty, Mary Elizabeth. *A Crack in the Wall.*

_____ Lee, Milly. *Landed.*

_____ Schotter, Roni. *Captain Snap and the Children of Vinegar Lane.*

Read and Chart

Read three of the books in the "Read and Chart" section and chart this information about each:

Title:

Author:

Main Character(s):

Bias:

Personal Response:

Read and Respond (Sample)

Open three Read and Respond book bags, read the books, read the response cards, and then answer the questions asked in your Literature journal:

Author: Leo Lionni

Title: *Tillie and the Wall*

What's interesting about the celebration pebble?

What's the <u>moral</u> of this story?

Why is Tillie a hero?

Is the wall in this book emotional or physical or both? Explain.

Additional Read and Respond Question Sets

Rose Blanche by Roberto Innocenti
1. Read the text.
2. In your literature log write the title, author.
3. How did this story make you feel?
4. Turn to page 27 of *Photographs that Changed the World* by Lorraine Monk. Read the message with the picture.
5. Find a similar picture in *Rose Blanche*.
6. Answer: Who? What? When? Where? Why? And how does it relate to the present?

The School is Not White! by Doreen Rappaport
1. Read the story.
2. In your literature log write the title, author.
3. Answer the following questions about the story:
    a. How did the text make you feel?
    b. Why did the Carters make their children go to the white school in Drew, Mississippi?
    c. Can you think of any virtues that we've studied that the Carter children exhibited? Name them.
    d. What kind of walls did the Carter children experience? Explain.
    e. At the end of the book, the author talks about each of the Carter children and their successes. Pick one and write about them.

The Rag Coat by Lauren Mills
1. Read the text.
2. In your literature log, write about the discrimination you see in this book.
3. Identify three pieces on Minna's coat. What do they represent?

The Bracelet by Yoshiko Uchida and *Baseball Saved Us* by Ken Mochizuki
1. Read both books.
2. In your literature log write titles, authors and what you remember from reading these two books.
3. What do these children suffer from in these two books? Explain.
4. How do they survive?
Be sure to look through the attached books on Manzanar.

What is a Wall, After All? by Judy Allen
1. Read the book.
2. In your literature log write title, author and what you remember from the book.
3. Reread. Look carefully; there's lots of information here.
4. List five new pieces of information.

Randall's Wall Evaluation Activities

I. Discuss the following questions: (2 pages)

- What events occurred in the story that helped Randall tear down his wall?

- Jean showed us in the story that one person really can make a difference. Discuss how you might be able to make a difference in someone's life.

II. Write a cinquain poem about Randall.

- Use his name for the first line, 2 adjectives to describe him in the second line, 3 words to explain his wall in the third line, 4 words in the fourth line explaining what helped him tear down his wall, and 1 word in the fifth line that you think best describes how Randall felt at the end of the book. Publish your poem in ink or word process.

III. Make a collage of pictures and words.

- Show the characteristics, traits, virtues, and talents of either Randall or Jean.

IV. Answer the following questions: (Write at least 1/2 page response)

- Of the three activities we did with this novel, which one did you enjoy the most?

- Which caused you to learn the most?

Title Pages Assignment

Note: *The essential questions in this assessment are tiered so that you can demonstrate thinking at lower and higher levels (F=factual, C=conceptual, P=philosophical).* [Remember, EPAIR=Economic, Political, Artistic, Intellectual, and Religious components of a civilization.]

1. To complete your Title Pages Assignment, answer the following:

- What causes conflict or walls? Why have cultures built walls? (F)

- Create at least 5 illustrations to answer the question. Be sure you have drawn one for each of the components of civilization (EPAIR). Be sure to use 4 colors! Add captions or labels to explain your illustrations.

2. Now choose one of the following questions and write a paragraph to complete your title pages work:

1. How can cultures tear down walls? (C)

2. How can a culture have walls within itself? (P)

3. Is world peace an ideal or can it become reality? (P)

Physical Walls Research Questions

Answer these questions about the wall of your choice and the country in which it is located.

Name of wall:_____

Country in which the wall is located:_____

Using an Atlas

1. What is the *capitol* of this country?

2. On what *continent* is your wall located?

Using an Almanac

3. What is the *population* of this country?

4. What is the *monetary unit* for this country?

5. What is the *literacy rate* for this country?

6. How many *Internet connections* per person are there in this country? What information about the country does this answer give?

7. What is the *life expectancy* for males and females in this country?

Using *CultureGrams*™

8. How might you *greet* someone in this country?

9. What *customs or gestures* are appropriate in this country?

10. When can a young person *marry* in this country?

11. What is the *official language* of this country?

12. What is the *major religion* in this country?

Using *Lands and Peoples*

13. Besides the wall, what other *places of interest* might one visit in this country?

14. Name a *mountain range* in this country?

15. Name a *famous river* or *body of water* in this country.

16. What is the most popular form of *recreation* in this country?

Walls Essential Questions

Directions: *In complete sentences, answer the corresponding essential question that pertains to the wall you researched for your KWL.*

Palestine/Israeli Wall, Gaza City – Why is this wall being built? Will it solve the problem?

Western Wall, Israel – Why, after some 2000 years, are people still drawn to this wall?

Great Wall, China – Is it ever wise to build a wall around your country or nation or city? Explain. Can you think of a modern day example of this?

Kaaba, Saudi Arabia – What makes a place sacred?

Vietnam War Memorial – Why do humans make or build memorials for war?

Berlin Wall, Germany – Why did the Berlin Wall finally fall?

Hadrian's Wall, Great Britain – Is it ever possible to build a wall that truly separates people? Explain.

Dog Wall, Japan – Why are pets so important to humans?

Guantanamo Bay Prison Walls, USA/Cuba – Can walls ever be controversial? Explain.

Belfast Peace Lines, Northern Ireland - Are you born prejudiced? Explain why this question is important to Northern Ireland.

DMZ, North/South Korea – Will the DMZ ever fall? Why or why not?

Wat Po, Thailand – Why do Buddhist boys have to become monks? Are you aware of other religions that demand this of their followers? Explain.

Social Studies Requirements Criteria Sheet

Each student will be responsible to complete a packet including:

_____Walls World Map (42 points)

_____Walls Chart (56 Points)

_____Physical Walls Research Questions Sheet (20 points)

_____Walls KWL (20 points)

_____Essential Question (5 points)

_____Bibliography (28 points)

_____Total (171 points)

Walls Chart

The class has 12 pictures of walls, four descriptive cards with each picture, three pictures to a table. In your table group, sort the cards and match the facts with the correct wall. Once everything is sorted correctly, the library media specialist will verify the correct identification of all walls and their locations by reading aloud short excerpts about each wall.

Now create and complete the following chart for all twelve walls, your own three and the nine from the other three groups:

Name of Wall	Location	Physical	Emotional	Political
The Western Wall	Jerusalem, Israel	X	X	X

Walls Map

Each group will locate the countries in which their walls are located on the large world map. After the walls are all identified on the map, you will complete an individual world map for your packet including the location of all twelve walls (the three from your group and the nine located by the other three groups).

KWL

On a separate sheet, complete a KWL on the wall of your choice. List at least five things for K (what you KNOW), five things for the W (what you WANT to know), and 10 things for the L (what you LEARNED) relying on your research in the Library Media Center. You must use at least **two sources** for the KWL. Use the **_Talking Walls CD-ROM set_** or **Internet sites** for five facts and a **book or periodical source** for five more facts for a total of 10 facts.

Essential Question

Answer the essential question for your wall in complete sentences. See Walls Essential Questions.

Physical Walls Research Questions

Complete the Physical Walls Research Questions by using an atlas, almanac, _CultureGrams_™, and _Lands and Peoples_. You may use the online or print versions of these sources.

Bibliography

Cite both sources used for the KWL in proper MLA format and in alphabetical order. You may use _Citation Machine_™ for your bibliography.

Communication Arts Assessment Rubric

CATEGORY	5	3	1
Literature Logs for Bias Books	The student has responded to all questions and relates the literature to his or her own experiences.	The student has responded to all questions but has not yet connected the literature to his or her own experiences.	The student has not yet responded to all questions.
Randall's Wall **Activities: Discussion Questions**	The student's written response demonstrates an understanding of situations that can create and tear down personal walls in his or her own life as well as the walls in the story.	The student demonstrates an understanding of circumstances in the story that created and tore down personal walls.	The student has not yet demonstrated an understanding of personal walls.
Randall's Wall **Activities: Cinquain Poem**	The student has demonstrated a deep understanding of the character through poetry structure.	The student has demonstrated knowledge of the character through poetry structure.	The student has not yet shown knowledge of the character through poetry structure.
Randall's Wall **Activities: Collage**	The student has shown a complete understanding of the main character.	The student has shown some understanding of the main character.	The student has not yet demonstrated understanding of the main character.
Randall's Wall **Activities: Reflection Questions**	The student has completed a thoughtful reflection that thoroughly answers the questions.	The student has completed the reflection.	The student has not yet completed the reflection.
Title Pages Assignment	The student has responded thoughtfully to the factual question and one philosophical question.	The student has responded accurately to the factual and the conceptual questions.	The student has not yet responded accurately to either the factual and/or the conceptual questions.

Research Assessment Rubric

CATEGORY	3	2	1
World Map	The student has located all the countries where the 12 walls are located and spelled the name of the wall correctly.	The student has attempted to locate the countries where the walls are located but has gotten three or more incorrect. All walls are spelled correctly.	The student has multiple misspellings and has not yet succeeded in marking half of the walls in the correct countries.
Walls Chart	The student has completed the Walls Chart and has all of the walls and countries listed. The wall and country are spelled correctly. An attempt has been made to classify the wall as political, emotional, and physical.	The student has completed the Walls Chart and has all of the walls and countries listed. However, some of the walls and countries are spelled incorrectly. An attempt has been made to classify the wall as political, emotional, and physical.	The Walls Chart is incomplete. Some of the walls and countries are misspelled and the student has not yet attempted to classify the walls as political, emotional, and physical.
Physical Walls Research Questions	The student has answered all of the questions correctly, using the multiple sources required.	The student has answered at least two questions from each source correctly.	The student has not yet answered one question from each source correctly.
Walls KWL and Essential Question	The student has completed a KWL for his/her chosen wall that includes Five Ks, Five Ws, and 10 Ls. He or she has answered the essential question in complete sentences.	The student has not met the requirements for completing the KWL for his or her chosen wall. His or her essential question is answered, but not in complete sentences.	The student is missing the K, W, or L on the KWL for his or her chosen wall. The essential question is not yet answered.
Required Sources	The student used the required two sources including the Walls CD or the Internet (depending on which wall they chose) and a print source.	The student used only one of the required sources.	The student has not yet used the required sources.
Bibliography	The student has cited both sources used for the KWL in proper MLA format and in alphabetical order.	The student has attempted to cite both sources used for the KWL in proper MLA format and in alphabetical order.	The student has not yet included a bibliography.

Allen, Debbie. Personal interview. 12 January 2007.

American Association of School Librarians. *Position Statement on Resource Based Instruction Role of the School Library Media Specialist in Reading Development.* Revised July 1999. 19 January 2007 <http://www.ala.org/ala/aasl/aaslproftools/positionstatements/aaslpositionstatementresource.htm >.

American Association of School Librarians. *Position Statement on the Value of Independent Reading in the School Library Media Program.* Revised July 1999. 13 January 2007 <http://www.ala.org/ala/aasl/aasl-proftools/positionstatements/aaslpositionstatement valueindependent.htm>.

American Association of School Librarians. *Your School Library Media Program and No Child Left Behind.* Chicago: American Library Association, 2004.

American Association of School Librarians, American Library Association, and Association for Educational Communication. *Media Programs: District and School.* Chicago: American Library Association, 1975.

American Association of School Librarians and Association for Educational Communication. *Information Power: Building Partnerships for Learning.* Chicago: American Library Association, 1998.

American Association of School Librarians and Association for Educational Communication. *Information Power: Guidelines for School Library Media Programs.* Chicago: American Library Association, 1988.

Becksvoort, Peg. Personal Interview. 04 January 2007.

Berger, Iris. "Broadening the Notions of Early Literacy." *BC Educational Leadership Research* (November 2005) 13 January 2007 <http://slc.educ.ubc.ca/eJournal/Issue2/Berger.pdf>.

Birkett, Mary. Personal interview. 12 January 2007.

Bishop, Kay and Nancy Larimer. "Literacy through Collaboration." *Teacher Librarian* 27:1 (October 1999): 15-20.

Brisco, Shonda. Personal interview. 13 January 2007.

Braverman, Nancy. Personal interview. 01 June 2006.

Brown, Carol. America's Most Wanted: Teachers Who Collaborate. *Teacher Librarian* 32:1 (October 2004): 13-18.

Bush, Gail. Every *Student Reads: Collaboration and Reading to Learn.* Chicago: American Association of School Librarians, 2005.

Butt, Rhonda and Christine Jameson. "Steps to Collaborative Teaching." *Oregon School Library Information System.* 13 January 2007 <http://www.oslis.k12.or.us/docs/steps_collab.pdf>.

Callison, Daniel and Keith Curry Lance. "Enough Already? Blazing New Trails for School Library Research: An Interview with Keith Curry Lance. *School Library Media Research* 8 (2005). 19 January 2007 <http://www.ala.org/ala/aasl/aaslpubsandjournals/slmrb/editorschoiceb/lance/interviewlance.htm>.

Church, Audrey P. *Leverage Your Library Program to Raise Test Scores: A Guide for Library Media Specialists, Principals, Teachers, and Parents.* Worthington, Ohio: Linworth, 2003.

Coatney, Sharon. "Building a Collaborative Culture." *Teacher Librarian* 32:4 (April 2005): 59.

Coles, Gerald. "Read Books in the Caboose." *Knowledge Quest* 33:2 (November/December 2004): 22-25.

"Collaborative Planning: Partnerships between Teachers and Library Media Specialists." *NEMA--Nebraska Educational Media Association.* 19 January 2007 <http://nema.k12.ne.us/CheckIt/coplan.html>.

Combes, Barbara. Personal interview. 16 January 2007.

Cunningham, Patricia M., James W. Cunningham, and Richard L. Allington. *Research on the Components of a Comprehensive Reading and Writing Instructional Program.* 11 September 2002 [Draft]. 13 January 2007 <www.wfu.edu/academics/fourblocks/ComLitInstr(Specific).doc>.

Danielsons, Jane E. Personal interview. 01 June 2006.

Delaney, Faith A. Personal interview. 10 January 2007.

Dervan, Josephine. Personal interview. 13 January 2007.

DeStefano, Kim. Personal interview. 31 May 2006.

Donham, Jean. "Collaboration in the Media Center: Building Partnerships for Learning." *NASSP Bulletin* 83:605 (March 1999): 20-26.

Dunson, Laura. Personal interview. 01 June 2006.

Eisenberg, Michael B. "It's All About Learning: Ensuring that Students are Effective Users of Information on Standardized Tests." *Library Media Connection* 22:6 (March 2004): 22-30.

"Elementary & Secondary Education: Subpart 4 – Improving Literacy through School Libraries." *U.S. Department of Education* 19 January 2007 <http://www.ed.gov/policy/elsec/leg/esea02/pg7.html>.

Farwell, Sybil. "Successful Models for Collaborative Planning." *Knowledge Quest* 26:2 (January/February 1998): 24-30.

Fisher, Bettie. Personal interview. 31 May 2006.

Fitzsimmons, C. Beth. Letter to President George W. Bush on behalf of NCLIS. 13 January 2007 <http://www.nclis.gov/info/LetterPresident-SchoolLibrariesWork.pdf >.

Georges, Fitzgerald. "The No Child Left Behind Act of 2001: What are the Implications for School Libraries?" *Library Media Connection* 23:1 (August/September 2004): 28-29.

Gniewek, Debra. Personal interview. 01 June 2006.

Gniewek, Debra. "Philadelphia Library Power: Collaboration Form." *Book Report* 18:2 (October 1999): 34-35.

Goldberg, Beverly. "Why School Libraries Won't Be Left Behind." *American Libraries* 36:8 (September 2005): 38-41.

Gorman, Michael. "President's Message: The Indispensability of School Libraries (and School Librarians)." *American Libraries* 36:9 (October 2005): 5.

Groff, Jennifer. Personal interview. 31 May 2006.

Grover, Robert. *Collaboration*. Chicago: American Association of School Librarians, 1996.

Hamilton, Wayne. "10 Things an Administrator Should Do to Support the School Library." *Teacher Librarian* 33:2 (December 2005): 71.

Hand, Dorcas. Personal interview. 10 January 2007.

Hassig, Ronda. Personal interview. 11 January 2007.

Haycock, Ken. "Collaborative Program Planning and Teaching." *Teacher Librarian* 27:1 (October 1999): 38.

Haycock, Ken. "Fostering Collaboration, Leadership and Information Literacy: Common Behaviors of Uncommon Principals and Faculties." *NASSP Bulletin* 83:805 (March 1999): 82-87.

Heimbrook, Debra. Personal interview. 01 June 2006.

Hirsh-Pasek and Robert Michnick-Golinkoff. "Getting Engaged through Reading." *Knowledge Quest* 33:2 (November/December 2004): 66-68.

International Reading Association. *Resolution: In Support of Credentialed Library Media Professionals in School Library Media Centers.* 13 January 2007 <http://www.reading.org/downloads/resolutions/resolution00_library_media_professionals.pdf>.

Johnston, Melissa P. Personal interview. 16 January 2007.

Kenney, Brian. "Ross to the Rescue!" *School Library Journal* 52:4 (April 2006): 44-47.

Krashen, Stephen D. *The Power of Reading: Insights from the Research.* 2nd ed. Westport, Connecticut: Libraries Unlimited, 2004.

Krebsbach, Vicki. Personal interview. 02 June 2006.

Krebsbach, Vicki. Personal interview. 16 January 2007.

Lance, Keith Curry. "Libraries and Student Achievement." *Threshold* (Winter 2004): 8-9.

Lance, Keith Curry, Christine Hamilton-Pennell, and Marcia J. Rodney. *Information Empowered; The School Librarian as an Agent of Academic Achievement in Alaska Schools, Revised Edition.* Juneau: Alaska State Library, 2000.

Lance, Keith Curry, Lynda Welborn, and Christine Hamilton-Pennell. *The Impact of School Library Media Centers on Academic Achievement.* San Jose: Hi Willow Research & Publishing, 1993.

Lance, Keith Curry, Marcia J. Rodney, and Christine Hamilton-Pennell. *How School Librarians Help Kids Achieve Standards: The Second Colorado Study.* San Jose: Hi Willow Research & Publishing, 2000.

Lance, Keith Curry, Marcia J. Rodney, and Christine Hamilton-Pennell. *Measuring Up to Standards: The Impact of School Libraries & Information Literacy in Pennsylvania Schools.* Greensburg, Pennsylvania: Pennsylvania Citizens for Better Libraries, 2000.

Leonard, Lawrence and Patricia Leonard. "The Continuing Trouble with Collaboration: Teachers Talk." *Current Issues in Education* 6:15 (2003). 19 January 2007 <http://cie.asu.edu/volume6/number15/index.html>.

"Lerner Outcomes: Adult Literacy." *National Center for Education Statistics.* 03 July 2007 <http://nces.ed.gov/programs/coe/2007/section2/indicator18.asp>.

Levine, Lesley. Personal interview. 01 June 2006.

"Library Power: A Report to the Community." *Philadelphia Education Fund.* 2006. 013 July 2007. Access at <http://www.philaedfund.org/pdfs/LP_Pub.pdf>.

Loertscher, David. "The Second Revolution: A Taxonomy for the 1980s." *Wilson Library Bulletin* 56 (February 1982): 417-421.

Loertscher, David V. *Taxonomies of the School Library Media Program.* 2nd ed. San Jose: Hi Willow Research & Publishing, 2000.

Logan, Debra Kay. *Information Skills Toolkit: Collaborative Integrated Instruction for the Middle Grades.* Worthington, Ohio: Linworth Publishing, Inc., 2000.

Mackey, Bonnie and Maureen White. "Conversations, Collaborations, and Celebrations." *Knowledge Quest* 33:2 (November/December 2004): 30-33.

Milbury, Peter. "Collaboration: Ten Important Reasons to Take it Seriously." *Knowledge Quest* 33:5 (May/June 2005): 30-32.

Miller, Donna. *The Standards-Based Integrated Library: A Collaborative Approach for Aligning The Library Program with the Classroom Curriculum.* 2nd ed. Worthington, Ohio: Linworth Publishing, 2004.

The Minnesota Early Literacy Training Project. "Creating Literacy-Rich Classrooms for Preschool Children." *Center for Early Education and Development.* 13 January 2007 <http://education.umn.edu/ceed/events/ceedsymposium/eltpsymp.pdf>.

Montiel-Overall, Patricia. "Toward a Theory of Collaboration for Teachers and Librarians." *School Library Media Research* 2005:8. 19 January 2007 <http://www.ala.org/ala/aasl/aaslpubsandjournals/slmrb/slmrcontents/volume82005/theory.htm>.

Morris, William, ed. *The American Heritage Dictionary of the English Language.* Atlanta: Houghton Mifflin, 1976.

Muronaga, Karen and Violet Harada. "The Art of Collaboration." *Teacher Librarian* 27:1 (October 1999): 9-14.

National Board for Professional Teaching Standards. *NBPTS Library Media Standards.* Arlington, Virginia: National Board for Professional Teaching Standards, 2001.

"NCLB: Narrowing the Curriculum?" *Center on Education Policy.* July 2005. 03 July 2007 <http://www.cep-dc.org/index.cfm>. Type title in Search box.

Oatman, Eric. "Overwhelming Evidence." *School Library Journal* 52:1 (January 2006): 56-59.

Obama, Barack. "Bound to the Word." *American Libraries* 34:7 (August 2005): 48-52.

Pickard, Patricia W. "Current Research: The Instructional Consultant Role of the School Library Media Specialist." *SLMQ* 21:2 (Winter 1993). 13 January 2007 <http://www.ala.org/ala/aasl/aaslpubsandjournals/slmrb/editorschoiceb/infopower/ selectpickard.htm>.

Pitcher, Sharon M. and Bonnie Mackey. *Collaboration for Real Literacy: Librarian, Teacher, and Principal.* Worthington, Ohio: Linworth Publishing, 2004.

Prince, Robyn M. "The Balanced Literacy Program and Library Media Centers." *School Library Media Activities Monthly* 20:4 (December 2003): 26-29.

Public Library Association. *Early Literacy Begins with You.* Chicago: Public Library Association, 2004. 13 January 2007 <http://www.ala.org/ala/pla/plaissues/earlylit/parentguidebrochures/bgeneric.pdf>.

Rasinski, Timothy and Nancy Padak. "Beyond Consensus – Beyond Balance: Toward a Comprehensive Literacy Curriculum." *Reading & Writing Quarterly* 20 (2004): 91-102.

"Reading First." *New York City Department of Education.* 13 January 2007 <http://schools.nyc.gov/Offices/TeachLearn/OfficeCurriculumProfessionalDevelopment/DepartmentofLiteracy/ReadingFirst/default.htm>.

Reed, Donna. "Marian the Librarian Meets NCLB." *Library Media Connection* 23:7 (April/May): 56-58.

Schomberg, Janie, Becky McCabe, and Lisa Fink. "TAG Team: Collaborate to Teach, Assess and Grow." *Teacher Librarian* 31:5 (October 2003): 8-11.

"School Libraries and Their Impact on Student Performance." *ResearchBrief* 18:1 (September 2, 2003) 13 January 2007. Access at <http://www.ascd.org/portal/site/ascd/menuitem.03e1753c019b7a9f989ad324d3108a0c/>.

School Libraries Work! New York: Scholastic Library Publishing, 2006.

Schuster, Ann. Personal interview. 24 September 2005.

Shannon, Donna. "The School Library Media Specialist and Early Literacy Programs." *Knowledge Quest* 33:2 (November/December 2004): 15-21.

Sherouse, Linda D. Personal interview. 11 January 2007.

Sigmon, Cheryl M. "The Media Center as the Hub of Four Blocks." *Teachers.Net.* 13 January 2007 <http://www.teachers.net/4blocks/article63.html>.

Simpson, Carol. "Damned If You Don't." *Library Media Connection* 23:3 (November/December 2004): 8.

Simpson, Carol. "The School Librarian's Role in the Electronic Age." *ERIC Digest.* 13 January2007 <http://www.ericdigests.org/1997-3/librarian.html>.

Small, Ruth V. "Collaboration: Where Does It Begin?" *Teacher Librarian* 29: 5 (June 2002): 8-11.

Smith, Jane Bandy. *Teaching and Testing Information Literacy.* Worthington, Ohio: Linworth Publishing, 2005.

Spellings, Margaret. "Straight Answers from Margaret Spellings." *American Libraries.* 36:8 (September 2005): 28.

St. Lifer, Evan. "Is NCLB Really 'The Da Vinci Code'?" *School Library Journal* 49:12 (December 2003): 13.

Strickland, Dorothy. "Balanced Literacy: Teaching the Skills and Thrills of Reading. *Instructor* 13 January 2007 <http://teacher.scholastic.com/professional/teachstrat/balanced.htm>.

Taylor, Rusty. Personal interview. 05 June 2006.

Thomas, Melody. "What is Collaboration to You?" *Library Talk* 15:2 (March/April 2002): 17-18.

Todd, Ross J. "School Libraries & Evidence." *School Library Journal* 22:1 (August/September 2003): 12-18.

Tomasso, Bernie. Personal interview. 11 January 2007.

Van Deusen, Jean Donham and Julie I. Tallman. "The Impact of Scheduling on Curriculum Consultation and Information Skills Instruction: Part One, The 1993-94 AASL/Highsmith Research Award Study." *School Library Media Quarterly* 23:1 (Fall 1994): 17-25.

Von Drasek, Lisa. Personal interview. 02 June 2006.

Von Drasek, Lisa. Personal interview. 12 January 2007.

Walker, Christine. "Are You the Gatekeeper or the Keymaster? The Role of the Library Media Specialist in Reading." *Knowledge Quest* 33:5 (May/June 2005): 46-47.

Wallace, Andy. Personal interview. 01 June 2006.

Weisburg, Hilda. Personal interview. 24 September 2005

Wells, Teresa. Personal interview. 02 June 2006.

Whelan, Debra Lau. "13,000 Kids Can't Be Wrong." *School Library Journal* 50:2 (February 2004) 46-50.

Whelan, Debra Lau. "A Golden Opportunity." *School Library Journal* 50:1 (January 2004): 40-42.

Whelan, Debra Lau. "Greatest Challenges for 2003." *School Library Journal* 49:1 (January 2003): 48-50.

Whelan, Debra Lau. "Why Isn't Information Literacy Catching On?" *School Library Journal* 49:9 (September 2003): 50-53.

Wright, Pam. Personal interview. 01 June 2006.

Youssef, Jennifer L. "Collaboration: It Really Does Work!" *Library Media Connection* 24:1 (August/September 2005): 40-41.

Zucker, Lauren. Personal interview. 10 January 2007.

Index